THE ROUGH GUIDE TO

MENORCA

Forthcoming titles include

Malta • Tenerife • Thai Beaches and Islands
US Rockies • Vancouver

Forthcoming reference guides include

Personal Computers • Videogaming • Web Directory

www.roughguides.com

Rough Guide Credits

Text editor: Ruth Blackmore
Series editor: Mark Ellingham
Production: Helen Prior and Julia Bovis
Cartography: Maxine Repath
Proofreading: Susannah Wight

Publishing Information

This first edition published July 2001
by Rough Guides Ltd,
62–70 Shorts Gardens, London, WC2H 9AH

Distributed by the Penguin Group:

Penguin Books Ltd, 27 Wrights Lane, London W8 5TZ
Penguin Putnam, Inc. 375 Hudson Street, New York 10014, USA
Penguin Books Australia Ltd, 487 Maroondah Highway,
PO Box 257, Ringwood, Victoria 3134, Australia
Penguin Books Canada Ltd, 10 Alcorn Avenue,
Toronto, Ontario, Canada M4V 1E4
Penguin Books (NZ) Ltd,
182–190 Wairau Road, Auckland 10, New Zealand

Typeset in Bembo and Helvetica to an original design by Henry Iles.
Printed in Spain by Graphy Cems.

© Phil Lee, 288pp, includes index
A catalogue record for this book is available from the British Library.

ISBN 1-85828-708-1

THE ROUGH GUIDE TO

MENORCA

by Phil Lee

with additional contributions by
Gavin Thomas

ROUGH
GUIDES

We set out to do something different when the first Rough Guide was published in 1982. Mark Ellingham, just out of university, was travelling in Greece. He brought along the popular guides of the day, but found they were all lacking in some way. They were either strong on ruins and museums but went on for pages without mentioning a beach or taverna. Or they were so conscious of the need to save money that they lost sight of Greece's cultural and historical significance. Also, none of the books told him anything about Greece's contemporary life – its politics, its culture, its people, and how they lived.

So with no job in prospect, Mark decided to write his own guidebook, one which aimed to provide practical information that was second to none, detailing the best beaches and the hottest clubs and restaurants, while also giving hard-hitting accounts of every sight, both famous and obscure, and providing up-to-the-minute information on contemporary culture. It was a guide that encouraged independent travellers to find the best of Greece, and was a great success, getting shortlisted for the Thomas Cook travel guide award, and encouraging Mark, along with three friends, to expand the series.

The Rough Guide list grew rapidly and the letters flooded in, indicating a much broader readership than had been expected, but one which uniformly appreciated the Rough Guide mix of practical detail and humour, irreverence and enthusiasm. Things haven't changed. The same four friends who began the series are still the caretakers of the Rough Guide mission today: to provide the most reliable, up-to-date and entertaining information to independent-minded travellers of all ages, on all budgets.

We now publish more than 200 titles and have offices in London and New York. The travel guides are written and researched by a dedicated team of more than 100 authors, based in Britain, Europe, the USA and Australia. We have also created a unique series of phrasebooks to accompany the travel series, along with an acclaimed series of music guides, and a best-selling pocket guide to the Internet and World Wide Web. We also publish comprehensive travel information on our Web site: **www.roughguides.com**

Help us update

We've gone to a lot of trouble to ensure that this Rough Guide is as up to date and accurate as possible. However, things do change and any suggestions, comments and corrections are much appreciated, we'll send a copy of the next edition (or any other *Rough Guide* if you prefer) for the best letters.

Please mark letters "**Rough Guide Menorca Update**" and send to:

Rough Guides, 62–70 Shorts Gardens, London WC2H 9AH, or Rough Guides, 4th Floor, 345 Hudson St, New York NY 10014.

Or send email to: mail@roughguides.co.uk
Online updates about this book can be found on
Rough Guides' website (see opposite)

The author

Phil Lee has been writing for Rough Guides for over a decade. His other books in the series include Norway, Toronto, Belgium & Luxembourg and Mallorca. He lives in Nottingham, where he was born and raised.

Acknowledgements

Particular thanks are due to Maria Peterson for her help with solving many island mysteries and for translating all sorts of Spanish bits and pieces; to Gavin Thomas, who did such an exemplary job in hiking the hikes; and to Ruth Rigby for her assistance with Basics. Special thanks also for a useful contribution by Joan Guiver; to Dominic Rigby for his help with the section on Menorcan birdlife; and to Chez Woodhead for help with restaurants. At Rough Guides, I am grateful to my thoughtful editor, Ruth Blackmore; Helen Prior for typesetting; and the Map Studio for cartography. Finally, a word of thanks to my stepdaughter Emma Rees, who somehow didn't get a mention for keeping me company during the research for the *Rough Guide to the Pacific Northwest* – and an excellent companion she was (and is) too.

CONTENTS

MAP LIST

Colour Maps at back of book

MAP SYMBOLS

———	Paved road	P	Parking
- - - ⇢	Unpaved road	★	Bus stop
- - - -	Foot path	✈	Airport
———	Walking route	⛺	Campsite
～	Cliffs	◉	Accommodation
♦	Point of Interest	▣	Restaurant
†	Church	▬	Building
♛	Castle	⊞	Church
▮	Tower	▦	Park
∴	Ruins	▦	National park
◠	Cave	▦	Beach
▲	Peak	✉	Post office
🏛	Mansion	ⓘ	Tourist office
🗼	Lighthouse		

Introduction

Often and unfairly maligned as an overdeveloped, package-tourist nightmare, boomerang-shaped **Menorca** is, in fact, the least developed – and second largest member of – the Balearic Islands, an archipelago to the east of the Spanish mainland which also comprises Mallorca, Ibiza and Formentera. Unlike its neighbours, Menorca remains essentially rural, its rolling fields, wooded ravines and humpy hills filling out the interior in between its two main – but still small – towns of Maó and Ciutadella. Much of this landscape looks pretty much as it did at the turn of the twentieth century – though many of the fields are no longer cultivated – and only on the edge of the island, and then only in parts, have its rocky coves been colonized by sprawling villa complexes. Nor is the development likely to spread: the resorts have been kept at a discreet distance from the two main towns, and this is how the Menorcans like it. Furthermore, determined to protect their island from the worst excesses of the tourist industry, the Menorcans have clearly demarcated development areas and are meanwhile pushing ahead with a variety of environmental schemes. The most prominent is the creation of a chain of conservation areas that will eventually protect much of the island, including the pristine coves that are one of its real delights. There are also plans to revamp the old mule track that once circled the entire island and turn it into a footpath.

Menorca stretches from the enormous natural harbour and island capital of **Maó** in the east to the smaller port of **Ciutadella** in the west, a distance of just 45km. These two towns, boasting over sixty percent of the population, have preserved much of their eighteenth- and early nineteenth-century appearance, though Ciutadella's labyrinthine centre, with its grandee mansions and Gothic cathedral, has the aesthetic edge over Maó's plainer, more mercantile architecture. Running through the interior between the two, the main **C721** highway forms the island's backbone, linking a trio of pocket-sized market towns – **Alaior**, **Es Mercadal** and **Ferreries** – and succouring what little industry Menorca enjoys, a few shoe factories and cheese-making plants. Branching off the highway, a sequence of asphalted side roads lead to the resorts that notch the north and south coasts. Mercifully, these tourist developments are largely confined to individual coves and bays, and only amongst the sprawling villa-villages of the southeast and on the west coast have they become overpowering.

The main highway also acts as a rough dividing line between Menorca's two distinct geological areas. In the north, sandstone predominates, giving a red tint to the low hills which roll out towards the bare, surf-battered coastline. One of the many coves and inlets along this stretch shelters the lovely fishing village and mini-resort of **Fornells**. To the south, all is limestone, with low-lying flatlands punctuated by bulging hills and fringed by a cove-studded coastline. Straddling the two zones, **Monte Toro**, Menorca's highest peak and the site of a quaint little convent, offers panoramic views which reveal the topography of the whole island. Clearly visible from here are the wooded ravines that gash the southern zone, becoming deeper and more dramatic as you travel west – especially around **Cala Santa**

Galdana, a popular resort set beneath severe, pine-clad sea-cliffs.

This varied terrain supports a smattering of minuscule villages and solitary farmsteads, present witnesses to an **agriculture** that had become, before much of it was killed off by tourism, highly advanced. Every field was protected by a dry-stone wall (*tanca*) to prevent the Tramuntana, the vicious north wind, from tearing away the topsoil. Even olive trees had their roots individually protected in little stone wells, while compact stone ziggurats sheltered cattle from both the wind and the blazing sun. Nowadays, apart from a few acres of rape and corn, many of the fields are barren, but the walls and ziggurats survive, as do many of the old twisted gates made from olive branches.

The landscape is further cluttered by hundreds of crude stone memorials, mostly dating from the second millennium BC. Yet, despite this widespread physical evidence, little is known of the island's prehistory. The most common monuments are thought to be linked to those of Sardinia and are attributed to the so-called Talayotic culture, which reached a peak of activity here in Menorca in around 1000 BC. **Talayots** are the rock mounds found all over the island. Popular belief has it that they functioned as watch-towers, but it's a theory few experts accept: they have no interior stairway, and only a few are found on the coast. Even so, no one has come up with a more convincing explanation. **Taulas** – huge stones topped with another to form a "T", around four metres high – are unique to Menorca and even more puzzling. They have no obvious function, and they are almost always found alongside a *talayot*. Some of the best-preserved *talayot* and *taula* remains are on the edge of Maó at **Talatí de Dalt**; another site, **Torrellafuda**, is near Ciutadella. The third kind of prehistoric monument found on Menorca is the **naveta**, a stone-slab construction shaped like an inverted loaf tin, dating

CATALAN AND CASTILIAN

Since the death of Franco and the subsequent federalization of Spain, the Balearics have formed their own autonomous region and asserted the primacy of their language, **Catalan** (*Català*). On Menorca it's spoken with a slight local variation as the dialect *Menorquín*. The most obvious sign of this linguistic assertiveness is the recent replacement of Castilian (Spanish) street names by their Catalan equivalents. In speech, though, the islanders are almost all bilingual, speaking Castilian and Catalan with equal fluency, and you'll find no shortage of people with perfect English or French either. In this book we've given the Catalan for everything to do with the islands – from town, street and beach names through to topographical features and food – as this is mostly what the visitor encounters.

from between 1400 and 800 BC. Many have false ceilings, and although you can stand up inside, they were clearly not living spaces, but rather communal tombs, or ossuaries. The prime example is the **Naveta d'es Tudons**, outside Ciutadella.

In more recent times, the deep-water channel of the port of Maó promoted Menorca to an important position in European affairs. The **British** saw its potential as a **naval base** and captured the island in 1708 during the War of the Spanish Succession – five years later it was ceded to them under the Treaty of Utrecht. Spain regained possession in 1783, but with the threat of Napoleon in the Mediterranean, a new British base was temporarily established under admirals Nelson and Collingwood until Britain finally relinquished all claims to the island in 1802. The British influence on Menorca, especially its architecture, is still manifest: the sash windows so popular in Georgian design are even now sometimes referred to as *winderes*, locals often part with a fond *bye-bye*, and there's a substantial expat community. The British also introduced the art of distilling juniper berries, and Menorcan gin (Xoriguer in particular) is now world-renowned.

Practicalities

Access to Menorca is easy from Britain and northern Europe, with plenty of charter flights and complete package deals, some of which drop to absurd prices out of season or through last-minute booking. From mainland Spain, both ferries and flights are frequent and comparatively inexpensive. The island has one airport (on the outskirts of Maó) and two ferry ports – Maó, with connections to the mainland and Mallorca, and Ciutadella with links just to Mallorca. From these points of arrival, the rest of the island is within easy striking distance by **car** – it only takes an hour or so to drive across Menorca – and to a large extent by **bus**.

The main constraint for independent travellers is **accommodation**. From mid-June to mid-September, sometimes later, rooms are in very short supply. If you go at this time – and especially in August – you're well advised to make a reservation several weeks in advance or to book a package. Out of season, things ease up and you can idle around, staying pretty much where you want, though many places close down from November to April. The best bases are Maó, Fornells and Ciutadella, each of which has a small cache of all-year hotels and *hostals*. In two weeks, you'll have more than enough time to explore the island – three and you'll be able to investigate its every nook and cranny.

Climate

Spring and autumn are the ideal times for a visit, when the **weather** is comfortably warm, with none of the oven-like temperatures which bake the island in July and August. It's well worth considering a winter break, too – even in January, temperatures are usually high enough during the day to sit out at a café in shirtsleeves. The island sees occasional rain in winter, but nothing too serious and anyway this is when the rain renders the fields bright green with none of the bare, brown, sunburnt appearance of summer. The main winter irritant is the wind, which often blows fiercely from the north.

MAÓ CLIMATE TABLE

	Jan	Apr	July	Oct
Highest recorded temp (°C)	22	26	39	31
Average daily max. temp (°C)	14	19	29	23
Average daily min. temp (°C)	6	10	20	14
Lowest recorded temp (°C)	-3	1	12	1
Average number of days with rain per day	8	6	1	9

BASICS

BASICS

Getting there from Britain and Ireland

The easiest and cheapest way to reach Menorca from Britain and Ireland is to **fly**. Non-stop flights from London take a little over two hours, from Manchester two and three-quarter hours, and from Dublin two and a half hours. All flights arrive at Menorca's one and only airport, which is located just outside the main town, Maó.

Numerous **charter flights** operate to Menorca during the summer season, and although they're heavily subscribed by package-tour operators well in advance, there are still usually spare seats left over for independent travellers. Last-minute returns can cost as little as £100, though often you have to be prepared to fly from any UK airport at any time of the day or night.

The new breed of **low-cost airlines** also offers competitive prices, though none flies direct to Menorca: the nearest airports are Palma and Barcelona, from where you can easily get a connecting flight. A flight with EasyJet to Palma, for example, will generally be around £50–70 each way from Luton, and £60–80 each way from Liverpool in mid-season. Lastly, it's worth checking out the special offers run from time to time by the bigger airlines, though again, none flies direct to the island.

Don't automatically rule out a **package holiday**: package prices can be so low – sometimes as little as £120 for a week – that they represent a reasonable deal for the flight alone.

Airlines

Air Europa ☎ 0870/240 1501, 🌐 www.air-europa.co.uk.

Air 2000 ☎ 0870/240 1402, 🌐 www.air2000.com.

British Airways ☎ 0345/773 3377, ☎ 1800/626747 (Eire), 🌐 www.britishairways.com.

British Midland ☎ 0870/607 0555, ☎ 01/283 8833 (Dublin), 🌐 www.britishmidland.com.

EasyJet ☎ 0870/600 0000, 🌐 www.easyjet.com.

Go ☎ 0845/605 4321, 🌐 www.go-fly.com.

Iberia ☎ 0845/601 2854, ☎ 01/407 3017 (Dublin), 🌐 www.iberia.com.

Discount flight agents

Aran Travel, Granary Hall, 58 Dominick St, Galway ☎ 091/562595, ✉ arantvl@ iol.ie. Well-informed and competitive holiday agent, with flight-only bargains.

Avro, Vantage House, 1 Weir Rd, London SW19 ☎ 020/ 8695 4440, 🌐 www. avro-flights.co.uk. Flight-only agent, specializing in charter flights.

Cheapflights, 🌐 www. cheap flights.co.uk. This UK website searches for the best fare bargains and offers online booking.

Dial-a-Flight, ☎ 0870/333 4488, ☎ 01/617 7556 (Dublin), 🌐 www.dial-a-flight.com. First-rate scheduled and charter-flight bargains with over-the-phone booking and a useful online price search.

Expedia UK, ⓦ *expedia.co.uk.* Microsoft's venture into the internet travel market, with a "flight wizard" listing many airline options, its own "special fares" and an online booking service.

First Choice, First Choice House, Peel Cross Road, Salford, Manchester M4 2AN ⓣ 0870/750 0499, ⓦ *www.holidays.co.uk.* Has a flight-only booking service.

www.flightline.co.uk A telephone-based outfit offering online searches for cheap, mainly charter, flights.

Joe Walsh Ltd, 8–11 Baggot St, Dublin 2 ⓣ 01/676 3053; 117 St Patrick St, Cork ⓣ 021/427 7959. General budget-fares agent.

www.lastminute.com The best-known of the cheap flight websites sells everything from holidays to mobile phones.

North–South Travel, Moulsham Mill Centre, Parkway, Chelmsford, Essex CM2 7PX ⓣ 01245/608291, ⓦ *www.northsouthtravel. co.uk.* Friendly, competitive travel agency, offering discount fares worldwide – profits are used to support projects in the developing world, especially the promotion of sustainable tourism.

STA Travel, London call centre ⓣ 020/7361 6145; northern England call centre ⓣ 0161/830 4713; ⓦ *www. statravel.co.uk.* Branches at many university campuses. Worldwide specialists in low-cost flights and tours for students and under-26s, though other customers are welcome.

Tom Mannion Travel, 71 O'Connell Street, Ennis, Co. Clare ⓣ 065/682 4211, ⓦ *www.travel.tmt.ie.* Discount-flight agents, with online booking facilities.

The Travel Bug, 125 Gloucester Rd, London SW7 4SF ⓣ 020/7835 2000; 597 Cheetham Hill Rd, Manchester M8 5EJ ⓣ 0161/721 4000; ⓦ *www.travel-bug.co.uk.* Large range of discounted tickets; their website offers a flight price "wizard", as well as a brochure-request service.

UsitCAMPUS, national call centre ⓣ 0870/240 1010,

@ *www.usitcampus.co.uk.*
Student/youth travel
specialists, with branches on
university campuses all over
Britain and also in YHA shops.
UsitNOW, 19–21 Aston Quay,
O'Connell Bridge, Dublin 2
☎ 01/602 1600; Fountain
Centre, Belfast BT1 6ET
☎ 028/9032 4073; branches
in Cork, Galway, Limerick and
Waterford; @ *www.usitnow.
com.* Ireland's main student
and youth travel specialists.

Package-tour operators

Celtic Holidays, 622 Pilgrims
Way, Wouldham, Kent, ME1
3RB ☎ 01634/868600,
@ *www.celticholidays.ltd.uk.*
Specialists in Menorcan
holidays, offering hotel
accommodation, villas and
apartments on the island, as
well as specialist sailing and
diving holidays.
Fahy Travel, 3 Bridge Street,
Galway ☎ 091/563055,
@ *fahytrav@iol.ie.* Has a good
selection of last-minute
bargains.
First Choice, First Choice
House, Peel Cross Rd,
Salford, Manchester M4 2AN
☎ 0870/750 0001, @ *www.
first-choice.com.* The standard
range of package-holiday fare,
with a flight-only booking
option. Late holiday and flight
offers on the website.

Ilkeston Co-op, 12 South St,
Ilkeston, Derbyshire DE7 5SG
☎ 0115/932 3546. A wide
range of package holidays,
often at extraordinarily cheap
prices, plus bargain-basement
charter flights to Menorca,
especially from Birmingham
and East Midlands airports.
Magic of Spain, 227
Shepherd's Bush Rd, London
W6 7AS ☎ 0870/027 0480.
Upmarket hotel and villa
holidays, often in out-of-the-
way places. Several lovely
fincas too. Highly
recommended.
Minorca Sailing Holidays, 58
Kew Rd, Richmond, Surrey
TW9 2PQ ☎ 020/8948 2106,
@ *www.minorcasailing.co.uk.*
Specializing in dinghy sailing
and windsurfing holidays with
a range of accommodation
options and tuition available.

Mundi Color, 276 Vauxhall Bridge Rd, London SW1V 1BE ⓣ0207/828 6021, ⓦ www.mundicolor.es. Small but well-chosen selection of classy and atmospheric hotels in both popular resorts and less familiar spots.

Naturetrek, Cheriton Mill, Cheriton, Alresford, Hants SO24 0NG ⓣ01962/733051, ⓦ www.naturetrek.co.uk. Tours, treks and cruises with birdwatching and botanical themes.

The Real Spain (Citalia), Marco Polo House, 3–5 Lansdowne Rd, Croydon CR9 1LL ⓣ0345/959922, ⓦ www.citalia.co.uk. High-quality hotels, villas and bungalows across the island.

Tony Roche Travel, Travel House, Walkinstown Cross, Dublin 12 ⓣ01/456 7311, ⓦ www.trtravel.com. Specialist in last-minute bookings.

Travel Club of Upminster, Station Rd, Upminster, Essex RM14 2TT ⓣ01708/225000, ⓦ www.travelclub.org.uk. Rents a number of villas and apartments on the island.

Twohigs Travel, 8 Burgh Quay, Dublin ⓣ01/677 2666; 13 Duke Street, Dublin ⓣ01/670 9750. Packages and flight agent.

Vintage Spain Limited, Milkmaid House, Rampton End, Willingham, Cambridgeshire CB4 5JB ⓣ01954/261431, ⓦ www.vintagetravel.co.uk. Specialists in renting country houses, most with pools, in "unspoilt" places.

GETTING THERE FROM BRITAIN AND IRELAND

●

Getting there from the US and Canada

here are no direct flights from North America to Menorca. The nearest you'll get are Iberia's one- or two-stop flights from Los Angeles, New York, Chicago, Miami and Montréal via Madrid to Palma, Mallorca. From here it's easy enough to get an onward flight to Menorca. The most obvious alternative is to search for the least expensive transatlantic fare offered by any airline to Madrid or Barcelona, from where an Iberia or Air-Europa domestic flight will shuttle you across to the island.

On Iberia's daily flights to Palma, Mallorca, via Madrid, the **Apex fare** (maximum stay one month, payment 21 days before departure) from Los Angeles (12hr) is \$1051 high season, \$730 low season; from New York (8hr) \$845 high, \$571 low; from Chicago (9hr) \$1075 high, \$688 low; and from Miami (8hr) \$927 high, \$575 low. From Montréal via Madrid to Palma the Iberia Apex fare is around CDN\$1252 in high season, CDN\$1008 in low, the same from Toronto, while from Vancouver expect to pay in the region of CDN\$1880 (high), CDN\$1390 (low). See

"Getting there from the rest of Spain" on p.16 for details of connecting flights on to Menorca.

If you want a **stopover in mainland Spain**, you'll need to purchase one ticket for the transatlantic leg and then a separate ticket for the onward flight to Menorca. The price of an Iberia Apex fare to Madrid from Los Angeles is $895 ($765 low); from New York $999 ($571 low); from Chicago $812 ($538 low); and from Miami $927 ($575 low). Flights from Montréal or Toronto to Madrid cost around CDN$1015 (high season) or CDN$911 (low), and from Vancouver approximately CDN$1515 (high) or CDN$1275 (low). You should also look out for special promotional offers.

North American travellers are hardly spoiled for choice when it comes to finding a **tour operator** offering deals to Menorca. Don't expect anything more imaginative than the basic air/hotel beach resort combo with maybe a sightseeing tour thrown in and the option of reduced-rate car rental. The companies listed below either have set packages available or will help you customize one of your own. As a very rough estimate of price, for a low-season six-night air-hotel package expect to pay upwards of $1040.

Airlines in North America

Air Europa ℡ 1-800/327 1225, Ⓦ www.air-europa.com.

Air France ℡ 1-800/237 2747; Canada ℡ 1-800/667 2747; Ⓦ www.airfrance.fr.

American Airlines/TWA ℡ 1-800/433 7300, Ⓦ www.americanair.com.

British Airways ℡ 1-800/247 9297; Canada ℡ 1-800/668 1059; Ⓦ www.britishairways.com.

Continental Airlines ℡ 1-800/231 0856, Ⓦ www.flycontinental.com.

Delta Airlines ℡ 1-800/241 4141, Ⓦ www.delta.com.

Iberia ℡ 1-800/772 4642; Canada ℡ 1-800/423 7421; Ⓦ www.iberia.com/ibusa.

Lufthansa ⓣ 1-800/645 3880,
  ⓦ *www.lufthansa-usa.com*.
Northwest/KLM ⓣ 1-800/447
  4747 or 1-800/374 7747,
  ⓦ *www.nwa.com*.

Sabena ⓣ 1-800/955 2000,
  ⓦ *www.sabena.com*.
TAP Air Portugal ⓣ 1-800/221
  7370,
  ⓦ *www.tap-airportugal.pt*.

Discount flight agents in North America

Air Brokers International, 150
  Post St, Suite 620, San
  Francisco, CA 94108, ⓣ 1-
  800/883 3273 or 413/397
  1383, ⓦ *www.airbrokers.com*.
  Consolidator and specialists
  in RTW tickets.
Air Courier Association, 191
  University Blvd, Suite 300,
  Denver, CO 80206 ⓣ 1-
  800/282 1202 or 303/215 0900,
  ⓦ *www.aircourier.org*. Lowest
  courier fares to Europe.
Airtech, 588 Broadway, Suite
  204, New York, NY 10017
  ⓣ 1-800/575 8324 or 212/219
  7000, ⓦ *www.airtech.com*.
  Stand-by seat broker, courier
  agent and consolidator.
Council Travel, 205 E 42nd St,
  New York, NY 10017 ⓣ 1-
  800/226 8624, 888/COUNCIL
  or 212/822 2700,
  ⓦ *www.counciltravel.com*.
  Other branches in San
  Francisco, Los Angeles,
  Boston, Chicago, Washington

DC. Nationwide specialists in
  student travel.
Educational Travel Center,
  438 N Frances St, Madison,
  WI 53703 ⓣ 1-800/747 5551
  or 608/256 5551,
  ⓦ *www.edtrav.com*.
  Student/youth and
  consolidator fares.
**International Association of
  Air Travel Couriers**, 8 South
  J St, PO Box 1349, Lake
  Worth, FL 33460 ⓣ 561/582
  8320, ⓦ *www.courier.org*.
  Courier flight broker.
STA Travel, 10 Downing St,
  New York, NY 10014
  ⓣ 1-800/777 0112 or 212/627
  3111, ⓦ *www.sta-travel.com*.
  Other branches in Los
  Angeles, Chicago, San
  Francisco, Philadelphia and
  Boston. Worldwide discount
  travel firm specializing in
  student/youth fares; also
  student IDs, travel insurance,
  car rental, train passes, etc.

TFI Tours International, 34 W 32nd St, New York, NY 10001 ⓣ 1-800/745 8000 or 212/736 1140. Consolidator.

Travac, 989 Sixth Ave, 16th floor, New York, NY 10018 ⓣ 1-800/872 8800 or 212/563 3303, ⓦ www.travac.com. Consolidator and charter broker mostly to Europe.

Travel Avenue, 10 S Riverside, Suite 1404, Chicago, IL 60606 ⓣ 1-800/333 3335 or 312/876 6866, ⓦ www.travel avenue.com. Discount travel company.

Travel Cuts, 187 College St, Toronto, ON M5T 1P7 ⓣ 1-800/667 2887 or 416/979 2406, ⓦ www.travelcuts.com. Branches in Montréal, Vancouver, Calgary and Winnipeg. Canadian discount travel organization, specializing in youth fares.

UniTravel, 11737 Administration Drive, Suite 120, St Louis, MO 63146 ⓣ 1-800/325 2222, ⓦ www. flightsforless.com. Consolidator.

Tour operators in North America

Auto Europe ⓣ 1-800/223 5555, ⓦ www.auto europe.com. Air-hotel deals and car rental.

Central Holidays, 120 Sullivan Ave, Englewood Cliffs, NJ 07632 ⓣ 1-800/227 5858, ⓦ www.centralholidays.com. Agents for the Iberia tour department's Discover Spain Vacations, offering escorted and independent tours.

EC Tours, 12500 Riverside Drive, Suite #210, Valley Village, CA 91607 3423 ⓣ 1-800/388 0877,

ⓦ www.ectours.com. A variety of package tours.

Escapade Tours, c/o Isram World of Travel, 630 Third Ave, New York, NY 10017 ⓣ 1-800/356 2405, ⓦ www. isram.com. Package trips.

International Gay Travel Association ⓣ 1-800/448 8550, ⓦ www.igita.org. Trade group with lists of gay-owned or gay-friendly travel agents and accommodation.

M.I. Travel, 450 Seventh Ave, Suite 1805, New York, NY 10123 ⓣ 1-800/848 2314 or

212/967 6565. Package and independent tours.

Petrabax Tours, 9745 Queens Blvd, Rego Park, NY 11374 ⓣ 1-800/634 1188, ⓦ *www.petrabax.com*. Escorted tours, hotels,

historic inns and property rentals on offer.

Saga Holidays, 222 Berkely St, Boston, MA 02116 ⓣ 1-800/343 0273, ⓦ *www.sagaholidays.com*. Group travel for seniors.

Getting there from Australia and New Zealand

There are no direct flights to any part of Spain from **Australia** or **New Zealand**, but various airlines offer one-stop services to Madrid and Barcelona. British Airways and Qantas (via London), KLM (via

Amsterdam), Alitalia (via Milan), Singapore Airlines (via Singapore) and Thai Airways (via Bangkok) have reasonably frequent flights and competitive fares; Lauda Air's connections (via Vienna) are less convenient, but may be worth checking for special offers. From Barcelona or Madrid you can easily get an onward direct flight to Menorca (see "Getting there from the rest of Spain", p.16). Alternatively, it may be worth considering a cheap flight to London, from where bargain fares to the island are generally easy to pick up (see "Getting there from Britain and Ireland", p.3). Any of the agents listed below can help with deals to Spain or London, or ticket you right through to the Balearics. Booking ahead as far as possible is the best way to secure the most reasonable prices.

The current lowest standard return fares to Spain are around A$1700/2300 (low/high season) from Australia, NZ$2000/2500 from New Zealand; to London, fares are around A$1400/2300 from Australia, NZ$2000/2500 from New Zealand. Though they charge heavily for cancellations or alterations, **discount agents** generally offer better deals than the airlines themselves. The internet can also be a good source of cheap flights: ⓦ *www.travel.com.au* offers discounted fares as does ⓦ *www.sydneytravel.com.*

Airlines in Australia and New Zealand

Alitalia Australia ⓣ 02/9244 2400; New Zealand ⓣ 09/302 1452; ⓦ *www.alitalia.it.*

British Airways Australia ⓣ 02/8904 8800; New Zealand ⓣ 09/356 8690; ⓦ *www.british-airways.com.*

Iberia c/o British Airways Australia ⓣ 02/8904 8800;

New Zealand ⓣ 09/356 8690.

Japan Airlines (JAL) Australia ⓣ 02/9272 1111; New Zealand ⓣ 09/379 9906; ⓦ *www.japanair.com.*

KLM Australia ⓣ 1300/303 747; New Zealand ⓣ 09/309 1782; ⓦ *www.klm.com.*

Lauda Air Australia ⓣ 1800/642

438, ℡ 02/9251 6155; New
Zealand ℡ 09/308 3368;
Ⓦ www.laudaair.com.
Three flights a week from
Sydney and Melbourne to
Barcelona, with a one-night
stopover in Vienna.

Qantas Australia ℡ 13/1313;
New Zealand ℡ 09/357 8900
or 0800/808 767;
Ⓦ www.qantas.com.au.

Singapore Airlines Australia
℡ 13/1011 or ℡ 02/9350
0262; New Zealand ℡ 09/303
2129 or 0800/808 909;
Ⓦ www.singaporeair.com.

Thai Airways Australia
℡ 1300/651 960; New
Zealand ℡ 09/377 3886 or
0800/100 992;
Ⓦ www.thaiair.com.

Travel and Discount agents in Australia and New Zealand

Anywhere Travel, 345 Anzac
Parade, Kingsford, Sydney
℡ 02/9663 0411,
Ⓔ anywhere@ozemail.com.au.

Budget Travel, 16 Fort St,
Auckland, plus branches
around the city ℡ 09/366
0061 & 0800/808040.

Destinations Unlimited, 220
Queen St, Auckland ℡ 09/373
4033.

Flight Centres Australia: 82
Elizabeth St, Sydney, plus
branches nationwide
℡ 02/9235 3522; nearest
branch ℡ 13/1600. New
Zealand: 350 Queen St,
Auckland ℡ 09/358 4310,
plus branches nationwide.
Ⓦ www.flightcentre.com.au.

Northern Gateway, 22
Cavenagh St, Darwin
℡ 08/8941 1394,
Ⓔ oztravel@norgate.com.au.

STA Travel Australia: 855
George St, Sydney; 256
Flinders St, Melbourne; other
offices in state capitals and
major universities; nearest
branch ℡ 13/1776; fastfare
telesales ℡ 1300/360960.
New Zealand: 10 High St,
Auckland ℡ 09/309 0458,
fastfare telesales ℡ 09/366
6673, plus branches in
Wellington, Christchurch,
Dunedin, Palmerston North,
Hamilton and at major
universities.
Ⓦ www.statravel.com.au.

Student Uni Travel, 92 Pitt St, Sydney ⓣ 02/9232 8444, ⓔ *sydney@backpackers.net* plus branches in Brisbane, Cairns, Darwin, Melbourne and Perth.

Trailfinders, 8 Spring St, Sydney (ⓣ 02/9247 7666); 91 Elizabeth St, Brisbane ⓣ 07/3229 0887; Hides Corner, Shield St, Cairns ⓣ 07/4041 1199.

Travel.com.au, 76–80 Clarence St, Sydney ⓣ 02/9249 5444 & 1800 000 447, ⓦ *www.travel.com.au.*

Usit Beyond, cnr Shortland St and Jean Batten Place, Auckland ⓣ 09/379 4224 or 0800/788336, ⓦ *www.usitbeyond.co.nz*, plus branches in Christchurch, Dunedin, Palmerston North, Hamilton and Wellington.

Specialist Travel Agents in Australia

IB Tours, 1/47 New Canterbury Rd, Petersham, Sydney ⓣ 02/9560 6932, ⓦ *www.ib-tours.com.au.* Offers a range of tours, accommodation and car rental in Menorca.

Ibertours, 1/84 William St, Melbourne ⓣ 03/9670 8388 & 1800/500016, ⓦ *www.ibertours.com.au.* Individually tailored packages to Menorca.

Silke's Travel, 263 Oxford St, Darlinghurst, Sydney ⓣ 02/9380 6244, ⓣ 1800/807 860, ⓦ *www.silkes.com.au.* Specially tailored packages for gay and lesbian travellers.

Getting there from the rest of Spain

Menorca is easily reached **by plane and ferry from mainland Spain and Mallorca**. Obviously, the main advantage of a flight over a ferry journey is its speed: Barcelona to Maó, for example, takes just forty minutes, compared to the ferry trip of nine hours. By plane, there's also the advantage of a wider range of jumping-off points: regular scheduled flights link many of Spain's major cities with Maó either direct or via Barcelona, whereas ferry and catamaran links are confined to five departure ports. These are Valencia and Barcelona on the mainland, and Palma, Cala Rajada and Port d'Alcúdia on Mallorca. While the ferry is less expensive, there's not that much in it and the saving is certainly not enough to justify the extra time and trouble – unless, that is, you're in or near one of the departure ports anyway. However, if you're taking your own vehicle over to Menorca, you will, of course, have to travel by boat.

BY AIR FROM MAINLAND SPAIN

The vast majority of **scheduled flights** to Menorca from the Spanish mainland are operated by the Iberia Regional/Air Nostrum partnership. The **Iberia** group has sales offices in every major Spanish city and most capital cities abroad. Seat availability isn't usually a problem and fares are very reasonable – a return flight from Madrid to Maó in the summer, for instance, costs around 36,400ptas/€219.27, and from Barcelona 26,520ptas/€159.75. There is also a variety of excursion fares available at discounted prices; the Air Nostrum website (Ⓦ *www.airnostrum.es*) and the Iberia site (Ⓦ *www.iberia.com*) are a good source for these. You could also try **Spanair**, the largest charter operator, which often undercuts Iberia by a significant margin. You can search for flights and make reservations on their website, Ⓦ *www.spanair.com*. They also have a nationwide number (Ⓣ 902 131 415) and an office at Palma airport (Ⓣ 971 745 020).

BY AIR FROM MALLORCA AND IBIZA

Getting to Menorca from Mallorca couldn't be simpler. Iberia, which has a monopoly on inter-island flights, operates eight **scheduled flights** daily from Palma to Maó. The journey takes 45 minutes and costs around 11,700ptas/€70.48 one-way, with a round-trip ticket costing about 18,980ptas/€114.33. To get to Menorca from Ibiza, you have to fly via Palma. There are eight flights daily of around 45 minutes between Ibiza and Palma, with prices being about the same as the Palma–Maó trip. There's usually no problem with seat availability, but you need to book ahead during the height of the season.

Iberia offices and flight frequencies

In addition to its many mainland offices, Iberia has a nationwide domestic flight reservation and information line in Spain on ☎ 902 400 500 (English spoken). The route frequencies given below cover direct flights to Menorca unless otherwise specified.

Barcelona Passeig de Gràcia 30 ☎ 934 013 387 and Plaça Espanya s/n ☎ 933 257 358 (6–10 daily; 45min).

Ibiza Town Passeig Vara de Rey 15 ☎ 971 302 580 (8 daily via Palma).

Madrid Velázquez 130 ☎ 915 878 787 or 915 874 747 (2 daily; 1hr 20min).

Maó Aeroport Menorca ☎ 971 369 016.

Palma, Mallorca Avgda Joan March 8 ☎ 971 757 151 (8 daily; 45min).

BY FERRY FROM MAINLAND SPAIN

Trasmediterranea operates **car ferry** services between mainland Spain and Menorca. These services run from **Barcelona to Maó** (3–8 weekly; 9hr) and **Valencia to Maó** (1 weekly; 17hr via Palma). There are no services from early December to the end of January.

Setting aside special deals and packages, a return ticket is about twice as much as a single. The **price** of a single passenger fare on a Trasmediterranea ferry from either Barcelona or Valencia to Maó is currently 6920ptas/€41.68 in mid-season, 10,350ptas/€62.34 return. Taking a car on the ferry will cost at least 19,000ptas/€114.45, but if there's a group of you, there are some car-plus-occupants deals that may work out cheaper. There are night-time sailings on most routes, when a **cabin** is extremely useful, especially if you're travelling with children. The inclusive cost of a double cabin starts at 18,690ptas/€112.59 per person one-way. On the same routes, the tariff for cars up to 2.4m long is

19,315ptas/€116.35. You might also consider Trasmediterranea's special all-in price for a car with up to four passengers. These packages start at around 47,000ptas/€283.13 one-way. **Tickets** can be purchased at the port of embarkation or in advance via both company's websites or Trasmediterranea's agents – see p.20.

BY FERRY FROM MALLORCA AND IBIZA

Trasmediterranea operates one or two **car ferries** per week from **Palma to Maó** (6hr). There are no car ferries direct from Ibiza to Menorca – you have to go via Palma. Trasmediterranea car ferries run from **Ibiza Town to Palma** three times weekly and take four and a half hours. The company's fast car-carrying **catamarans** (3 weekly from mid-June to mid-Sept; 2hr 15min) ply the same route and charge about forty percent more.

Advance bookings are strongly recommended on ferry and catamaran summer services – all year if you are taking a vehicle or need a cabin.

Two other ferry companies link Mallorca and Menorca. The first, **Cape Balear de Cruceros** (℡971 818 517, Ⓦ www.cape-balear.com) operates a passenger-only catamaran service from **Mallorca's Cala Rajada to Ciutadella** (1–3 daily; 75min), which costs around 8000ptas/€48.19 return, a single fare half that. The second is **Iscomar** (℡902 119 128, Ⓦ www.iscomar.com), whose car ferries run from **Port d'Alcúdia to Ciutadella** (1–2 daily; 3hr 30min). The single fare is 4400ptas/€26.44 and vehicles up to 4.5m in length cost an additional 7800ptas/€46.88. Remember, however, that car-rental firms in the Balearics do not allow their vehicles off their home island. More detailed information on sailings can be found in the tourist offices in Maó and Ciutadella, as well as in Menorca's daily newspaper, the *Menorca – Diario Insular*.

Ferry company details

Trasmediterranea Information and reservation line for all passenger enquiries within Spain and the Balearic Islands, ⓣ 902/454645, ⓦ *www.trasmediterranea.com*.

UK and Ireland agents for Trasmediterranea: Southern Ferries, First Floor, 179 Piccadilly, London W1V 9DB ⓣ 020/7491 4968, ⓕ 020/7491 3502.

Visas and red tape

British citizens need a valid passport to enter Spain for up to ninety days. Citizens of other EU countries (and Norway and Iceland) need only a valid national identity card. US, Australian, New Zealand and Canadian citizens don't need a visa, but do require a passport valid for the entire period of the visit – and can stay for up to ninety days. **Visa requirements** do change, however, and it is always advisable to check the current situation. For further information, contact your nearest embassy or consulate (see below).

Spanish embassies and consulates abroad

Australia 15 Arkana St, Yarralumla, Canberra, ACT 2600 (ⓣ 02/6273 3555); Level 24, 31 Market St, Sydney, NSW 2000 (ⓣ 02/9261 2433); 4th floor, 540 Elizabeth St, Melbourne, VIC 3000 (ⓣ 03/9347 1966).

Canada 74 Stanley Ave, Ottawa, Ontario K1M 1P4 (ⓣ 613/747 2252, ⓦ www.docuweb.ca/SpainIn Canada); 1 Westmount Square #1456, Montréal, Québec H3Z 2P9 (ⓣ 514/935 5235, ⓦ www.total.net/~consular/); Simcoe Place, 200 Front St, #2401, PO Box 15, Toronto, Ontario M5V 3K2 (ⓣ 416/977 1661).

Ireland 17A Merlyn Park, Ballsbridge, Dublin 4 (ⓣ 01/269 1640).

New Zealand No representation.

UK 39 Chesham Place, London SW1X 8SB (ⓣ 020/71235 5555); Suite 1a, Brook House, 70 Spring Gardens, Manchester M2 2BQ (ⓣ 0161/236 1213); 63 North Castle St, Edinburgh EH2 3LJ (ⓣ 0131/220 1843). Premium-rate visa-information line ⓣ 0891/600123.

USA 2375 Pennsylvania Ave NW, Washington, DC 20037 (ⓣ 202/728 2330); 150 E 58th St, New York, NY 10155 (ⓣ 212/355 4080); 545 Boylston St 803, Boston, MA 02116 (ⓣ 617/536 2506); 180 N Michigan Ave #1500, Chicago, IL 60601 (ⓣ 312/782 4588); 1800 Berins Drive #660, Houston, TX 77057 (ⓣ 713/783 6200); 5055 Wilshire Blvd #960, Los Angeles, CA 90036 (ⓣ 323/938 0158); ⓦ www.spainemb.org.

VISAS AND RED TAPE

21

Insurance

As an EU country, Spain has free reciprocal health agreements with other member states. To take advantage of this, British citizens will need to complete self-certification form E111, available over the counter from main post offices. Other EU countries have comparable forms. However, treatment within this scheme is only provided by practitioners within the Spanish healthcare system, the Instituto Nacional de la Salud, whereas most doctors on Menorca are more accustomed to – or only deal with – private insurance work. Taking out your own **travel insurance** means you won't have to hunt around for a doctor who will treat you for free, and will also cover the cost of items not within the EU scheme's purview, such as dental treatment and repatriation on medical grounds. It will usually also cover your baggage and tickets in case of theft, as long as you get a report from the local police. Non-EU residents will need to insure themselves for all eventualities, including medical costs. For further details of what to do and where to go in a medical emergency, see the section on "Health" (p.28).

If you need to make a claim, you should keep receipts for medicines and medical treatment, and in the event you have anything stolen, you must obtain an official statement from the police. Bank and **credit cards** often have certain levels

ROUGH GUIDE TRAVEL INSURANCE

Rough Guides now offers its own **travel insurance**, customized for our readers by a leading UK broker and backed by a Lloyd's underwriter. It is available to anyone, of any nationality, travelling anywhere in the world, and we are convinced that this is the best-value scheme you'll find.

There are two main Rough Guide insurance plans: Essential, for effective, no-frills cover, starting at £11.75 for two weeks; and Premier – more expensive but with more generous and extensive benefits. Each offers European or worldwide cover, and can be supplemented with a "Hazardous Activities Premium" if you plan to engage in sports considered dangerous, such as windsurfing or trekking. Unlike many policies, the Rough Guides schemes are calculated by the day, so if you're travelling for 27 days rather than a month, that's all you pay for. You can alternatively take out annual multi-trip insurance, which covers you for all your travel throughout the year (with a maximum of sixty days for any one trip).

For a policy quote, call the Rough Guide Insurance Line on UK freefone ☎0800/015 0906, US freefone ☎1-866/220 5588, or, if you're calling from elsewhere on (☎+44) 1243/621 046. Alternatively, get an online quote at ⓦ*www.roughguides. com/insurance*.

of medical or other insurance included and you may automatically get travel insurance if you use a major credit card to pay for your trip.

In the **UK and Ireland**, travel agents and tour operators are likely to require some sort of insurance when you book a package holiday. If you have a good all-risks home insurance policy it *may* cover your possessions against loss or theft even when overseas. Many private medical schemes such as BUPA or PPP also offer coverage plans for abroad, including baggage loss, cancellation or curtailment and cash replace-

INSURANCE

ment, as well as sickness or accident. **Americans** and **Canadians** should also check that they're not already covered. Canadian provincial health plans usually provide partial cover for medical mishaps overseas. Holders of official student/teacher/youth cards are entitled to meagre accident coverage and hospital in-patient benefits. Homeowners' or renters' insurance often covers theft or loss of documents, money and valuables while overseas, though conditions and maximum amounts vary from company to company. In **Australia** and **New Zealand**, travel insurance is put together by the airlines and travel agent groups (see p.14) in conjunction with insurance companies.

Information and maps

The **Spanish National Tourist Office (SNTO)** gives away a useful range of pamphlets and leaflets on Spain as a whole, but has precious little on Menorca. The exception is the booklet listing all the Balearic Islands' hotels, *hostals* and campgrounds. As this is printed in Madrid and can be difficult – if not impossible – to obtain on the island itself, it's best to get this from the tourist office before you go.

There are efficient year-round **tourist offices** in Menorca's two main towns, Maó and Ciutadella, and a seasonal office at the airport, but nowhere else. All three will provide free maps of Menorca, Maó and Ciutadella, plus leaflets detailing all sorts of island-wide practicalities – from bus and train timetables to lists of car-rental firms, ferry schedules and boat-excursion organizers. In addition, the island's own daily **newspaper**, the *Menorca – Diario Insular*, has a useful information page detailing the day's bus, boat and plane schedules.

SNTO offices abroad

General website:
Ⓦ *www.tourspain.es.*

Australasia c/o Spanish Tourism Promotions, 178 Collins St, Melbourne Ⓣ 03/9650 7377, Ⓔ *sales@ spanishtourism.com.au.*

Canada 2 Bloor St West, Suite 3402, Toronto, Ontario M4W 3E2 Ⓣ 416/961 3131, Ⓦ *www. docuweb.ca/SpaininCanada.*

UK 22–23 Manchester Square, London W1M 5AP. General enquiries Ⓣ 020/7486 8077; brochure requests, 24hr premium line Ⓣ 09063 /640630, Ⓦ *www.tourspain. co.uk.*

USA 666 Fifth Ave, New York, NY 10103 Ⓣ 212/265 8822, Ⓔ *nyork@tourspain.es*; Water Tower Place, Suite 915 East, 845 N Michigan Ave, Chicago, IL 60611 Ⓣ 312/642 1992, Ⓔ *chicago@tourspain.es*; 8383 Wilshire Blvd, Suite 960, Beverly Hills, Los Angeles, CA 90211 Ⓣ 323/658 7188, Ⓔ *losangeles@tourspain.es.*

MENORCA ON THE INTERNET

The **internet** has not, as yet, really taken off in Menorca. Currently, most sites originating from the island are rudimentary and many are not regularly updated. Furthermore, the majority are only available in Castilian (Spanish) or Catalan, though you can get help via any internet translation service – for Spanish try *babelfish.altavista.com/translate.dyn.*

 www.baleares.com A tourist guide to all the islands, but with a separate section for Menorca. The site's poorly presented, but the information it contains is good – once you find it.

Govern Balear *www.caib.es/kfcont.htm* The official site of the Balearic provincial government. A well-presented source of general information. The tourist information section is presented in several languages, including English, and has links to sites offering information on things like accommodation, eating and drinking and sports.

Maó City Council *www.mao-menorca.net* The island's capital has a surprisingly useful site with street maps, a guide to local places of interest, an events diary (although very out-of-date) and some suggested walks around the town. The whole site is available in both Spanish and English.

Menorca Virtual *www.menorcavirtual.com* A good starting point, this well-organized portal will link you to most of the Menorcan business and official websites. There's a high proportion of sites offering accommodation for rent, car rental and other potentially useful contacts. Many listings are in English, as well as Spanish.

Menorca-info *www.menorca-info.de* A German guide to the island, partly translated into Spanish and English. It's particularly useful for its comprehensive links to watersports activities, but also contains the more standard

listings of accommodation
and eateries.

**Spanish Meteorological
Institute Weather
Information** Ⓦ *www.inm.
es/wwb* A source of daily
weather forecasts for the
whole of Spain.

MAPS

For most visitors, the **maps** in this guide – possibly supplemented by the free maps issued by the tourist offices – will
suffice, though if you're planning to explore the islands'
nooks and crannies by bike or car, you'll need a more
detailed road map. The most detailed and up-to-date is the
Menorca (1:75,000) produced by Distrimapas Telstar; it's
produced in several languages – so be sure to get the
Catalan edition. The language of the map should be clearly
displayed, but if it isn't, check a couple of Catalan spellings
– Maó (Mahón in Castilian) and Port de Maó (Puerto de
Mahón in Castilian). The map shows all the island's major
and most of the minor roads, though sometimes it doesn't
effectively indicate which country lanes are easily driveable
and which aren't. It is sold at leading bookshops and many
larger newsagents for around 375ptas/€2.25, but is not
readily available outside of Menorca. To buy one before you
go, consult a specialist map shop.

Serious **hikers** are poorly provided for, as there are simply no really reliable hiking maps. The IGN (Instituto
Geográfico Nacional) issues **topographical maps** of the
Balearics at the 1:25,000 and 1:50,000 scales, based on an
aerial survey of 1979, but many minor roads and footpaths
simply don't appear and even crags and cliffs are not always
shown. Nevertheless, they are the best product on the market. IGN maps are available in island bookshops (such as the
two listed below) and newsagents, though supplies are not

INFORMATION AND MAPS

particularly consistent or reliable; it's best to purchase them before you go from a specialist map shop.

Map outlets/bookshops on Menorca

Maó

Librería Fundació, facing Plaça Colón at Costa de Sa Plaça 14 (Mon–Fri 9.30am–1.30pm & 5–8pm, Sat 9.30am–1.30pm; ☎ 971 363 543). Stocks a fair selection of English-language guidebooks and is strong on birdwatching guides. It also has general maps of Menorca – including the Distrimapas Telstar – plus a reasonable, though far from exhaustive, assortment of IGN walking maps.

Ciutadella

Punt i Apart, c/Roser 14, or Libreria Pau, c/Nou de Juliol 23. Good for island walking maps from the IGN series, as well as more general maps and travel books.

Health

No inoculations are required for Menorca and the only likely blight to your holiday may be an upset stomach or a ferocious hangover. To avoid the former, wash fruit and avoid *tapas* dishes that look like they were cooked last week. Many islanders also refrain from consuming mayonnaise during the summer.

If you should fall ill, for minor complaints it's easiest to go to a **farmàcia** – there are plenty of them and they're listed in the Menorca yellow pages (details of several in Maó and Ciutadella are given in the *Guide*. Pharmacists are highly trained, willing to give advice (often in English) and able to dispense a number of drugs which would be available only on prescription in many other countries. Most keep usual shop hours (ie 9am–1pm & 4–7pm), but in Maó some open late and at weekends, and a rota system keeps at least one open 24 hours a day. In theory at least, the rota is displayed in the window of every pharmacy, or you can check at reception in one of the better hotels. Outside the towns, you'll find a *farmàcia* in most of the larger villages, though there's not much chance of late-night opening or of an English-speaking pharmacist unless you're staying in a resort area. In more serious cases you can get the address of an **English-speaking doctor** from your consulate, hotel, local *farmàcia* or tourist office.

In medical **emergencies**, telephone the general emergency number, ☏112 and an ambulance will – if required – be dispatched. If you're reliant on free treatment within the EU health scheme, try to remember to make this clear to the ambulance staff and, if you're whisked off to hospital, to the medic you subsequently encounter. It's a good idea to hand over a photocopy of your E111 on arrival at hospital, or else you may be mistaken for a private insurance job and billed accordingly (see p.22 for more information on insurance). Hospital charges are as much as 25,000ptas/€150 per visit.

Dentists are all private – you'll pay around 6000ptas/€36.14 for having a cavity filled. A comprehensive list of *dentistas* can be found in the yellow pages, or ask at your hotel or *hostal* reception.

HEALTH

Condoms no longer need to be smuggled into Spain as they did during the Franco years. They're available from most *farmàcias*, and from all sorts of outlets – like bars and vending machines – in the resorts.

Money and costs

In terms of food, wine and transport, Menorca remains a budget destination for northern Europeans, North Americans and Australasians. However, Balearic hotel prices have increased considerably over the last few years, so independent travellers on any kind of budget will have to plan their accommodation carefully and, in summer, when vacant rooms are scarce, reserve well in advance.

The box on p.41 will give you general guidelines on accommodation prices. On average, if you're prepared to buy your own picnic lunch, stay in inexpensive *hostals* and hotels, and stick to the cheaper bars and restaurants, you could get by on around £20–25 (approximately US$30–35) a day per person. If you intend to stay in three-star hotels and eat at quality restaurants, then you'll need more like £50/$75 a day per person, with the main variable being the cost of your room – and bear in mind that room prices rise steeply as the season progresses. On £80/$120 a day and upwards, you'll be limited only by your energy reserves – unless you're planning to stay in a five-star hotel, in which case this figure won't even cover your bed. **Eating out** is excellent value, and even in a top-notch restaurant in Maó a superb meal will only set you back around £17/US$25 – though, of course, you may pay well over the odds for food and drink in the tourist resorts.

One other cost is **IVA**, a seven percent sales tax levied on most goods and services. In most cases, notices clearly indicate whether IVA is included in the price or not, but if you aren't certain – and especially on bigger purchases – be sure to ask; otherwise, especially in more expensive hotels and restaurants, you may be in for a bit of a shock.

MONEY AND THE EXCHANGE RATE

Spain is one of twelve European Union countries which have opted to join a single currency, the **euro** (€). The transition period, which began on January 1, 1999, is lengthy, however: euro notes and coins are not scheduled to be issued until January 1, 2002, with **pesetas** remaining in place for cash transactions, at a fixed rate of 166.386 pesetas to 1 euro, until they are scrapped entirely on February 28, 2002.

Even before euro cash appears in 2002 you can opt to pay in euros by credit card, and you can get travellers' cheques in euros. You should not be charged commission for changing them in any of the twelve countries in the euro zone. Neither should you be charged for changing from any of their old currencies to any other (Deutschmarks to pesetas, for example).

All prices in this book are given in both pesetas (ptas) and the euro equivalent. **Peseta coins** come in denominations of 1, 5, 10, 25, 50, 100, 200 and 500 pesetas; notes as 1000, 2000, 5000 and 10,000 pesetas. Once in circulation, the euro will come in coins of 1 to 50 cents, €1 and €2, and notes of €5 to €500.

The **exchange rate** for the peseta at the time of writing was around 260 to the pound sterling, 210 to the Irish punt, 190 to the US dollar, 130 to the Canadian dollar, 100 to the Australian dollar and 80 to the NZ dollar. You can take in as much money as you want (in any form), although amounts over five million pesetas must be declared; coming out, you'll need to declare sums over one million pesetas.

TRAVELLERS' CHEQUES, CREDIT CARDS AND BANKS

The most reliable way of carrying your money is in travellers' cheques, as they offer the security of knowing that lost or stolen cheques will be replaced. American Express cheques, sold through most North American, Australasian and European banks, are the most widely accepted cheques in Spain. When you cash your cheques, guard against outrageous **commissions** (usually they're 400–500ptas/€2.4–3 per transaction); if commission is waived, make sure that the exchange rate doesn't deteriorate drastically to compensate the bank.

Note also that many Visa, MasterCard and British bank/cash cards, as well as US cards, can be used for withdrawing cash from **ATMs** in Spain; check with your bank to find out about these reciprocal arrangements – the system is highly sophisticated and can often give instructions in a variety of languages. Make sure you have a personal identification number (PIN) that's designed to work overseas.

Credit cards are particularly useful for car rental, cash advances (though these attract a high rate of interest from the date of withdrawal) and hotel bills. American Express, Visa and MasterCard are all widely accepted.

Banks can be found in all but the smallest Menorcan village. **Opening hours** are generally Monday to Friday 9am–2pm and Saturday (except in summer) 9am–1pm.

Getting around

You're spoiled for choice when it comes to **transport** on the island. There's a reliable bus network between all the major settlements, reasonably priced taxis, a plethora of car-rental firms and plenty of bicycles and mopeds to rent. Distances are small and consequently the costs of travel limited, whether in terms of petrol or the price of a ticket. Indeed, Menorca's one and only major road, the C721, which traverses the island from Ciutadella in the west to Maó in the east, is just 45km long.

BUSES

The island's extensive network of **bus services** links the main towns – Maó and Ciutadella – with most of the villages and resorts of the coast and interior. These main bus

MENORCA BUS SERVICES

A bus **timetable** is readily available from most tourist offices and bus times are also detailed daily on page 2 of the island's newspaper, the *Menorca – Diario Insular*, available at all newsagents. The following, however, will give you some idea of frequency and journey times:

From **Ciutadella** to: Alaior (Mon–Sat 6 daily, 4 on Sun; 40min); Cala Blanca (May–Oct hourly, Nov–April 2–4 daily; 15min); Cala en Forcat (May–Oct hourly, Nov–April 2–4 daily; 15min); Cap d'Artrutx (May–Oct hourly, Nov–April 2–4 daily; 25min); Es Mercadal (Mon–Sat 6 daily, 4 on Sun; 30min); Ferreries (Mon–Sat 8 daily, 5 on Sun; 20min); Maó (Mon–Sat 6 daily, 4 on Sun; 1hr); Sant Tomàs (May–Oct Mon–Fri 1 daily; 40min).

From **Es Mercadal** to: Fornells (May–Oct Mon–Fri 1 daily; Nov–April 1 daily on four days a week; 15min).

From **Es Migjorn Gran** to: Ferreries (1 daily; 15min); Maó (1 daily; 45min).

routes are supplemented by more intermittent local services between smaller towns and between neighbouring resorts. Ticket **prices** are reasonable: the one-way fare from Maó to Ciutadella is just 575ptas/€3.46. On all island bus services, destinations are marked on the front of the bus. Passengers enter the bus at the front and buy tickets from the driver, unless they've been bought in advance at a bus station. Bus stops are mostly indicated with the word *parada*. All the island's buses are operated by Transportes Menorca. Information on journey times and frequency of services is given in the box above. The Catalan words to look out for on timetables are *diari* (daily), *feiners* (workdays, including Saturday), *diumenge* (Sunday) and *festius* (holidays).

From **Ferreries** to: Alaior (Mon–Sat 6 daily, 4 on Sun; 20min); Cala Santa Galdana (May–Oct 10 daily; 20min); Ciutadella (Mon–Sat 6 daily, 4 on Sun; 20min); Es Mercadal (Mon–Sat 6 daily, 4 on Sun; 10min); Es Migjorn Gran (1 daily; 15min); Maó (Mon–Sat 6 daily, 4 on Sun; 40min).

From **Fornells** to: Es Mercadal (May–Oct Mon–Fri 1 daily; Nov–April 1 daily on four days a week; 15min); Maó (May–Oct 2 daily except on Sun; Nov–April 2 daily on four days a week; 35min).

From **Maó** to: Alaior (Mon–Sat 6 daily, 4 on Sun; 20min); Arenal d'en Castell (May–Oct 1–2 daily except on Sun; Nov–April 1 daily on four days a week; 20min); Ciutadella (Mon–Sat 6 daily, 4 on Sun; 1hr); Es Mercadal (Mon–Sat 6 daily, 4 on Sun; 30min); Es Migjorn Gran (1 daily; 45min); Ferreries (Mon–Sat 6 daily, 4 on Sun; 40min); Fornells (May–Oct 1–2 daily except on Sun; Nov–April 1 daily on four days a week; 35min); Sant Tomàs (May–Oct Mon–Sat 1 daily; 35min); Son Bou (May–Oct 5 daily; 35min); Son Parc (May–Oct 1–2 daily except on Sun; Nov–April 1 daily on four days a week; 35min).

On the whole, buses are reliable and comfortable enough. The only significant problem is that some country towns and villages do not have a bus station or even a clearly marked *parada*, which can be very confusing, as in some places buses leave from the most obscure parts of town.

TAXIS

The excellence of the island's bus services means it's rarely necessary to take a **taxi**, though it is a fast and easy way of reaching your resort from the airport and, perhaps more importantly, of getting back to your hotel after a day's hiking. In the latter case, you should arrange collection details

GETTING AROUND

before you set out – there's no point wandering round a tiny village hoping a taxi will show. Local journeys are all metered, though there are supplementary charges for each piece of luggage and for night and Sunday travel. For longer journeys there are official prices, which are displayed at some taxi stands and are available at both Maó and the airport tourist office. Naturally, you're well advised to check the price with the driver *before* you set out. Fares are reasonable, but not cheap: the journey from the airport to downtown Maó, a distance of around 5km, will cost you in the region of 1200ptas/€7.22, Maó to Ciutadella (45km) 5700ptas/€34.33 and Maó to Fornells 3900ptas/€23.49.

DRIVING AND VEHICLE RENTAL

Getting around on public transport is easy enough, but you'll obviously have a great deal more freedom if you have your own vehicle and, predictably, most of the more secluded (and attractive) beaches are only accessible under your own steam. Major roads are generally good, though side roads are very variable – unpaved minor roads are particularly lethal after rain. Signage is variable too: all major roads are well and clearly signed, but out in the sticks – especially in the network of country lanes in central Menorca – signs are few and far between. The principle here seems to be that signs are unnecessary, as everyone knows the way, don't they. This can be considered a charming reminder of an earlier, pre-tourist era – but it's hard to feel much warmth when you are completely lost.

Fuel (*gasolina*) comes in three main grades. Different companies use different brand names, but generally Super Plus is 97-octane fuel, selling at about 155ptas/€0.93 per litre, and Super is 95-octane, equivalent to four-star in the UK, selling at about 144ptas/€0.86 per litre, and always without lead (*sense plom*). Diesel (*gasoleo* or *gasoil*) costs about 130ptas/€0.78 per litre.

Throughout Menorca speed **limits** are posted – the maximum on urban roads is 60kph, on other roads 80kph – and on the main highway, the C721 from Maó to Ciutadella, speed traps are not infrequent. If you're stopped for any violation, the Spanish police can (and usually will) levy a stiff on-the-spot fine of up to 10,000ptas/€60 before letting you go on your way, their draconian instincts reinforced by the fact that few tourists are likely to appear in court to argue the case. Most **driving rules** and regulations are pretty standard (seat belts are compulsory and "Stop" signs mean exactly that), but remember that a single, unbroken white line in the middle of the road means no overtaking, even if the rule is frequently ignored. You yield to traffic coming from the right at all junctions, whether or not there's a giveway sign; and be prepared for road signs that give very little, if any, warning of the turning you might require. On busier roads, turnings that take vehicles across oncoming traffic are being phased out and replaced by semicircular minor exits that lead round to traffic lights on the near side of the major road. Finally, drivers do not have to stop (and usually don't) at zebra crossings, which merely indicate a suitable pedestrian crossing place. If you come to an abrupt stop at a crossing, as you might do in Britain, the pedestrians will be amazed and someone may well crash into your rear end. The exceptions are in the case of ramped zebra crossings and – of course – where there's a stop light connected to the crossing. As ever, don't drink and drive.

CAR RENTAL

Dozens of companies offer **car rental** (still rendered in Castilian, *coches de alquiler*): most of the major international players have outlets, and a bevy of small companies make up

the remainder. Several useful addresses are given at the Maó and Ciutadella "Getting around" accounts, and comprehensive lists are available from the island's tourist offices. To rent a car, you need to be 21 or over (and have been driving for at least a year), and you'll probably need a credit card – though some places will accept a hefty deposit in cash and some smaller companies simply ignore all the normal regulations. If you're planning to spend much time driving the island's rougher tracks, you'll probably be better off with a moped, or even a four-wheel drive (about thirty percent more expensive than the average car and available from larger rental agencies).

Rental **charges** vary enormously: out-of-season costs for a standard car can come down to as little as 2000ptas/€12 per day with unlimited mileage; in July and August, by comparison, the same basic vehicle could set you back 6000ptas/€36.14 a day (though weekly prices are slightly better value, and special rates operate at the weekend). The big companies all offer competitive rates, but you can often get a better deal through someone in contact with local vehicle rental firms, such as Autos Abroad (see below). **Fly-drive** deals are well worth investigating. In Britain, for example, Iberia offers Avis cars from around £100 a week in the low season, £170 in high season, as long as you book your flight with them.

Car rental companies

GETTING AROUND

UK

Autos Abroad ⓣ 0870/066 7788, ⓦ www.autosabroad. co.uk.

Avis ⓣ 0870/606 0100, ⓦ www.avisworld.com.

Budget ⓣ 0800/181181, ⓦ www.go-budget.co.uk.

Europcar ⓣ 0845/722 2525, ⓦ www.europcar.com.

Hertz ⓣ 0870/844 8844, ⓦ www.hertz.co.uk.

Holiday Autos ⓣ 0870/400
0000, ⓦ *www.holiday
autos.com*.
National ⓣ 0870/536 5365,
ⓦ *www.
nationalcar-europe.com*.
Thrifty ⓣ 01494/751600,
ⓦ *www.thrifty.co.uk*.

Republic of Ireland
Avis ⓣ 01/605 7555,
ⓦ *www.avis.com*.
Budget ⓣ 1850/575757,
ⓦ *www.budget.ie*.
Europcar ⓣ 01/614 2800,
ⓦ *www.europcar.ie*.
Hertz ⓣ 01/676 7476,
ⓦ *www.hertz.com*.
Holiday Autos ⓣ 01/872 9366,
ⓦ *www.holidayautos.com*.

North America
Avis International ⓣ 1-800/331
1084, ⓦ *www.avis.com*.
Budget ⓣ 1-800/527 0700,
ⓦ *www.budget.com*.
Hertz International
ⓣ 1-800/654 3001,
ⓦ *www.hertz.com*.

Australia and New Zealand
Avis, Australia ⓣ 13/6333;
New Zealand ⓣ 0800/655111;
ⓦ *www.avis.com*.
Hertz, Australia
ⓣ 1800/550067;
New Zealand ⓣ 0800/655955;
ⓦ *www.hertz.com*.

MOPED RENTAL

Widely available, **mopeds** are a popular means of transport,
especially for visiting remoter spots. Prices start at about
2000ptas/€12 per day, including insurance and crash hel-
mets, which must be worn. Be warned, however, that the
insurance often excludes theft – always check with the
company first. You will generally be asked to show some
kind of driving licence (particularly for mopeds over 50cc),
and to leave a deposit on your credit card, though most
places will accept cash as an alternative. We've listed names
and addresses of rental companies throughout the *Guide*
where most appropriate; in addition, tourist offices on the
island will provide comprehensive lists of suppliers.

GETTING AROUND

CYCLING

Cycling can be an inexpensive and flexible way of getting around Menorca, and of seeing a great deal of the countryside that would otherwise pass you by. The Spanish are keen cycling fans, which means that you'll be well received and find reasonable facilities. In general terms, the island is – give or take the odd hill and ravine – comparatively flat. In addition, traffic is passably light once you're off the main arterial roads. **Renting a bike** is straightforward, as there are dozens of suppliers (there's usually at least one in every resort), and tourist offices will provide a list or advise you of the nearest outlet; we've also listed a few in the *Guide*. As for **costs**, a mountain bike will cost around 1200ptas/€7 a day, 7000ptas/€42.16 for a week. Ordinary bicycles are a good deal cheaper – reckon on about 900ptas/€5.42 a day, 5000ptas/€30.12 for the week.

Accommodation

Although package-tour operators have a virtual stranglehold on thousands of hotel rooms, villas and apartments in Menorca, reasonably priced rooms are still available to the independent traveller. Options are severely limited, however, at the height of the season. Off season, you should be able to get a simple, medium-sized double room with shower and sink for around 3500ptas/€21, whereas in August the same double, if available, can set you back as much as 6000ptas/€36.14 – though this still compares reasonably well with much of the rest of Europe. You can, however, comfortably spend 15,000ptas/€90 and upwards in hotels with three or more stars – some of them being very firmly in the super-luxury class.

Vacant rooms are at their scarcest from late June to early September, when advance **reservations** are strongly recommended. Most hoteliers speak at least a modicum of English, so visitors who don't speak Catalan or Spanish can usually book over the phone, but a confirming letter, fax or email is always a good idea. The easiest places to get a room are Maó and Ciutadella, with Fornells lagging some way behind.

ACCOMMODATION PRICE CODES

After each accommodation entry in this guide you'll find a symbol that corresponds to one of nine price categories. These categories represent the minimum you can expect to pay for a double room in high season; for a single room, expect to pay around two-thirds the price of a double. Note that in the more upmarket *hostals* and *pensions*, and in anything calling itself a hotel, you'll pay a tax (IVA) of seven percent on top of the room price.

❶ Under 3000ptas/€18
❷ 3000–4000ptas/€18–24
❸ 4000–6000ptas/€24–36
❹ 6000–8000ptas/€36–48
❺ 8000–10,000ptas/€48–60
❻ 10,000–14,000ptas/€60–84
❼ 14,000–20,000ptas/€84–120
❽ 20,000–25,000ptas/€120–150
❾ Over 25,000ptas/€150

ACCOMMODATION

It's often worth **bargaining** over room prices outside peak season and at fancier hotels, since the posted tariff doesn't necessarily mean much. Many hotels have rooms at different prices, and tend to offer the more expensive ones first. Families can make real savings by asking for a room with three or four beds – most hotels offer larger rooms at not a great deal more than the double-room price. On the other hand, people travelling alone invariably get the rough end of the stick. We've detailed where to find places to stay in most of the destinations listed in the *Guide*, from the most basic of rooms to luxury hotels, and given a price range for each (see box on p.41). We've also indicated where an establishment closes over the winter – this is common (but not universal) practice in all the resorts.

Finally, note that the **stars** the Spanish government allocates to accommodation in all the different categories are only useful as a general guideline. Establishments tend to be assessed in terms of facilities rather than aesthetics, so, for example, a basic hotel in a workaday area of Maó might be allocated three stars, whereas a fine old mansion nearby might end up with two.

FONDAS, CASAS DE HUÉSPEDES, PENSIONS, HOSTALS AND HOTELS

There is an elaborate diversity of types of places to stay on Menorca – though in practice the various categories often overlap. The least expensive places are **fondas**, **casas de huéspedes** and **pensions** (*pensiones* in Castilian), though in fact, these are few and far between on the island. Food is usually served at *fondas* and *pensions* (some will only rent rooms on a meals-inclusive basis), while *casas de huéspedes* – literally "guesthouses" – are often used as long-term lodgings. Confusingly, the name of many *pensions* does not

ACCOMMODATION SIGNS

The various categories of accommodation in Spain are identifiable by square blue signs inscribed with the following letters in white.

F fonda

CH casa de huéspedes

P pensió

Hˢ hostal

HRˢ hostal-residencia

H hotel

follow their designation – lots of *pensions* call themselves *hostals* and vice versa. As a result, the name isn't always a reliable guide to the establishment's price, though the sign outside usually is (see box above).

Slightly more expensive are **hostals** (*hostales* in Castilian) and **hostal-residencias**, categorized from one to three stars; a one-star *hostal* generally costs about the same as a *pensió*. Many *hostals* offer good, functional rooms, often with a private shower; the *residencia* designation means that no meals other than breakfast are served.

A notch up the scale, **hotels** are also star-graded by the authorities, from one to five stars. One-star hotels cost no more than three-star *hostals* (sometimes they're cheaper), but at three stars you pay a lot more, and at four or five you're in the luxury class with prices to match.

It's safe to assume that bedrooms in a hotel will be adequately clean and furnished, but in the lower categories you're well advised to ask to see the room before you part with any money. Standards vary greatly between places in

ACCOMMODATION

the same category (even between rooms in the same *hostal*) and it does no harm to check that there's hot water if there's supposed to be, or that you're not being stuck at the back in an airless box.

A word about **complaints**: by law, each establishment must display its room rates and there should be a card on the room door showing the prices for the various seasons. If you think you're being overcharged, take it up first with the management; you can usually produce an immediate resolution by asking for one of the *hojas de reclamaciones* (complaints forms) that all places are obliged by law to keep. The threat of filling in a form is usually in itself enough to make the proprietor back down.

FINCAS

Many of Menorca's old stone **fincas** (farmhouses) have been snaffled up for use as second homes, and some are now leased by the owners to package-tour operators for the whole or part of the season; The Magic of Spain (see p.6) has one of the best selections. Alternatively – and preferably well in advance of your holiday – you might consider approaching the Associació Agroturisme Balear, Avgda Gabriel Alomar i Villalonga 8A–2A, 07006 Palma, Mallorca (℡971 721 508, ℱ971 717 317, ⓦ*agroturismo@mallorcanet. com*), which issues a booklet detailing most of the finest *fincas* and takes bookings. Some of the *fincas* are very luxurious and situated in remote, beautiful spots – though others form part of a working farm – and they're not cheap: prices range from 6000ptas/€36.14 to 12,000ptas/€72 per person per night, and a minimum length of stay is often stipulated.

CAMPING

There are just two official **campsites** (*càmpings*) on Menorca: the well-appointed *Son Bou*, a Class 1C establishment just outside the south-coast resort of Son Bou, and the plainer *S'Atalaia*, a Class 3C campground, near the resort of Cala Santa Galdana. The Son Bou can accommodate about four hundred campers, the *S'Atalaia* just one hundred – and both take tents, trailer caravans and motor caravans. Although neither has a seashore location, they are both very popular, heaving with campers in the height of the summer, when it's best to make a reservation well ahead of time. Prices and specific details of each site are given in the relevant chapters (see p.144 and p.159).

Backcountry camping is legal, but not encouraged, and has various restrictions attached. Spanish regulations state that you're not allowed to camp "in urban areas, areas prohibited for military or touristic reasons, or within 1km of an official campsite". What this means in effect is that you can't camp on resort beaches (though there is some latitude if you're discreet), but you can camp out almost anywhere in the countryside, providing you act sensitively and use some common sense. Whenever possible, ask locally first and/or get the permission of the landowner.

Eating and drinking

Traditional Balearic **food** has much in common with Catalan food and is far from delicate, but its hearty soups and stews, seafood dishes and spiced meats can be delicious. In common with other areas of Spain, this regional cuisine has, after many years of neglect, experienced something of a renaissance, and nowadays restaurants offering *Cuina Menorquína* (Castilian *Cocina Menorquína*) are comparatively commonplace and should not be missed. Neither should a visit to one of the island's many pastry shops (*pastelerias/pastisserias*), where you'll find the sweetest of confections and the Balearics' gastronomic pride and joy, *ensaimadas* (spiralled flaky pastries).

Most restaurants, cafés and bars have **multilingual** menus (including English), but out in the sticks, in the cheaper cafés and restaurants, there may only be a **Catalan** (or Castilian) menu, or maybe no menu at all, in which case the waiter will rattle off the day's dishes in Catalan. Though Catalan is the islands' first language, Castilian (ie Spanish) is also used or understood by almost all restaurateurs. With these factors in mind, we've given the **Castilian** names alongside the Catalan names in this section wherever it's useful.

CAFÉS, BARS AND RESTAURANTS

Across the island, the distinction between **cafés** (or *cafeterias*) and **restaurants** is blurred. The bulk serve both light snacks and full meals, with the best deals often appearing as the *menú del día* (menu of the day). This consists of three or four courses, including bread, wine and service, and usually costs 1000–1500ptas/€6–9. At either end of the market, however, the differences become more pronounced: in the more expensive restaurants, there is usually a *menú del día*, but the emphasis is on à la carte; by contrast, the least expensive cafés only serve up simple snacks, and in their turn are often indistinguishable from the island's **bars**, also known as *cellers* or *tavernas*. Before the tourist boom, these snacks always consisted of traditional dishes prepared as either *tapas* (small snacks) or *racions* (larger ones). Today, it's often chips, pizzas and sandwiches, though *tapas* have become increasingly popular with tourists in the last three or four years. This has produced one or two anomalies: some cafés, bars and restaurants sell *tapas* that are in fact full meals, and *racions* per se have all but disappeared. The prime spot for traditional (ie smallish) *tapas* is Maó, where a reasonably lively *tapas* scene allows you to move from place to place sampling a wide range of local specialities. A *tapas* portion on average costs 700–900ptas/€4.2–5.4.

MENORCAN CUISINE

In terms of **cuisine**, many restaurants, *cafeterias* and bars, especially those in the resort areas, are reliant on the tourist industry and many ignore the strong flavours of traditional Balearic and Spanish food for the blandness of pizzas, hamburgers and pastas, or else dish up a hotchpotch of sanitized local favourites such as omelettes, paella and grilled meats. However, there are still plenty of places – highlighted in the

Guide – where the food is more distinctive and flavour-some. Fresh **fish and seafood** can be excellent, though it's almost always expensive – much of it is imported, despite the local fishing industries around the Balearics and on the Catalan coast. Nevertheless, you're able to get hake, cod (often salted) and squid at very reasonable prices, while fish stews and rice-based *paellas* are often truly memorable. **Meat** can be outstanding too, usually either grilled and served with a few fried potatoes or salad, or – like ham – cured or dried and served as a starter or in sandwiches. Veal is common, served in stews, while poultry is often mixed with seafood (chicken and prawns) or fruit (chicken/duck with prunes/pears).

Vegetables rarely amount to more than a few chips or boiled potatoes with the main dish, though there are some splendid vegetable concoctions to watch out for, such as *tumbet* (pepper, potato, pumpkin and aubergine stew with tomato purée). It's more usual to start your meal with a **salad**, either a standard green or mixed affair, or one of the island's own salad mixtures, which come garnished with various vegetables, meats and cheeses. **Dessert** in the cheaper places is nearly always fresh **fruit** or *flam*, the local version of *crème caramel*; look out also for *crema Catalana*, with a caramelized sugar coating, the Catalan version of *crème brûlée*, and *música*, dried fruit-and-nut cake.

BREAKFAST, SNACKS AND SANDWICHES

Unless you're staying in a top-flight hotel or marooned in a resort, **breakfast** is best taken in a bar or café. A traditional Balearic breakfast (or lunch) dish is *pa amb tomàquet* (*pan con tomate* in Castilian) – a massive slice of bread rubbed with tomato, olive oil and garlic, which you can also have topped with ham – washed down with a flagon of wine. *Pa amb oli* (bread rubbed with olive oil) arrives in similar style, but dispenses with the tomato. If that sounds like gastric madness, other breakfast standbys are *torradas* (*tostadas*; toasted rolls) with oil or butter and jam, and *xocolata amb xurros* (*chocolate con churros*) – long, fried tubular doughnuts that you dip into thick drinking chocolate. Most places also serve *ou ferrat* (*huevo frito*; fried egg) and cold *truita* (*tortilla*; omelette), both of which make an excellent breakfast.

Coffee and **pastries** (*pastas*), particularly croissants and doughnuts, are available at some bars and cafés, though for a wider selection of cakes you should head for a *pastisseria* (pastry shop) or *forn* (bakery), which have an excellent reputation here as in the rest of Spain. These often sell a wide array of appetizing baked goods besides the obvious bread, croissants and *ensaimadas*. For ordering coffee see "Soft drinks and hot drinks" (p.61).

Some bars specialize in **sandwiches** (*bocadillos*), both hot and cold, and as they're usually outsize affairs in French bread they'll do for breakfast or lunch. In a bar with *tapas* (see below), you can have most of what's on offer put in a sandwich, and you can often get sandwiches prepared at grocery shops too. Menorcan cheese (*formatge*) is a real island favourite and comes in various stages of maturity.

TIPPING AND OPENING HOURS

In all but the most rock-bottom establishments it is customary to leave a small **tip**; the amount is up to you, though ten to fifteen percent of the bill is sufficient. Service is normally included in a *menú del día*. The other thing to take account of is **IVA**, a sales tax of seven percent, which is either included in the given prices (in which case it should say so on the menu) or added to your bill at the end.

Opening hours vary but, as a general rule, cafés and *tapas* bars open from around 9am until at least early in the evening, many till late at night; restaurants are open from

SNACKS AND TAPAS

Some common fillings for bocadillos are:

Catalan	Castilian	English
Butifarra	*Butifarra*	Catalan sausage
Cuixot dolç	*Jamón York*	Cooked ham
Formatge	*Queso*	Cheese
Llom	*Lomo*	Loin of pork
Pernil salat	*Jamón serrano*	Cured ham
Salami	*Salami*	Salami
Salxitxó	*Salchichón*	Sausage
Tonyina	*Atún*	Tuna
Truita	*Tortilla*	Omelette
Xoriç	*Chorizo*	Spicy sausage

Tapas and racions

Catalan	Castilian	English
Anxoves	*Boquerones*	Anchovies
Bollit	*Cocido*	Stew
Calamars	*Calamares*	Squid, usually deep fried in rings
Calamars amb tinta	*Calamares en su tinta*	Squid in ink
Cargols	*Caracoles*	Snails, often served in a spicy sauce
Cargols de mar	*Berberechos*	Cockles
Calamarins	*Chipirones*	Whole baby squid
Carn amb salsa	*Carne en salsa*	Meat in tomato sauce
Croqueta	*Croqueta*	Fish or chicken croquet
Empanada petita	*Empanadilla*	Fish/meat pasty
Ensalada Russa	*Ensaladilla*	Russian salad (diced vegetables in mayonnaise)

Catalan	Castilian	English
Escalibada	*Escalibada*	Aubergine and pepper salad
Faves	*Habas*	Broad beans
Faves amb cuixot	*Habas con jamón*	Beans with ham
Fetge	*Hígado*	Liver
Gambes	*Gambas*	Prawns
Musclos	*Mejillones*	Mussels (steamed, or served with diced tomatoes and onion)
Navallas	*Navajas*	Razor clams
Olives	*Aceitunas*	Olives
Ou bollit	*Huevo cocido*	Hard-boiled egg
Patates amb all i oli	*Patatas alioli*	Potatoes in mayonnaise
Patates cohentes	*Patatas bravas*	Fried potato cubes with spicy sauce and mayonnaise
Pilotes	*Albóndigas*	Meatballs
Pinxo	*Pincho moruno*	Kebab
Pop	*Pulpo*	Octopus
Prebes	*Pimientos*	Peppers
Ronyons amb Xeres	*Riñones al Jerez*	Kidneys in sherry
Sardines	*Sardinas*	Sardines
Sípia	*Sepia*	Cuttlefish
Tripa	*Callos*	Tripe
Truita Espanyola	*Tortilla Española*	Potato omelette
Truita Francesa	*Tortilla Francesa*	Plain omelette
Tumbet	*Tumbet*	Pepper, potato, pumpkin and aubergine stew with tomato purée
Xampinyons	*Champiñones*	Mushrooms, usually fried in garlic
Xoriç	*Chorizo*	Spicy sausage

EATING AND DRINKING

BALEARIC DISHES AND SPECIALITIES

Many of the specialities that follow come from the Balearics' shared history with Catalunya (Catalonia). The more elaborate fish and meat dishes are generally found in fancier restaurants.

Cocaroll	Pastry containing vegetables and fish
Ensaimada	Flaky spiral pastry with fillings such as *cabello de ángel* (sweetened citron rind)
Panades sobrasada	Pastry with peas, meat or fish

Soup (Sopa)

Carn d'olla	Mixed meat soup
Escudella	Mixed vegetable soup
Sopa d'all	Garlic soup
Sopas Mallorquínas	Vegetable soup, sometimes with meat and chick peas

Salad (Amanida)

Amanida Catalana	Salad with sliced meat and cheese
Escalivada	Aubergine, pepper and onion salad
Esqueixada	Dried cod salad with peppers, tomatoes, onions and olives

Starters

Entremesos	Hors d'oeuvres of mixed meat and cheese
Espinacs a la Catalana	Spinach with raisins and pine nuts
Fideus a la cassola	Baked vermicelli with meat
Llenties guisades	Stewed lentils

| *Samfaina* | Ratatouille-like stew of onions, peppers, aubergine and tomato |
| *Truita (d'alls tendres de xampinyons, de patates)* | Omelette/tortilla (with garlic, mushrooms or potato); don't order trout (*truita*) by mistake – ask for a tortilla |

Rice dishes

Arròs negre	"Black rice", cooked with squid ink
Arròs a banda	Rice with seafood, the rice served separately
Arròs a la marinera	Paella: rice with seafood and saffron
Paella a la Catalana	Mixed meat and seafood paella; Catalana sometimes distinguished from a seafood paella by being called *Paella a Valencia*

Meat (Carn)

Albergínies en es forn	Stuffed aubergines with grilled meat
Botifarra amb mongetes	Spicy blood sausage with white beans
Conill (all i oli)	Rabbit (with garlic mayonnaise)
Escaldum	Chicken and potato stew in an almond sauce
Estofat de vedella	Veal stew
Fetge	Liver
Fricandó	Veal casserole
Frito Mallorquín	Pigs' offal, potatoes and onions cooked with oil
Mandonguilles	Meatballs, usually in a sauce with peas
Perdius a la vinagreta	Partridge in vinegar gravy
Pollastre (farcit, amb gambas, al cava)	Chicken (stuffed, with prawns, or cooked in cava)

Continues over

Porc (rostit)	Pork (roast)
Sobrasada	Finely minced pork sausage, with paprika

Fish (Peix) and shellfish (marisc)

Bacallà (amb samfaina)	Dried cod (with ratatouille)
Caldereta de llagosta	Lobster stew
Cloïsses	Clams, often steamed
Espinagada de Sa Pobla	Turnover filled with spinach and eel
Greixonera de peix	Menorcan fish stew, cooked in a pottery casserole
Guisat de peix	Fish and shellfish stew
Llagosta (amb pollastre)	Lobster (with chicken in a rich sauce)
Lluç	Hake, a common dish either fried or grilled
Musclos al vapor	Steamed mussels
Pop	Octopus
Rap a l'all cremat	Monkfish with creamed garlic sauce
Sarsuela	Fish and shellfish stew
Suquet	Fish casserole
Tonyina	Tuna
Truita	Trout (sometimes stuffed with ham, a la Navarre)

Sauces and terms

Salsa mahonesa	Mayonnaise
Allioli	Garlic mayonnaise
Salsa romesco	Spicy tomato and wine sauce to accompany fish (from Tarragona)
A la planxa/a la brasa	Grilled
Rostit	Roast
Fregit/frit	Fried
Farcit	Stuffed/rolled
Guisat	Casserole

EATING AND DRINKING

Desserts (Postres)

Arròs amb llet	Rice pudding
Crema Catalana	Crème caramel
Gelat	Ice cream
Mel i mató	Curd cheese and honey
Postres de músic	Cake of dried fruit and nuts
Turrón	Almond fudge
Xurros	Deep-fried doughnut sticks (served with hot chocolate)
Yogur	Yoghurt

Market shopping

Vegetables (Verdures/Llegumes)

Albergínies	Aubergines
Cebes	Onions
Concombre	Cucumber
Espàrrecs	Asparagus
Mongetes	Beans
Pastanagues	Carrots
Patates	Potatoes
Pèsols	Peas
Tomàquets	Tomatoes
Xampinyons	Mushrooms

Fruit (Fruita)

Maduixes	Strawberries
Meló	Melon
Pera	Pear
Pinya	Pineapple
Plàtan	Banana
Poma	Apple
Préssec	Peach
Raïm	Grapes
Taronja	Orange

EATING AND DRINKING

around noon until 2, 3 or sometimes 4pm, before reopening in the evening from around 6pm or 7pm – 7pm or 8pm in winter – until 10pm or 11pm. Those restaurants with their eye on the tourist trade often stay open all day and can be relied upon on Sundays, when many local spots close. **Reservations** are rarely essential, but popular spots are best booked ahead of time: where it's advisable, we have said so in the *Guide*.

WINE

Wine (*vi* in Catalan, *vino* in Castilian), either red (*negre*, *tinto*), white (*blanc*, *blanco*) or rosé (*rosada*, *rosado*), is the invariable accompaniment to every meal and is, as a rule, inexpensive. In bars, cafés and budget restaurants, it may be whatever comes out of the barrel, or the house bottled special (ask for *vi/vino de la casa*). In a bar, a small glass of wine will generally cost anything from 60ptas/€0.3 to 160ptas/€1; in a restaurant, prices start at around 750ptas/€4.5 a bottle, and even in the poshest of places you'll be able to get a bottle of house wine for under 2500ptas/€15. If you're having the *menú del día*, house wine will be included in the price.

Across Menorca, all the more expensive restaurants, the supermarkets, and some of the cheaper cafés and restaurants carry a good selection of Spanish wines. The thing to check for is the appellation **Denominació d'Origen (DO)**, which indicates the wine has been passed as of sufficiently high quality by the industry's watchdog, the Instítuto Nacional de Denominaciónes d'Origen (INDO). Over forty regions of Spain currently carry DO status, including the north central region that produces Spain's most famous and widely distributed **red wine**, **Rioja**. Even though there's now a profusion of reds being produced all over the country, it's hard to match Rioja for reliability and finesse.

SOME COMMON CATALAN AND CASTILIAN FOOD TERMS

English	Catalan	Castilian
Basics		
Bread	*Pa*	*Pan*
Butter	*Mantega*	*Mantequilla*
Cheese	*Formatge*	*Queso*
Eggs	*Ous*	*Huevos*
Oil	*Oli*	*Aceite*
Pepper	*Pebre*	*Pimienta*
Salt	*Sal*	*Sal*
Sugar	*Sucre*	*Azúcar*
Vinegar	*Vinagre*	*Vinagre*
Garlic	*All*	*Ajo*
Rice	*Arròs*	*Arroz*
Fruit	*Fruita*	*Fruta*
Meals		
to have breakfast	*Esmorzar*	*Desayunar*
to have lunch	*Dinar*	*Almorzar*
to have dinner	*Sopar*	*Cenar*
In the restaurant		
Menu	*Menú*	*Carta*
Bottle	*Ampolla*	*Botella*
Glass	*Got*	*Vaso*
Fork	*Forquilla*	*Tenedor*
Knife	*Ganivet*	*Cuchillo*
Spoon	*Cullera*	*Cuchara*
Table	*Taula*	*Mesa*
The bill	*El compte*	*La cuenta*

EATING AND DRINKING

The wines are generally made of the *tempranillo* and *garnacha* grapes and are classified according to their age. At one end of the scale, *joven* indicates a young, inexpensive, straightforward wine which has spent no time in wood. Wines labelled *con crianza* (with breeding) or *reserva* have received respectively moderate and generous ageing in oak casks and in the bottle. At the top of the scale, in both price and quality, are the *gran reserva* wines, which are only produced in the best years and which have to spend at least two years in the cask followed by three in the bottle before being offered for sale. The names to look for in red Rioja include **Martínez-Bujanda**, **Tondonia** and **Monte Real**.

The region of **Navarra** also produces excellent wine using similar techniques and grape varieties at a fraction of the price. The labels to watch for here are **Chivite** and **Señorío de Sarría**. The wines that have attracted most attention recently are the reds of the **Ribera del Duero** region, 120km north of Madrid, with wines such as **Protos, Viña Pedrosa** and **Pesquera** offering the smooth integration of fruit and oak that is the hallmark of good Spanish wine.

Spain's **white wines** have not enjoyed the same reputation as the reds. Traditionally, they tended to be highly alcoholic and over-oaked. Spain's best white, the **Rioja Blanca** made by **Marquès de Murrieta**, descends from this tradition, but it offers a smooth-tasting marriage of oak and lemony fruit. The demands of the export market have recently led to new approaches to white wine-making, and the result has been clean, fruity and dry wines that tend to be competent rather than memorable. The best of this style has to be **Marquès de Riscal Blanco** from Rueda, just south of Valladolid.

Spain's growing reputation for **sparkling wine** is built on the performance of two producers, Freixenet and Codorníu, which hail from a small area west of Barcelona.

Local grape varieties are used and the best examples, known as **cava**, are made by the same double-fermentation process as is used in champagne production.

OTHER ALCOHOLIC DRINKS

Fortified wines and spirits in the Balearics are those you can find throughout Spain. The classic Andalucian wine, **sherry** – *vino de Jerez* – is served chilled or at room temperature, a perfect drink to wash down *tapas*. The main distinctions are between *fino* or *Jerez seco* (dry sherry), *amontillado* (medium), and *oloroso* or *Jerez dulce* (sweet), and these are the terms you should use to order. In mid-afternoon – or even at breakfast – many islanders take a *copa* of **liqueur** with their coffee. The best – certainly to put *in* your coffee – is **coñac**, excellent Spanish brandy, mostly from the south and often deceptively smooth. If you want a Balearic brandy, try the mellow, hard-hitting Suau from Mallorca. Other good brands include Magno, Veterano and Soberano. Most other spirits are ordered by brand name, too, since there are generally cheaper Spanish equivalents for standard imports. Larios **gin** from Málaga, for instance, is about half the price of Gordons, but around two-thirds the strength and a good deal rougher. The Menorcans, who learnt the art of gin-making from the British, still produce their own versions of the liquor, in particular the waspish Xoriguer. Always specify *nacional* to avoid getting an expensive foreign brand.

Almost any **mixed drink** seems to be collectively known as a *Cuba Libre* or *Cubata*, though strictly speaking this is rum and Coke. For mixers, ask for orange juice (*suc de taronja* in Catalan) or lemon (*llimona*); tonic is *tònica*.

Cervesa, pilsner-type beer (more usually seen in Castilian, *cerveza*), is generally pretty good, though more expensive than wine. The two main brands you'll see

EATING AND DRINKING

DRINKS

English	Catalan	Castilian

Alcohol

English	Catalan	Castilian
Beer	Cervesa	Cerveza
Wine	Vi	Vino
Champagne	Xampan/Cava	Champan/Cava

Hot drinks

English	Catalan	Castilian
Coffee	Café	Café
Espresso coffee	Café sol	Café solo
White coffee	Café amb llet	Café con leche
Decaff	Descafeinat	Descafeinado
Tea	Te	Té
Hot chocolate	Xocolata	Chocolata

Soft drinks

English	Catalan	Castilian
Water	Aigua	Agua
Mineral water	Aigua mineral	Agua mineral
(sparkling)	(amb gas)	(con gas)
(still)	(sense gas)	(sin gas)
Milk	Llet	Leche
Juice	Suc	Zumo
Tiger nut drink	Orxata	Horchata

everywhere are San Miguel and Estrella, though keep an eye out for draught *cerveza negra* – black fizzy beer with a bitter taste. Beer generally comes in 300ml bottles or, for a little bit more, on tap – a *cana* of draught beer is a small glass, a *cana gran* larger. Equally refreshing, though often deceptively strong, is **sangría**, a wine-and-fruit punch which you'll come across at *festas* and – ad nauseam – in tourist resorts.

SOFT DRINKS AND HOT DRINKS

Soft drinks are much the same as anywhere in the world, but one local favourite to try is *orxata* – *horchata* in Castilian – a cold milky drink made from tiger nuts. Also, be sure to try a *granissat* (iced fruit-squash); popular flavours are *granissat de llimona* or *granissat de café*. You can get these drinks from **orxaterias** and from **gelaterias** (ice-cream parlours; *heladerías* in Castilian). Although you can drink the **water** almost everywhere, it usually tastes better out of the bottle – inexpensive *aigua mineral* comes either sparkling (*amb gas*) or still (*sense gas*).

Coffee – served in cafés, bars and restaurants – is invariably espresso, slightly bitter and, unless you specify otherwise, served black (*café sol*). A slightly weaker large black coffee is called a *café Americano*. If you want it white, ask for *café cortado* (small cup with a drop of milk) or *café amb llet* (*café con leche* in Castilian) made with hot milk. For a large cup ask for a *gran*. Black coffee is also frequently mixed with brandy, cognac or whisky, all such concoctions being called *carajillo*; liqueur mixed with white coffee is a *trifásico*. **Decaffeinated** coffee (*descafeinat*) is increasingly available, though in fairly undistinguished sachet form. Tea (*te*) comes without milk unless you ask for it, and is often weak and insipid. If you do ask for milk, chances are it'll be hot and UHT, so your tea isn't going to taste much like the real thing. Better are the **infusions** that you can get in some of the more fashionable bars, like mint (*menta*), camomile (*camamilla*) and lime (*tiller*).

Bar opening hours are difficult to pin down, but you should have little difficulty in getting a drink somewhere until at least 11pm, sometimes midnight. Some bars close on Sundays and operate limited opening hours in the winter, when the resorts pretty much close down.

Opening hours, public holidays and festivals

Although there's been some movement towards a North European working day in Menorca's resorts, most shops and offices still close for a siesta of at least two hours in the hottest part of the afternoon. There's a lot of variability, but basic **working hours** are generally Mon–Fri 9am–1pm and 4–7pm, plus Sat 9am–1pm.

Nearly all **museums** take a siesta, closing between 1pm and 3pm, while many close on Mondays and some on Saturdays and Sundays too. **Churches** are generally open every weekday and sometimes on the weekend, but nearly all close for a three- or four-hour siesta. Entry is usually free, but sometimes a donation is requested. Almost all of Menorca's many **prehistoric sites** are open access – and free.

PUBLIC HOLIDAYS

Public holidays – as well as local festivals (see opposite) – may well disrupt your travel plans at some stage. There are ten annual Spanish national holidays and these are supplemented by five local holidays. In the Balearics, the resorts are generally oblivious to public holidays, but elsewhere almost all businesses and shops close, and it can prove difficult to find a room. Similarly, vacant seats on planes and buses (which are in any case reduced to a skeleton service) are at a premium.

Public holidays

January 1 New Year's Day (Año Nuevo)
January 6 Epiphany (Reyes Magos)
March 19 St Joseph's Day (Sant Josep)
Good Friday (*Catalan* Divendres Sant; *Castilian* Viernes Santo)
May 1 Labour Day (Dia del Trabajo)
Early or mid-June Corpus Christi
June 24 St John's Day (Sant Joan, the king's name-day)
June 29 St Peter and St Paul (Sant Pere i Sant Pau)
July 25 St James's Day (Santiago)
August 15 Assumption of the Virgin (Asunción)
October 12 Discovery of America Day (Día de la Hispanidad)
November 1 All Saints (Todos los Santos)
December 6 Constitution Day (Día de la Constitución)
December 8 Immaculate Conception (Inmaculada Concepción)
December 25 Christmas Day (*Catalan* Nadal; *Castilian* Navidad)

FESTIVALS

It's hard to beat the experience of arriving in a town to discover the streets decked out with flags and streamers, a band playing in the square and the entire population out celebrating the local *festa* (in Castilian, *fiesta*). Everywhere in

FESTIVAL CALENDAR FOR MENORCA

January

16 The *Revetla de Sant Antoni Abat* (Eve of St Antony's Day) is celebrated by the lighting of bonfires (*foguerons*) in Sant Lluís. The locals move from fire to fire, dancing round in fancy dress and eating traditional eel and vegetable patties.

17 *Procesó d'els Tres Tocs* (Procession of the Three Knocks). Held in Ciutadella, this procession commemorates the victory of Alfonso III over the Muslims here on January 17, 1287. There's a mass in the cathedral first and then three horsemen lead the way to the old city walls, where the eldest of the trio knocks three times with his flagstaff at the exact spot the Catalans first breached the walls.

February

Carnaval Towns and villages live it up during the week before Lent with marches and fancy-dress parades.

March/April

Setmana Santa (Holy Week) is as widely observed here as elsewhere in Spain. There are solemn Good Friday (*Divendres Sant*) processions in several villages, with the most important taking place in Maó. In Ciutadella, there's also the *Matança dels bruixots* (the Slaughter of the Wizards) in which puppets representing well-known personalities are hung in the streets.

May

8 The *Festa de la Verge del Toro* (The Festival of the Virgin of the Bull). The day of the patron saint of the island begins with a special mass at the hilltop shrine of Monte Toro and continues with a shindig down in the little town of Es Mercadal.

June

23–25 In Ciutadella, the midsummer *Festa de Sant Joan* has

been celebrated since the fourteenth century. There are jousting competitions, folk music, dancing and processions following a special mass held in the Cathedral on the 24th. Another highlight is on the Sunday before the 24th, when the *S'Homo d'es Bé* (the Man of the Lamb) leads a party of horsemen through the town. Clad in animal skins and carrying a lamb in honour of St John, he invites everyone to the forthcoming knees-up.

July

16 *Festes de la Mare de Déu del Carme*. The day of the patron saint of seafarers and fishermen is celebrated in many towns, but especially in Maó, with parades and the blessing of boats.
Third Sunday The *Festa de Sant Martí in Es Mercadal* celebrates the feast day of St Martin with a popular religious procession followed by dancing and all sorts of fun and games.
24–25 *Festa de Sant Jaume in Es Castell*. Parades and processions in Es Castell.

August

Second weekend High jinks on horseback through the streets of Alaior in the *Festa de Sant Llorenç*.
Last week Three days of fun and games in Ferreries during the *Festa de Sant Bartomeu*.

September

7–9 In Maó, the three-day *Festa de la Mare de Déu de Gràcia* celebrates the Virgin of Grace, the city's patron saint, and begins with a pilgrimage to the chapel of the Virgin. Thereafter, there are processions and parades along with horseback games in which the horses are trained to rear up on their hind legs.

December

Christmas (*Nadal*) is especially picturesque in Ciutadella, where there are Nativity plays in the days leading up to the 25th.

Menorca takes at least one day off a year to devote to party-ing. Usually it's the local saint's day, but there are celebra-tions, too, of harvests, and of safe return from the sea – any excuse will do.

Each **festival** is different, with a particular local empha-sis, but there is always music, dancing, traditional costume and an immense spirit of enjoyment. The main event of most *festas* is a parade, either behind a revered holy image or a more celebratory affair with fancy costumes and *gigan-tones*, giant carnival figures that rumble down the streets to the delight, or terror, of children.

Although these *festas* take place throughout the year, **Holy Week** (*Setmana Santa*) stands out, its passing celebrat-ed in many places with magnificent processions.

The highlights of Menorca's festival year are listed above; for information about less prominent festivals, try local tourist offices.

Directory

ADDRESSES These are usually abbreviated to a standard format – c/Nou 7 translates as Nou Street (*carrer*) no. 7; Plaça Espanya 9 as Espanya Square (*plaça*) no. 9; Plaça Espanya 5, 2è means second floor at no. 5 Plaça Espanya; Plaça Espanya 15, 1–C means suite C, first floor, at no. 15; Plaça Espanya s/n (*sense número*) means without a number. In Franco's day, most avenues and boulevards were named after Fascist heroes and, although the vast majority were redesignated years ago, there's still some confusion. Another source of bafflement can be house numbers: some houses carry more than one number (the by-product of half-hearted reorganizations), and on many streets the sequence is impossible to fathom.

CHILDREN Most *hostals*, *pensions* and hotels welcome children and many offer rooms with three or four beds; restaurants and cafés almost always encourage families too. Many package holidays have child-minding facilities as part of the deal. For babies, food seems to work out quite well (some places will prepare food specially) though you might want to bring powdered milk – babies, like most Spaniards, are pretty contemptuous of the UHT stuff generally available. Disposable nappies and other basic supplies are widely available in the resort areas and both Maó and Ciutadella.

ELECTRICITY The current is 220 volts AC, with standard European-style two-pin plugs. Brits will need an adaptor to connect their appliances, North Americans both an adaptor and (some sort of) transformer.

EMAIL Sending and receiving emails in Menorca is becoming increasingly easy. There are internet cafés in Maó and Ciutadella (see p.76 and p.166) and many of the more expensive hotels have already installed internet connections in their rooms.

EMERGENCY TELEPHONE NUMBERS

Medical emergencies, fire & police ☏ 112.

Fire brigade ☏ 971 351 011.

Guardia Civil ☏ 062.

Local police (Policía Local) ☏ 092.

Maritime emergencies ☏ 900/202 202.

National police (Policía Nacional) ☏ 091.

Ambulance (Ambulància) ☏ 913 354 545.

LAUNDRIES Although there's the occasional self-service launderette (usually rendered in Castilian, *lavandería automática*), mostly you'll have to leave your clothes for a full (and somewhat expensive) laundry service. A dry cleaner is a *tintorería* (also Castilian).

POST There are post offices (*correus*) in Maó and Ciutadella and many of the island's larger villages and resorts. Opening hours are usually Mon–Fri 9am–2pm, though the main post office in Maó is open through the afternoon and on Saturday mornings too. You can buy stamps (*segells*) at tobacconists, as well as at post offices. Postal rates are inexpensive, with postcards and small letters attracting two tariffs: one to anywhere in Europe; the other worldwide.

SPORTS All of Menorca's larger resorts offer a wide range of watersports – from pedaloes through to water skiing and scuba diving. The best windsurfing (along with rental facilities) is to be had at Fornells with Windsurf Fornells (☏ 971 376 400) being one of the more reliable operators.

TELEPHONES International phone calls can be made from any public phone box. They take peseta coins and usually credit cards and will soon be reconfigured to take the euro. Phonecards are sold at newsagents and tobacconists. To make an international call dial ⊺ 00, then the country code followed by the area code, omitting the initial zero, and lastly the number. Making a reverse-charge call (*cobro revertido*) on ⊺ 1009 can be a bit of a hassle, especially if your Spanish – the language in which the phone company conducts its business – is poor: it's best to ring the international directory enquiries for advice: ⊺ 025.

TIME Spain is one hour ahead of the UK, six hours ahead of Eastern Standard Time, nine hours ahead of Pacific Standard Time, nine hours behind Australian Eastern Standard Time and eleven behind New Zealand except for brief periods during the changeovers made in the respective countries to and from daylight saving. In Spain the clocks go back on the last Sunday of March and forward again on the last Sunday of October.

TOILETS Public toilets, which remain rare, are averagely clean, but almost never have any paper (best to carry your own).

THE GUIDE

Maó and the southeast

espite its status as island capital, **MAÓ** (in Castilian, Mahón) has a comfortable, small-town feel – the population is just 20,000 – and wandering around the ancient centre, with its long-established cafés and old-fashioned shops, is a relaxing and enjoyable way to pass a few hours. Nowadays, most visitors approach Maó from its landward side, but this gives the wrong impression. The town has always been a port and it's only from the water that the logic of the place becomes apparent, with its centre crowding a steeply inclined ridge set tight against the south side of the harbour. From this angle, Maó is extraordinarily beautiful, its well-worn houses stacked high up on the crest of the ridge interrupted by bits and pieces of the old city walls and the occasional church. It is, however, the general flavour of the place that appeals rather than any individual sight, particularly the town's striking and unusual hybrid architecture: tall, monumental Spanish mansions stand alongside classical Georgian sash-windowed town houses, elegant reminders of the British occupation.

Port it may be, but there's no seamy side to Maó, and the

harbourfront is home to a string of excellent **restaurants and cafés** that attract tourists in their droves. Few, however, stay the night, preferring the purpose-built resorts close by. As a result, Maó has surprisingly few *hostals* and hotels, which means that you can base yourself here and – if you avoid the waterfront – escape the tourist throngs with the greatest of ease. Nonetheless, rooms are still in short supply in July and August, and reserving in advance during this period is pretty much essential.

Once you've explored the town, it's well worth taking a boat trip out along the **Port de Maó**, as the islanders commonly call the 5.4km-long inlet that stretches east to the ocean, comprising the Mediterranean's finest natural harbour. The scenery isn't exactly fabulous, but each of the several islets dotting the seaway has its own distinctive history and you do get a sense of Maó's past nautical importance. The inlet's southern shore has its historic moments too, notably in the old garrison town of **Es Castell** and the subterranean galleries of eighteenth-century **Fort Marlborough**, located in the picturesque little fishing village of **Sant Esteve**.

Of much less interest are the purpose-built resorts and villa complexes that fill out a goodly proportion of **southeast Menorca**, whose boundary is the road between Maó and Cala en Porter. The development is at its most dispiriting along the harsh flatlands backing onto the south coast between **Punta Prima** and **Binidalí** and again at **Cala en Porter**, but there are one or two pleasant spots hereabouts, especially the agreeable little town of **Sant Lluís** and the mini-resort of **Cala d'Alcaufar**, which huddles around the prettiest of coves.

MAÓ AND THE SOUTHEAST

Maó

Map 2, G1.

With its good-looking mansions and grand churches, the oldest and most diverting part of **MAÓ** rolls along the clifftop above the harbour for roughly 1km. Behind, immediately to the south, the predominantly nineteenth-century town clambers up the hill, its complicated pattern of tiny squares and short lanes bisected by the principal shopping street and pedestrianized main drag – this goes under various names, with **Costa de Sa Plaça** and **c/Moreres** being the longest individual strips. It takes five to ten minutes to walk from one end of the main street to the other and you emerge at **Plaça S'Esplanada**, the mundane main square, site of an underground car park and the local bus terminus.

On the outskirts of Maó lie two prehistoric sites, **Trepucó** and the more extensive **Talatí de Dalt**, one of the island's most satisfying Talayotic remains.

ARRIVAL AND INFORMATION

Menorca's **airport** (☎971 157 000), just 5km southwest of Maó, is a smart, compact affair with a handful of car-rental outlets, currency-exchange facilities and a **tourist information desk**, which has a good selection of free literature (May–Oct daily 8.30am–11pm; ☎971 157 115). There are no buses into town, but the taxi fare will only set you back about 1200ptas/€7.22.

Ferries from Barcelona and Palma sail right up the Port de Maó inlet to Maó harbour, mooring next to the Trasmediterranea offices, which are located directly beneath the town centre. From behind the ferry dock, it's a brief walk up the wide stone stairway of Costa de Ses Voltes to Plaça Espanya and the oldest part of town.

Local buses, which shuttle up and down the southeast coast, stop on the main square, the Plaça S'Esplanada, just across from the tourist office. **Island-wide buses** arrive at the stands along Avinguda J. M. Quadrado, a few metres to the west of the tourist office.

For more information on ferries see p.18 in *Basics*.

Driving the labyrinthine lanes of the centre of Maó is well-nigh impossible and you're better off **parking** on the periphery. The obvious – and easiest – spot is the underground car park below Plaça S'Esplanada, though this is a good deal more expensive than on-street parking (when you can find a place). On-street parking is metered during shopping hours: Mon–Fri 9am–2pm & 4.30–7.30pm (mid-June to mid-Sept 5.30-8.30pm) plus Sat 9am–2pm. The maximum stay is two hours and costs 200ptas/€1.20. At other times, it's free – and there's more chance of a space. Note that if the time you've paid for overlaps into a free period, then your ticket will be valid (for the time you've got left) when the next restricted period begins.

Information and services

The **Oficina d'Informació Turistica** in Plaça S'Esplanada (June–Aug Mon–Fri 8.30am–7.30pm, Sat 9am–2pm; Sept–May Mon–Fri 9am–1.30pm & 5–7pm, Sat 9am–1pm; ☏971 363 790) provides maps of the island and free leaflets giving the lowdown on almost everything you can think of, from archeological sites and beaches to bus timetables, car rental, accommodation and banks. They will not, however, help you find accommodation.

Maó's **post office** (*correu*) is at c/Bon Aire 11–13, near Plaça Bastió (Mon–Fri 9am–5pm, Sat 9am–1pm). You can check your **email** at Webera, opposite the Església de Santa

Maria at c/Església 1B (Mon–Fri 10am–2pm & 4–9pm, Sat 6–10pm; ☎971 356 873); the rate is 480ptas/€2.89 per hour. The main **banks** are Banco de Credito Balear, Plaça S'Esplanada 2; Banca March, c/Sa Ravaleta 7; and Banco de Santander, c/Moreres 46 and 69. Among several downtown **pharmacies**, there's one at c/Sa Ravaleta 5 and another at c/Moreres 28.

GETTING AROUND

Exploring Maó's meandering lanes is best done on foot. When it comes to trips further out, regular local **buses** serve points on the southeast coast, leaving from the main square, Plaça S'Esplanada. The **taxi** rank is on Plaça S'Esplanada. Alternatively, telephone Radio Taxis ☎971 367 111. There's no shortage of vehicle-rental outlets in town. For **bikes**, try VRB, c/S'Arraval 52 (☎971 353 798), which rents out ordinary and mountain bikes at reasonable rates. Advance booking is recommended. **Cars** can be rented from Avis (☎971 361 576) and Atesa (☎971 366 213) from the airport, while downtown there's another Avis outlet at Plaça S'Esplanada 53 (☎971 364 778), plus many smaller concerns – the tourist office has an exhaustive list. **Mopeds** are available at Motos Gelabert, Avinguda J. A. Clavé 12 (☎971 360 614).

For times and frequency of buses to
and from Maó, see box on p.34.

ACCOMMODATION

Maó has a limited supply of **accommodation**, but, along with Ciutadella it remains the best bet on Menorca for bargain lodgings. There's a cluster of inexpensive **hostals** (and

ACCOMMODATION PRICE CODES

After each accommodation entry in this guide you'll find a symbol that corresponds to one of nine price categories. These categories represent the minimum you can expect to pay for a double room in high season; for a single room, expect to pay around two-thirds the price of a double. Note that in the more upmarket *hostals* and *pensions*, and in anything calling itself a hotel, you'll pay a tax (IVA) of seven percent on top of the room price.

❶ Under 3000ptas/€18
❷ 3000–4000ptas/€18–24
❸ 4000–6000ptas/€24–36
❹ 6000–8000ptas/€36–48
❺ 8000–10,000ptas/€48–60
❻ 10,000–14,000ptas/€60–84
❼ 14,000–20,000ptas/€84–120
❽ 20,000–25,000ptas/€120–150
❾ Over 25,000ptas/€150

one hotel) a short walk east of the centre among the narrow streets beyond Plaça Princep and two more just to the south of the centre near Plaça Reial. None of these places is especially inspiring, but they're reasonable enough and convenient – unlike Maó's two quality **hotels**, which are stuck out on the edge of town. **Prices** vary considerably according to season, with rates in July and August about thirty percent more than in winter; advance reservations are advised from June to October and are pretty much essential in July and August.

HOSTALS

Hostal La Isla
c/Santa Caterina 4
℡ 971 366 492.
At the corner of
c/Concepció, a recently

refurbished, reasonably comfortable one-star with 22 rooms, all with showers, and its own bar and restaurant. ❸.

Hostal-residencia Jume
c/Concepció 6 ⊕ 971 363 266,
Ⓕ 971 364 878.
Centrally located on a narrow
side street, this large, one-star
hostal occupies a five-storey
modern block and has thirty-
five frugal rooms. ❸.

Hostal-residencia Orsi
c/Infanta 19
⊕ & Ⓕ 971 364 751.
In a large old terrace house a
couple of minutes' walk from
Plaça Reial, this unassuming
hostal has seventeen rooms,
with mostly shared showers,
and a rooftop terrace. The
owners are English-speakers –

one an American, the other a
Scot. ❹.

Hostal Reynes
c/Comerç 26 ⊕ 971 364 059.
A one-star *hostal* in an
undistinguished modern
block in a quiet residential
area, five minutes' walk from
Plaça Reial. ❸.

Hostal-residencia Roca
c/Carme 37 ⊕ 971 350 839.
At the corner of c/Santa
Caterina, this *hostal* offers
fourteen no-frills rooms in a
plain but reasonably cheerful
modern block with a
ground-floor café. ❸.

**All Maó hotels and restaurants recommended in this chapter
are marked on map 3 at the back of the *Guide*.**

HOTELS

Hotel del Almirante
Carretera de Maó ⊕ 971 362
700, Ⓕ 971 362 704.
Once the residence of British
admiral Lord Collingwood,
this maroon-and-cream
Georgian house has a
delightful, antique-crammed

interior, though some of the
bedrooms are modern affairs
overlooking the swimming
pool round the back. Several
package-tour operators use
the place, but there are
sometimes vacancies. It is
located about 2km east of

MAÓ: ACCOMMODATION

79

Maó beside the coastal road to Es Castell. To get there, take a bus or taxi towards Es Castell and ask to be dropped off. Open May to October. ❻.

Hotel-residencia Capri
c/Sant Esteve 8 ☎ 971 361 400, ℻ 971 350 853.
Routine, modern, three-star hotel with plain but perfectly adequate rooms in the centre of Maó, a brief walk west of the tourist office – head down Avinguda J. M. Quadrado and take the first turn on the left. ❼.

Hotel Port-Mahón
Avgda Fort de L'Eau s/n ☎ 971 362 600, ℻ 971 351 050.
Situated a twenty-minute walk east of the town centre via c/Carme or c/Barcelona at the corner of Avinguda Fort de L'Eau and Avinguda Port de Maó. An elegant colonial-style hotel of columns, pediments and circular windows in a superb location overlooking Port de Maó. There's a swimming pool and a smart patio café, and each of the eighty-odd rooms has air conditioning. The hotel has recently been refurbished in a crisp modern style with Art Deco flourishes. Room prices vary enormously, with the top whack a hefty 30,000ptas/€180.72. ❽.

Hotel Sheila
c/Santa Cecília 41
☎ 971 364 855.
At the corner of c/Sant Nicolau, this old terraced house has been intelligently refurbished in ultra-modern style to hold nineteen spick-and-span, en-suite rooms. There's car parking space and a café here too. ❻.

THE TOWN

Maó's setting and architecture are delightful, but it musters few sights of specific interest. The highlights are the exquisite Churrigueresque chapel in the church of **St Francesc** and, next door, the prehistoric and classical artefacts of the

Museu de Menorca. These two attractions are in the town centre above the **harbour**, the location of the enjoyable **Xoriguer gin distillery**, where you can sample as many of the island's liquors as you like.

Plaça Espanya

Map 3, G3.

From just behind the ferry terminal, a graceful stone stairway and a narrow, twisting street – the Costa de Ses Voltes – tangle together as they climb up the hill to emerge in the old town at the compact **Plaça Espanya**. On the north side of the square, a sociable little **fish market** is plonked on top of a sturdy bastion that was originally part of the **Renaissance city wall**; this mighty zigzag of fortifications, bridges and gates once encased the whole city and replaced the city's **medieval walls**, portions of which also survive – look back up from the foot of the stairway and several chunks are clearly visible. Constructed of sandstone blocks and adobe, the earlier fortifications depended on their height for their efficacy, with a gallery running along the top from which the defenders could fire at the enemy. By the middle of the fifteenth century, however, the development of more effective artillery had shifted the military balance in favour of offence, with cannons now able to breach medieval city walls with comparative ease. The military architects of the day soon evolved a new design in which walls were built much lower and thicker to absorb cannon shot, while four-faced bastions – equipped with artillery platforms – projected from the line of the walls, providing the defenders with a variety of firing lines. The costs of re-fortifying the major cities of western Europe were astronomical, but every country joined in the rush. In Maó, the Habsburgs ordered work to start on the new Renaissance walls in the middle of the

MAÓ: THE TOWN

sixteenth century, though the chain of bastions took over one hundred years to complete.

Plaça Espanya is the starting point for the four-hour hike along the coast described on p.99.

Plaça Carme

Map 3, G3.

Immediately to the east of the fish market, **Plaça Carme** is overshadowed by the massive facade of the eighteenth-century **Església del Carme**, a Carmelite church whose barn-like interior is almost entirely devoid of embellishment. The adjoining cloisters, the **Claustre del Carme**, have, after long service as the municipal courts, been refurbished to house the town's fresh meat, fruit and vegetable market, with the market stalls set against sculpted angels and religious carvings. The cloisters were originally taken from the Carmelites in 1837 under the terms of a national edict that confiscated church property, passing vast estates and buildings to the state in what was the largest redistribution of land since the *Reconquista*. For the liberals, who pushed the edict through, the church was the acme of reaction, and its monks and priests, who usually opposed progressive reform, the representatives of arcane medievalism. Their legislation was, as might be expected, bitterly resented by the church, but it caught the popular mood, a volatile mix of anti-clericalism and self-interest, with many small farmers hoping to buy the confiscated land from the state at knock-down prices. The confiscation was just one aspect of the prolonged struggle between conservatives and progressives that destabilized Spain throughout the nineteenth century, but it had permanent effects: later conservative administrations did return some of the ecclesiastical property, but most of the land was lost to the church for good.

A narrow, dead-end alley on the right-hand side of the Plaça Espanya fish market offers fine views back down over the port and is home to the chic, pastel-painted *Mirador Café* (reviewed on p.92).

Plaça Conquesta, Plaça Constitució and the Església de Santa Maria

North of Plaça Espanya lies slender **Plaça Conquesta**, whose full-length but poorly crafted statue of Alfonso III, the Aragonese king who expelled the Menorcan Moors, was donated by Franco in a typically nationalist gesture. At the far end of the square, turn left along the cobbled lane – c/Alfons III – and you'll soon spy the genteel arcades, bull's-eye upper windows and wrought-iron grilles of the seventeenth-century **Ajuntament** (town hall). This was built by the Spanish, but subsequently occupied by the island's first colonial governor, Sir Richard Kane (see box on p.138), who donated its distinctive clock as well as the portraits of King George III and Queen Charlotte, which still hang in the entrance hall.

The Ajuntament is on the northern edge of **Plaça Constitució**, a narrow piazza overshadowed by the **Església de Santa Maria** (map 3, F3; 7.30am–1pm & 6–8.30pm), a heavy-duty pile founded in 1287 by Alfonso III to celebrate the island's reconquest. Rebuilt in the middle of the eighteenth century and remodelled on several subsequent occasions, the church is an enjoyable architectural hybrid. The Gothic features of the exterior are encased within later Neoclassical additions, while inside, the **nave** is all Catalan Gothic, a hangar-like, aisle-less,

MAÓ: THE TOWN

single-vaulted construction designed to make the high altar visible to the entire congregation – and indeed there's no missing it: its larger-than-life Baroque excesses shoot up to the roof flanked by spiral columns. Unfortunately, the nave is dark and gloomy, as most of the windows are bricked up – in contradiction to the original design in which kaleidoscopic floods of light would have poured in through soaring, stained-glass windows.

In contrast to the clean lines of the nave, the truncated **transepts** and the ceiling above the high altar sport intricate stuccowork, with dozens of cherubs peering out from a swirling, decorative undergrowth. Several side chapels exhibit similar Baroque flourishes, but the church's pride and joy is really its **organ**, a monumental piece of woodwork filling out the elevated gallery above the south entrance. The instrument, with its trumpeting angels, four keyboards and three thousand pipes, was made in Austria in 1810 and lugged across half of Europe at the height of the Napoleonic wars. Britain's Admiral Collingwood helped with the move, probably as a crafty piece of appeasement: defiance of their new Protestant masters had played a large part in the locals' decision to rebuild the church during the British occupation.

The British occupied Menorca on three occasions:
1708–56, 1763–82 and 1798–1802. For a brief biography
of the first (and most enlightened) British governor,
Richard Kane, see p.138.

Carrer Isabel II

Map 3, D2.

Georgian doors and fanlights, sash and bay windows and fancy ironwork distinguish **Carrer Isabel II** as it runs west

from Plaça Constitució. This narrow, elongated street, lined
by a string of fine patrician mansions backing onto the cliffs
above the harbour, once lay at the heart of the British
administration. Halfway along, the present **Gobierno
Militar** (military governor's house) is the most distinctive
building today, with its elaborate paintwork and shaded,
colonial-style arcades.

There's a useful – and extremely pleasant – shortcut down to
the harbour from c/Isabel II: Costa d'es General, an alley at
the foot of c/Rector Mort, tunnels through the old city wall
before snaking its way down the cliff to the waterside below.

The Església de St Francesc

Map 3, C2.

At the end of c/Isabel II the Baroque facade of the
Església de St Francesc appears as a cliff-face of pale
golden stone set above the rounded, Romanesque-style
arches of its doorway. The church was a long time in the
making, its construction spread over the seventeenth and
eighteenth centuries, following the razing of the town by
Barbarossa in 1535 – a random piece of piracy during the
protracted struggle for control of the Mediterranean
between the Ottomans and the Habsburgs which lasted
until the destruction of the Turkish fleet at the Battle of
Lepanto in 1571. Inside, the mighty nave, with its lofty
vaulted roof, encloses a crude but flamboyant high altar
with panels of biblical scenes designed to edify the (illiter-
ate) congregation. The nave is poorly lit, but it's still possible to pick out the pinkish tint in much of the stone and
the unusual spiral decoration of the pillars. In contrast, the
Chapel of the Immaculate Conception, tucked away
off the north side of the nave, is flooded with light: an

MAÓ: THE TOWN

octagonal wonderland of garlanded vines and roses in the Churrigueresque style. The chapel is attributed to Francesc Herrara, the painter, engraver and architect who trained in Rome and worked in Menorca before moving on to Palma in Mallorca.

The Museu de Menorca

Map 3, C2. Tues–Sat 10am–1pm & 4–6pm, Sun 10am–2pm; free.

The monastic buildings adjacent to the Església de St Francesc now house the **Museu de Menorca**, easily the island's biggest and best museum, with multilingual labels to explain most of the exhibits. Entry to the collection is through the cloister, whose sturdy pillars and vaulted aisles illustrate the high point of the Menorcan Baroque.

The first floor holds a wide sampling of prehistoric artefacts, beginning with bits and pieces left by the Neolithic pastoralists who were well established here by about 4000 BC. There's also an extensive range of material from the **Talayotic period**. The early stuff, household objects and the like, is pretty crude, but the displays ably illustrate the increasing sophistication of the Talayotic people, both in their homemade goods and in their use of imported items. In particular, look out for the dainty, rather quizzical-looking bronze bull, probably of Phoenician manufacture, found at the Torralba d'En Salord Talayotic site. Other imported items include several enormous amphorae and a few pieces of charming, multicoloured Punic jewellery. These reflect the final flourishing of Talayotic culture when Menorca became a major port of call for ships sailing between Italy and Spain.

The Torralba d'En Salord Talayotic
site is described on p.142.

On the second floor, the collection deteriorates. A series of skimpy displays gallop through the Moorish period and continue to 1900, but without much conviction. The only items of interest are a small selection of majolica pottery and the folkloric wooden figurines carved by the **Monjo Brothers**. These whimsical representations of various *Menorquín* characters date from the late nineteenth century.

Plaça Bastió

Map 3, E3.

From the Museu de Menorca it's a brief walk southeast along narrow side streets to **Plaça Bastió**, an expansive square that holds Maó's one remaining medieval gateway, the **Portal de Sant Roc**. A sturdy affair of roughly hewn stone comprising two turrets and a connecting arch, the gateway's projecting parapet has survived. It is named after Saint Roch, a fourteenth-century hermit who was popular hereabouts as a talisman to ward off the plague: Christian legend asserted that he both recovered from a bout of the plague and cured fellow sufferers, a good recommendation at a time when every city in Europe feared an outbreak.

Plaça S'Esplanada

Map 3, D4.

From Plaça Bastió, it's a few paces along narrow c/Alaior to the steeply sloping main street: this section is known as **Costa de Sa Plaça**, and its old-fashioned shops and tiny piazzas form the town's commercial centre. There are more shops up the hill along **c/Moreres**, which brings you to the flowerbeds and benches of the principal square, **Plaça S'Esplanada**. The main excitement here is at the weekend, when the square becomes a social hub, with crowds converging on its ice-cream vendors and kiddies' swings. The

MAÓ: THE TOWN

square is overlooked from the west by an unpleasant reminder of Fascist days in the form of a monumental Civil War memorial endowed with Francoist insignia. The column is inscribed with the old fable, *Honor todos los que dieron su vida por Espanya* (Honour to all those who gave their life for Spain). The army barracks behind the monument is still in use.

Costa de Sa Plaça is also signed c/Hannover, its earlier name, after the Hanoverian regiment that garrisoned the town on behalf of the British for most of the first occupation.

The quayside

Below the town stretches the three-kilometre-long **quayside**, in the middle of which lies Maó's ferry terminal. To the west, beyond a few bars and restaurants, are the fishing boats and jetties, followed by an industrial area, which extends round the murky waters at the head of the inlet. To the east, it's a couple of hundred metres to the departure point for **boat tours** of Port de Maó (see box opposite) and then comes the town's elongated marina, where flashy chrome yachts face a string of restaurants, bars and cafés. By day, the half-hour stroll east along the quayside is tame verging on boring; at night, with tourists converging on the restaurants, it's slightly more animated, but not much.

There is, however, one enjoyable attraction a couple of minutes' walk west of the ferry terminal. This is the showroom of the **Xoriguer gin distillery** (map 3, E2; June–Aug Mon–Fri 8am–7pm, Sat 9am–1pm; Sept–May Mon–Fri 9am–1pm & 4–7pm; free), where you can help yourself to free samples of gin, various liqueurs and other spirits. Multilingual labels give details of all the different types, and there are some pretty obscure examples, such as

PORT DE MAÓ BOAT TRIPS

Departing from the jetty near the foot of Costa de Ses Voltes, Yellow Cats (☎971 352 307) – as in yellow catamarans – organize regular boat trips along the Port de Maó inlet. Their basic trip is an hour-long scoot down and around the port costing 1200ptas/€7.22 per person, though they also do several other, longer tours, most notably a three-hour excursion that includes an hour's visit to the Illa del Llatzeret; this costs 2500ptas/€15.06. Frequency depends on the season: in the summer there are departures every hour or so, whereas in January there is only a handful of sailings every week.

These boat trips are the only way to get close to the three islets that dot the Port de Maó – four if you count tiny Illa Pinto, just opposite the Yellow Cat jetty; it's used by the military and is attached to the north shore by a causeway. The first of the three islands is the Illa del Rei, whose dilapidated buildings once accommodated a military hospital and where Alfonso III landed at the start of his successful invasion of Muslim Menorca in 1287. Next comes tiny Illa Plana, also known as Illa Quarentena, a pancake-flat islet that's variously been a quarantine station, a US and now a Spanish naval base, and then there's the larger Illa del Llatzeret. Built of stone retrieved from Fort Sant Felip (see p.105), the imposing walls of this former hospital for infectious diseases are a tribute to provincial superstition – the Menorcans were convinced that contagion could be carried into town by the wind, so they built the walls to keep the germs inside. In addition, internal walls separated patients suffering different diseases for precisely the same reason. The hospital was in operation until 1917, since when – oddly enough – it has been used as a holiday retreat for health workers. Llatzeret was only separated from the mainland in 1900 when a canal was cut on its landward side to provide a more sheltered route to the daunting La Mola (see p.118) fortress.

calent, a sweet, brown liqueur with aniseed, wine, saffron and cinnamon; and *palo*, a liquorice-tasting spirit supposedly of Phoenician provenance. The lime-green *hierbas*, a favourite local tipple, is a sweet and sticky liqueur, partly made from camomile collected on the headlands of La Mola outside Maó (see p.118). In all its guises, it is, however, gin which remains the main product, and *pomada*, a gin cocktail with lemonade, is now as near as damn it Menorca's national drink. Gin was first brought to the island by British sailors in the late eighteenth century, but a local businessman, a certain Beltran, obtained the recipe in obscure circumstances and started making the stuff himself. Nowadays, Xoriguer is the most popular island brand, mostly sold in modern versions of the earthenware bottles once used by British sailors, which are known locally as *canecas*.

EATING, DRINKING AND NIGHTLIFE

Maó has a place in culinary history as the eighteenth-century birthplace of **mayonnaise** (*mahonesa*). Various legends, all of them involving the French, claim to identify its inventor: take your pick from the chef of the French commander besieging Maó; a peasant woman dressing a salad for another French general; or a housekeeper disguising rancid meat from the taste buds of a French officer. The French also changed the way the Menorcans bake their bread, while the British started the dairy industry and encouraged the roasting of meat. Traditional Balearic food is, however, not very much in evidence these days, as most of Maó's **restaurants** specialize in Spanish, Catalan or Italian dishes. These tourist-oriented establishments are mainly spread out along the quayside – the Moll de Ponent west of the main stairway, the Moll de Llevant to the east. There's also a smattering of more economical **cafés** and

café–bars, both down on the quayside and in the town centre, though surprisingly few *tapas* bars.

As far as **opening hours** are concerned, almost all the town's cafés and restaurants open daily during high season, though restaurants usually take a siesta between 4pm and 7pm or 8pm. Out of season, many places shut completely, others close early.

Nightlife is not Maó's forte, but some fairly lively bars dot the harbourfront, staying open till around 2am on the weekend. There's a cluster near the ferry_terminal and another towards the east end of the harbour on Moll de Llevant.

- -

All Maó hotels, restaurants, cafés and bars recommended in this chapter are shown on map 3 at the back of the *Guide*.

- -

CAFÉS AND CAFÉ-BARS

- - - - - - - - - - - - - - - - - -

Café Baixamar
Moll de Ponent 17.
An attractively decorated little café–bar, with old-fashioned mirrors and soft-hued paintwork, serving tasty traditional Menorcan snacks and *tapas* – island cheese and sausage, for example, costing just 475ptas/€2.86.

Cafeteria Consey
Plaça S'Esplanada 72.

Amongst the string of mundane cafés on the main square, this is probably the best option for its reasonably priced snacks and small selection of *tapas* at around 400ptas/€2.40 per portion. It's a popular spot with the locals, but you do have to contend with some pretty naff musak and ersatz wood and marble decor.

Cafeteria La Bombilla
c/Sant Roc 31.
This modest little café in the town centre on Plaça Bastió

offers a good range of *tapas*, averaging about 500ptas/€3 per portion.

Café–bar La Farinera
Moll de Llevant 84.
Located near the ferry port, this is a spruce and modern café–bar offering tasty snacks. It also has a selection of interesting photographs of old Menorca stuck on the walls. Usually open from 6am.

Mirador Café
Plaça Espanya s/n.
Located just footsteps from the fish market, at the top of the main stairway leading from the harbour to the town centre, this little café–bar offers tasty snacks, and its terrace has great views over the harbour. Jazz is the favoured background music.

Varadero
Moll de Llevant 4.
Close to the ferry terminal – and adjacent to the Yellow Cats jetty – this smart, modern place has a restaurant on one side and a café–bar on the other. The café–bar is the place to aim for – a stylish

spot to nurse a drink and sample a small range of *tapas*. Very popular with tourists in the summer.

RESTAURANTS

L'Arpó
Moll de Llevant 124
℡ 971 369 844.
A cosy and intimate restaurant featuring a superb selection of fish dishes from 1800ptas/€10.84. Try the paella.

Gregal
Moll de Llevant 306
℡ 971 366 606.
The decor of the *Gregal*, near the east end of the harbourfront, may be uninspired – just run-of-the-mill modern and comfortable – but the food is outstanding, with mouthwatering seafood dishes prepared in all sorts of delicious (and often traditional) ways. Try, for instance, the John Dory in leek sauce at 4500ptas/€27.10 or the sea-anemone fritters at 1600ptas/€9.63.

Jàgaro

Moll de Llevant 334

℡ 971 362 390.

At the east end of the waterfront, an ambitious restaurant with a smart, traditional interior and a terrace packed with greenery. The menu is perhaps a little too wide-ranging for its own good, featuring everything from hamburgers to paella. It's best to stick to the fish at between 2000/€12.04 and 3000ptas/€18.07 per main course.

Mesón del Puerto

Moll de Ponent 66

℡ 971 352 903.

Just west of the ferry terminal, this pleasant, old-fashioned bodega-style café–restaurant, with big wooden tables and agricultural bric-a-brac pinned on the walls, has a good, very Spanish, menu. The squid and the cod – both at 1700ptas/€10.24 – are especially tasty.

La Minerva

Moll de Llevant 87

℡ 971 351 995.

One of – if not the – smartest restaurants in town, with glossy furnishings and fittings, a harbourside terrace, and a menu that features dishes with a Mediterranean slant. The paella is outstanding and so is the *menú del día*, a relative snip at 2000ptas/€12.04. Save room for the desserts, which are little short of wonderful – the vanilla custard boats in syrup speak for themselves.

Pilar

c/Forn 61 ℡ 971 366 817.

A very intimate and cosy family-run place featuring traditional Menorcan cuisine, with main courses costing around 1800ptas/€10.84. It's near Plaça S'Esplanada: leave the square along c/Pi, a short pedestrianized alley on its north side, take the first right and then the first left. Recommended. Closed Mon, sometimes Sun too.

Il Porto

Moll de Llevant 225 ℡ 971 354 426.

An enjoyable place to eat, with a fountain and an

arcaded terrace. The cooks perform in full view, turning out tasty fish and meat dishes from a wide-ranging menu that features Italian fare – the pizzas are particularly good. Popular with families. Closed in winter.

Roma

Moll de Llevant 295.

Popular, fast-service eatery specializing in well-prepared Italian food at bargain prices, with pasta and pizzas from 900ptas/€5.42. The decor is a tad old-fashioned, but that seems to suit the clientele. Closed in winter.

For a Menorcan food glossary see pp.50–57.

BARS AND NIGHTCLUBS

Bar Akelarre

Moll de Ponent 41.

Probably the best – and certainly the most fashionable – bar in town, down on the waterfront near the ferry terminal. It occupies an attractively renovated ground-floor vault with stone walls and a miniature garden-cum-terrace at the back, right at the foot of the old city walls. Jazz and smooth modern sounds are the backcloth, with occasional live acts.

Café Blues

c/Santiago Ramon i Cajal 3.

An amenable basement bar featuring jazz through to R&B. A favourite with local twenty-somethings, it's located a couple of minutes' walk south of Plaça Reial, along c/Infanta then first right up c/Verge de Gràcia and it's dead ahead at the first intersection.

Mambo

Moll de Llevant s/n.

Amongst the several bars that dot the waterfront east of the ferry terminal, this is one of the best – a busy little spot in pleasantly converted old premises with stone walls and beamed ceiling. Stand-up only.

Café Marès

Plaça Conquesta s/n.

Down a narrow alley off Plaça Conquesta and with fine views over the port, this smart café–bar, with its lean modern furnishings and pastel-painted walls, is one of Maó's chicest spots.

Nou Bar

c/Nou 1.

The ground-floor café here, at the corner of Costa de Sa Plaça, with its ancient armchairs and gloomy lighting, is a dog-eared old place much favoured by locals.

Salsa Bar

Moll de Ponent 29.

Tiny, lively, first-floor bar playing mostly Latin sounds.

Sí

c/Verge de Gràcia 16.

Low-key, locals' late-night bar south of Plaça Reial. Usually open from 11.30pm to around 3am.

AROUND MAÓ: TREPUCÓ AND TALATÍ DE DALT

Two notable prehistoric sites are located close to Maó, both with open access and no entry charge. One of them, **Trepucó**, is on the southern edge of town near the ring road, the other – the more appealing **Talatí de Dalt** – is about 4km to the west of Maó beside the C721. If you've ventured this far, you may as well drop by a third site, **Rafal Rubí**, about 3km further west on the C721 and the site of two *navetas*. All three sites are signed.

Trepucó

Map 2, G2.

It takes about thirty minutes to walk to **Trepucó** from the Plaça S'Esplanada. Follow c/Moreres from the northeast

MENORCA'S TALAYOTIC SITES

Menorca's **Talayotic sites** conform to a common pattern, though there are of course differences in the condition in which each has been preserved. The tallest structure on each site is generally the **talayot**, a cone-shaped tower between 5m and 10m high. These are positioned a few metres from the **taula**, a T-shaped structure up to 4.5m high. Some sites may contain several *talayots*, but there's only ever one *taula*, and this almost always sits in the middle of a circular enclosure whose perimeter is (or was) marked by a low wall. Archeologists have unearthed objects in these enclosures and the remains of firepits have been found against the perimeter wall, both of which seem to imply a religious function, though this is only conjecture – there's certainly insufficient evidence to justify referring to these enclosures as "shrines", as they've sometimes been called. There's general agreement, however, that the *taula* and its enclosure formed the public part of the settlement, and on many sites the remains of circular family dwellings surround them.

Archeologists divide the Talayotic period into several different periods, but as far as the non-specialist is concerned, the only significant difference between the various phases is the encircling **wall**, a dry-stone affair often several metres high and made up of large stones. These walls were for defence and probably reflect an increase in piracy across the western Mediterranean: the earlier settlements don't have them; the later ones – from around 1000 BC – do. For further details see pp. 196–198.

corner of the square, take the first right onto c/Cós de Gràcia and then go straight on down c/Verge de Gràcia to the ring road. Here, go over the traffic island and follow the twisting lane directly ahead, past the cemetery. Thereafter the route is not, at present, clearly signed. After 200m, go straight at the fork, and then – 500m later – veer left at the fork and, after a further 100m, turn right. Surrounded by olive trees and dry-stone walls, the tiny site's focal point is a 4.2-metre-high and 2.75-metre-wide **taula**, one of the largest and best-preserved of these T-shaped monoliths on the island. The *taula* stands inside a circular compound which is edged by the remains of several broadly circular buildings. These were thoroughly excavated by a team of archeologists from Cambridge University in the late 1920s, but even they couldn't work out how the complex was structured. There are two cone-shaped **talayots** close by, the larger one accessible, the other not. The shape of the larger *talayot* is, however, not entirely authentic, as, during the invasion of 1781, the French increased its width to mount their guns.

Talatí de Dalt and Rafal Rubí

Another illuminating Talayotic remnant, **Talatí de Dalt** (map 2, E1), lies 4km from Maó, just south of the main C721 highway. If you're driving, take the short and sign-posted country lane on the left; by public transport, take any Alaior bus, but check first that the driver is prepared to let you off. Much larger than Trepucó, the site is partly enclosed by a Cyclopean wall and features an imposing *taula* set within a circular precinct. The *taula* here appears to be propped up by a T-shaped pillar, though it's generally agreed that this is the result of an accidental fall, rather than by prehistoric design. Next to the *taula* are the heaped stones of the main *talayot* and all around are the meagre remains of prehistoric dwellings. The exact functions of these are not known, but there's no doubt that the *taula* was the village centrepiece, and probably the focus of religious ceremonies. The rustic setting is charming – olive and carob trees abound and a tribe of hogs roots around the undergrowth.

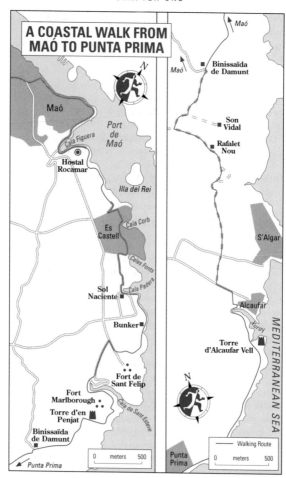

A COASTAL WALK FROM MAÓ TO PUNTA PRIMA

Maó

Port de Maó

Cala Figuera

Hostal Rocamar

Illa del Rei

Cala Corb

Es Castell

Calas Fonts

Cala Padera

Sol Naciente

Bunker

Fort de Sant Felip

Fort Marlborough

Torre d'en Penjat

Cala de Sant Esteve

Binissaïda de Damunt

↙ Punta Prima

0   meters   500

Maó ↗

Maó

Binissaïda de Damunt

Son Vidal

Rafalet Nou

S'Algar

Alcaufar

Àrroy

Torre d'Alcaufar Vell

MEDITERRANEAN SEA

Punta Prima

Walking Route

0   meters   500

A COASTAL WALK FROM MAÓ TO PUNTA PRIMA

16km; 100m ascent; 4–4hr 30min.

Starting in the centre of Maó, this long and varied walk winds around the southeastern corner of the island. Initially, it follows the Port de Maó, then detours inland before rejoining the coast to finish at the resort of Punta Prima, from where buses run (May–Oct) back to Maó. The coastal scenery is magnificent throughout, while the walk also gives a good impression of the successive layers of fortification that grew up to protect Maó's seaward approaches. The going is generally easy, except for one brief section of overgrown track, and is almost entirely flat – but be sure to check bus schedules back from Punta Prima before setting out.

Beginning in Maó's Plaça Espanya, descend Costa de Ses Voltes and turn right along the waterfront, walking around the headland and the narrow inlet of Cala Figuera to reach, after 1.5km, the Hostal Rocamar. Just past here, before the road turns into a slipway and disappears under water, a flight of steps (arrowed up to "13D") ascends to the right. Climb these, go through the gap in the wall at the top and you'll find yourself in an area of overgrown scrub, divided into tiny fields by a lattice of stone walls. Follow the clifftop path, from where there are expansive views across the Port de Maó – of the Illa de Rei and its eighteenth-century British hospital buildings in the middle of the channel and of the elegant pastel-painted Golden Farm mansion (see p.116) behind, on the northern shore. Ahead in the distance, stacked up above the mouth of the seaway, are the imposing barracks of La Mola (see p.118).

Continue along the cliffs to reach the pink apartment building at the edge of the old garrison town of Es Castell (see p.103). Follow the road in front to a T-junction, head left for

Continues over

50m, then right down c/San Cristòfol to reach Cala Corb. Cross the *cala* using the steps, and carry on ahead to Es Castell's main square, Placa S'Esplanada, then continue straight on to rejoin the waterfront **Cales Fonts** with its string of restaurants. Head right here for 50m, then left onto c/Llevant (opposite the *Cafeteria Can Omi*) and follow this road for 200m, across a T-junction, to reach the top of **Cala Padera**. Continue to the *Sol Naciente* restaurant ahead, then turn left along the road behind it, passing a block of memorably kitsch pueblo-style develop-ment. After 50m, opposite a (nameless) *supermercat*, a narrow path heads off along the low clifftops, rounding a line of desir-able holiday villas to reach open country.

Continue along, passing a walled enclosure marked "Propriedad de La Armada Español" and containing a Civil War bunker. The path zigzags through the scattered outer remains of the **Fort de Sant Felip**, Port de Maó's main defensive emplacement until Carlos III had it demolished, allowing the British to retake the island in 1798 without any casualties. Carry on until you reach the barbed-wire fence of the Sant Felip military zone, still off limits, then follow the path round the fence and, when it runs out, bear right across a field past two huge cairns to reach the road leading to the fort entrance.

Turn right briefly, then go left down the road with the dead-end sign for 400m to reach a second dead-end sign, where a track heads off right – the solid-looking cobbles underfoot here are reputedly of Roman provenance, part of a road that once stretched back to Maó. Follow this track down to reach the sequestered inlet of **Sant Esteve** (see p.105), then rejoin the road and head round the cove, passing the subterranean entrance to **Fort Marlborough** (see p.106), built by the British to complement the firepower of Fort de Sant Felip.

When the road ends, head left (literally) through the bushes and scramble up to the top, then continue around the clifftop through further decaying military remains until you hit, more or less simultaneously, the high stone wall of the **Villa Eugenia** *finca* and the **Torre d'en Penyat** ("The Hanging Tower"). Built by the British in 1798 at the beginning of their third and final occupation of the island, the tower has acquired a lurid reputation as a place in which local miscreants were executed – you can go inside to enjoy the fine acoustics and a large collection of Balearic trash. Continue inland behind the tower, where the path swings left, following the walls of Villa Eugenia to reach an old donkey trail between high stone walls. This, the **Camí de Cavalls**, was once a major agricultural thoroughfare that extended around the entire coast of the island, but today it just looks rather forlorn.

Turn left, following the *camí* for 1km, straight over the access road at the entrance to Villa Eugenia, after which the track becomes increasingly overgrown. Push your way through the branches to reach the handsome farmstead of **Binissaida de Damunt**, where the path emerges onto a track. Go right, past the farm entrance, then left onto a gravel road and right at the next junction at the Camí de Cavalls sign.

Follow this track past the entrance to Son Vidal and onto a T-junction and the gate to **Rafalet Nou** farm. Go left, climbing over the gate (it's usually locked), heading past the farmhouse and straight on through another gate. Continue 150m to a fork, then go right 200m to a T-junction. Turn right again (the left turn has been walled off), following the path over a treacherous cattlegrid and past the drab outlying buildings of **S'Algar** until you reach a metalled road. Head straight across for 500m to reach a second road. Turn left, then right, following the signs down to tiny **Xuroy** beach, where there's a bar in summer.

Walk to the top of the beach, then go left through the gap in the wall and up around the clifftop, heading to the right of the large **Torre d'Alcaufar Vell**, constructed by the Spanish in 1787 and recently restored. Conclude by walking a final 2km along the magnificently unspoilt coast to **Punta Prima**.

Back on the C721 and heading west, it's about 2.5km more to **Rafal Rubí** (map 4, G5), where two smallish *navetas* occupy adjacent fields just north of the main road. Made of large stones and resembling bread tins, they hardly set the pulse racing, but if you visit on a moonlit night they really are very spooky. For more on *navetas*, see p.198.

Port de Maó

Port de Maó, as Menorcans term the whole of the extended inlet that links Maó with the Mediterranean, is one of the finest natural harbours in the world. No less than 5.4km long and a maximum of 900m wide, the channel also boasts the narrowest of deep-sea entrances, strategic blessings that have long made it an object of nautical desire. The high admiral of the Holy Roman Emperor Charles V opined that "June, July, August and Mahon are the best ports in the Mediterranean", and after Barbarossa's destruction of Maó in 1535, his master finally took the point and had the harbour fortified. Later, the British eyed up the port as both a forward base for Gibraltar and a lookout against the French naval squadron in Toulon. Using the War of the Spanish Succession as their excuse, they occupied Menorca in 1708 and, give or take occasional French and Spanish interventions, stayed in control until 1802. They poured vast resources into the harbour defences and, since their departure, the Spaniards have updated and remodelled the fortifications on several occasions.

Nowadays, both shores, as well as a trio of mid-channel islets, carry the marks of all this military interest and are pocked by ruined **fortifications**, thick-walled affairs hugging the contours of the coast. The seaway is best explored by boat from Maó (see p.89), but both shores do offer great views and possess, in their own right, several modest attractions.

Highlights of Port de Maó's south shore include the garrison town of **Es Castell**, purpose-built by the English in the 1770s, and the unusual subterranean fortress of **Fort Marlborough**, located in one of the island's prettiest fishing villages, **Sant Esteve**.

Port de Maó's north shore is
described in Chapter 2, pp.115–118.

To explore the south shore thoroughly you'll need your own transport, though there is a frequent **bus** service from Maó to Es Castell.

ES CASTELL

Map 2, H2.

Tucked in tight against the shore just 3km from Maó, the gridiron streets of **ES CASTELL** (formerly known as Villa Carlos) have a militaristic and very English air. Originally called Georgetown, the town is ranged around **Plaça S'Esplanada**, the old parade ground-cum-plaza. The square's Georgian-style town hall, graced by a stumpy, toy-town clock tower, and the elongated facades of its three barracks, bear witness to British influence. Elsewhere, sash windows, doors with glass fanlights, and wrought-iron work adorn many of the older houses, though nowadays the centre looks rather bedraggled. As a garrison town, the fortunes of Es Castell have always been tied to those of the military, and, with Franco gone, the army no longer has the same prestige. This is reflected in the town's general demeanour – and especially on the main

PORT DE MAÓ

square, where two of the barracks stand abandoned and neglected.

Nevertheless, Es Castell is still worth a brief wander, beginning in the Plaça S'Esplanada, where one of the barracks houses a modest military **museum**, equipped with a motley collection of old rifles and uniforms (Mon, Thurs & first Sun in the month 11am–1pm; 400ptas/€2.40). From the plaza, it's a couple of minutes' walk east down c/Stuart to the harbour, a pretty spot occupying the thumb-shaped cove of **Cales Fonts**. Stroll north along the waterside and you'll pass a string of **restaurants**, two of the best being the *Vell Parrander* at Moll de Cales Fonts 52 (☎971 369 419), and the *Siroco* at no. 39 (☎971 367 965); both serve tasty seafood at reasonable prices. At the north end of the harbour, a sullen **bastion** is all that remains of the town's fortifications and from here c/Bellavista leads south back towards the main square – hang a left at either c/Sant Ignasi or c/Victori.

Buses from Maó stop on c/Gran, footsteps away from the main square along c/Victori.

At Es Castell, you can pick up the
coastal hike described on p.99.

EAST TO SANT ESTEVE

Beyond Es Castell, the main coastal road clips down towards the mouth of Port de Maó before veering right for Sant Lluís (see p.107). Keeping straight, you'll come to a narrow country lane that leads past the turning to Sant Esteve (see opposite) and then reaches – in about 300m more – a dead end at the *zona militar*. This restricted military area sprawls over the inlet's final headland, where the Emperor Charles V built an imposing star-shaped fortress in the 1550s, naming it **Fort Sant Felip** (map 2, I2) after his son, later Philip II. Once Menorca's greatest stronghold, the fort was adopted and adapted by the British, who controlled the seaway from here. This irritated the Spanish no end and so, when Menorca was returned to them in 1782, at the end of the second British occupation, they promptly destroyed it – which, in retrospect, seems more than a little defeatist. After all, although it's true that no colonial power could use it again, neither could the Spanish and a few years later the British captured the island with the greatest of ease. Today, nothing survives except the most fragmentary of ruins, though rumours persist of secret tunnels.

Sant Esteve

Map 2, I3.

Doubling back from Fort Sant Felip, you've a short hop to **SANT ESTEVE**, an extraordinarily picturesque little village, whose old whitewashed houses are strung out along a slender cove with a turquoise sea lapping against crumbly dark cliffs. On the far side of the cove, near the end of the village, a tunnel burrows into the hillside to enter what was once **Fort Marlborough** (June–Sept Tues–Sat 10am–1pm & 5–8pm, Sun 10am–1pm; Oct–May Tues–Sun 10am–1pm; 500ptas/€3), an intricate, largely subterranean stronghold built to guard the southern approach to Fort Sant Felip by the British between 1710 and 1726. The fort, which was named after one of Britain's most talented generals, Sir John Churchill, the Duke of Marlborough, is a complicated affair, beginning with a long gallery dug into the soft rock with counter-galleries cut at right angles to detect enemy attempts to mine into the fortress. In addition, the main gallery encircles an interior moat – dry now, but once filled with water – and comes complete with gun slits that would have been used to fire on the moat from every angle. In turn, the moat encircles a small fortified hillock, the most protected part of the fortress and once the site of an artillery battery that had this stretch of the coast in its sights. Fort Marlborough was besieged twice – once by the French in 1756 and once by the Spanish in 1781 – and on both occasions it was captured, but only after a prolonged siege. Indeed, one of the advantages of this type of fortress was that it could tie up a large enemy force for weeks and yet require a minuscule garrison – the British put just sixty men here.

The self-guided tour round Fort Marlborough takes about forty minutes.

Southeast Menorca

Beyond Port de Maó, the **southeast corner** of Menorca, delineated by the road between Maó and Cala en Porter, consists of a low-lying limestone plateau fringed by a rocky shoreline with a string of craggy coves. In recent years, this stretch of coast has been extensively developed and today thousands of villas cover what was once empty scrubland. The result is not pretty and, although many prefer this low-rise architecture to the high-rise hotels of the 1960s, it's difficult to be enthusiastic, especially in **Cala en Porter**, the biggest and perhaps the ugliest *urbanització* of the lot. That said, the coast itself can be beautiful, and the resort of **Cala d'Alcaufar**, one of the earliest developments, fringes a particularly picturesque cove. Inland, lies an agricultural landscape crisscrossed by country lanes and dotted with tiny villages, plus one town – mildly diverting **Sant Lluís**.

Most of the district is devoted to villa-style **accommodation** and package-tour operators rule the local roost, so it's lean pickings for the independent traveller. That said, there's a reasonable chance of finding a room here and there amongst the southeast's scattering of hotels and *hostals*, with Cala d'Alcaufar being the best bet.

From May to October, getting around by **bus** is fairly straightforward. There are hourly buses from Maó to Sant Lluís and Punta Prima, as well as regular services to Cala en Porter and Cala d'Alcaufar; in winter, there's a good bus service from Maó to Sant Lluís and Cala en Porter, but nothing at all to Punta Prima and Cala d'Alcaufar. Bear in mind, however, that, with the exception of compact Cala d'Alcaufar, all of these resorts spread for miles, and if you've rented a villa you could be facing a very long, hot and confusing trek from the nearest bus stop. To avoid exhaustion, ring for a **taxi** from Maó's Radio Taxis on ☏971 367 111.

For more information on frequency and journey times of buses from Maó, see box on p.34.

SANT LLUÍS

Map 2, G4.

It's just 4km south of Maó along the main road to **SANT LLUÍS**, a trim, one-square, one-church town of brightly whitewashed terraced houses. As at Es Castell (see p.103), the town's grid plan betrays its colonial origins. A French commander, the Duc de Richelieu, built Sant Lluís to house his Breton sailors in the 1750s, nam-

SOUTHEAST MENORCA

ing the new settlement after the thirteenth-century King Louis IX, who was beatified for his part in the Crusades. The French connection is further recalled by the trio of coats of arms carved on the west front of the **church** – those of the royal household and two French governors.

Buses from Maó stop at the north end of town beside Plaça Nova. There are no *hostals* here, but the *Biniarroca Hotel Rural*, occupying a lavishly renovated *finca* just east of town on the road to Es Castell, at Camí Biniarroca 57 (☎971 150 059, ✆971 151 250; ❽), is one of the island's most luxurious hotels. It has twelve plush guest rooms, an outside swimming pool and a first-rate **restaurant** (reservations required), serving from an international menu. Two other good places to eat hereabouts are *La Venta* (☎971 150 995), beside the traffic island at the south end of town, where the speciality is suckling pig, and the *Sa Parereta* (☎971 150 303), a smart restaurant with a wide-ranging international menu and an outside terrace located in the nearby hamlet of **Torret**. Torret is just south of Sant Lluís along the main road – but be sure to ring for reservations and directions.

S'ALGAR AND CALA D'ALCAUFAR

At the south end of Sant Lluís, keep on the main road (the PM702) and you'll soon reach the turning for Punta Prima (see below) and then the fork that leads to either **S'ALGAR** (map 2, I5), where rank upon rank of suburban-looking villas sprawl along the coast, or – a far better option – the pretty little resort of **CALA D'ALCAUFAR** (map 2, H5). The development here is restrained: a smattering of holiday homes and old fishermen's cottages set beside a handsome inlet of flat-topped limestone cliffs and a turquoise sea. You can stroll out across the surrounding headlands, one of which has a Martello tower, or just enjoy the sandy beach. The main footpath down to the beach runs through the *Hostal Xuroy* (☎ & ⓕ 971 151 820; ❼; May–Oct), a pleasant two-star establishment, with 46 modern rooms – though most of them are booked up months in advance by package-tour companies.

The hike from Maó to Punta Prima described on p.99 threads along the southeast coast and can – amongst other possibilities – be picked up at Cala d'Alcaufar.

PUNTA PRIMA

Map 2, H6.

Hogging a barren stretch of seashore, **PUNTA PRIMA** is a sprawling, standard-issue resort whose villas and super-markets back onto a wide and windy beach at the island's southeastern tip. Frankly, the place doesn't have much going for it, though at least the view from the beach does take in the offshore **Illa de l'Aire**, an inaccessible and uninhabited chunk of rock equipped with an automatic lighthouse. The problem with the island is that it funnels the ocean into the choppy channel between itself and the shore, and this can make swimming dangerous – watch for the green or red flags. Inevitably, the wind attracts the windsurfers, and windsurfing equipment is available for rent, as are pedaloes and sunbeds.

The resort has two **hotels**: the three-star *Xaloc Playa*, with its own swimming pool (☎ 971 159 080, ⓕ 971 159 165; ❻; May–Oct), and the nearby 500-room *Pueblo de Menorca* (☎ 971 159 070, ⓕ 971 159 211; ❼; April–Oct), also with its own pools, plus sports facilities and disco, though it's rather too large for many tastes.

- -
**Punta Prima is at the end of the
coastal walk described on p.99.**
- -

WEST TO BINIDALÍ AND SANT CLIMENT

Travelling Menorca's south coast from Punta Prima to
Binidalí, a distance of around 10km, is a depressing experience: poorly signposted roads meander across the coastal
scrubland traversing patches of undistinguished tourist
development. On the map, it looks as if there are about half
a dozen resorts, but on the ground it's impossible to deter-
mine where one settlement ends and another begins. The
only vague light in the architectural gloom is **Binibeca
Vell**, a purpose-built settlement of second homes at
BINIBECA (map 2, F6); the narrow whitewashed alley-
ways, wooden balconies and twisting flights of steps, are
designed to resemble an old Mediterranean fishing village.
At the end of the coastal road is scrawny **BINIDALÍ** (map
2, D5), from where (with relief) you can head inland to
SANT CLIMENT (map 2, D2), a tiny village with a
minuscule main square and a dinky little church. The village is also home to the *Restaurant-bar Casino* (☎ 971 153
418), where there's live jazz a couple of nights a week (usually Tues & Thurs). Unfortunately for the inhabitants, the
village is also within earshot of the airport and bisected by
the busy Maó–Cala en Porter road.

SON VITAMINA AND THE CALES COVES CAVES

It's hard to understand quite why anyone thought the villa
complexes of **SON VITAMINA** and **CALES COVES**,
off the main road 3km west of Sant Climent, would prosper
– they're simply too far from the sea. Nonetheless, ambi-

tious plans were laid and a wide access road was constructed. But the plot buyers failed to materialize and it took ages for either place to limp into life – and even today it's all rather forlorn, an untidy smattering of villas surrounded by waste ground. That said, this is the starting point for the 2.5-kilometre hike down to the coast to the remote prehistoric **Cales Coves caves** (map 2, A3). The walk begins at the wide asphalted circle located 150m off the main road at the entrance to the two complexes. From here, take the (unsigned) lane that exits diagonally to the right – it's too rough to drive in an ordinary car – and proceed down through the scrubland to the seashore, where a pair of pebbly beaches edge an attractive forked inlet; a sketchy footpath climbs the rocks to link the two. The surrounding cliffs are punctured by over one hundred man-made caves, the earliest of which date back to Neolithic times when they served as both funerary chambers and troglodytic dwellings, equipped with circular living quarters. Later, in the Talayotic period, the caves were used exclusively as burial chambers and, though the necropolis was abandoned as a burial site long before the end of the Iron Age, several engraved stones discovered here indicate a continued interest well into Roman times. Indeed, it appears that the Romans regularly visited the caves during pagan festivals. It's easy to explore the caves by clambering around the cliffs, though there's nothing specific to see once you're inside.

Just west of Son Vitamina, before you reach Cala en Porter, the main road passes the turning to the prehistoric ruins of Torralba d'en Salord (see p.142) and Alaior (see p.139).

CALA EN PORTER

Map 2, A2.

Back on the main road, it's a short haul west to **CALA EN PORTER**, a sprawling *urbanització* that has engulfed a bumpy plateau with hundreds of villas of such similar appearance and proportions that it soon becomes disorienting. Nor is there any focus to the development, which is limited to the south by plunging seacliffs and in the west by a steep bluff that flanks a deep ravine with marshes at the back and a wide sandy beach at the front. Access to the beach is either by road down into the ravine or by flights of steps running down the bluff. One redeeming feature – and the resort's most popular attraction – is the **Cova d'en Xoroi**, a large cave stuck in the cliff-face high above the ocean. A stairway from the entrance on the clifftop winds down to the cave, offering stirring views along the coast. You can also visit at night, as a local businessman has installed a bar and disco in the cave, which warms the place up from about midnight onwards. The cave is the subject of one of the island's best-known folk tales. Legend has it that a shipwrecked Moor named Xoroi (literally, "One Ear") hid out here, raiding local farms for food. Bored and lonely, he then kidnapped a local virgin – the so-called "Flower of Alaior" – and imprisoned her in his cave. Eventually, Xoroi's refuge was discovered when locals picked up his tracks back after a freak snowstorm. Cornered, Xoroi committed suicide by throwing himself into the ocean, while the girl (and her children) were taken back to Alaior, where they lived happily ever after.

From June to September, the Cova d'En Xoroi is open
daily 11am–9pm; 450ptas/€2.70. The bar–disco is open
nightly from 10pm until around dawn, with entry about
1000ptas/€6. Restricted hours apply in winter.
Further details on ⓣ 971 377 236.

CALA EN PORTER

●

Fornells and the northeast

Menorca's **northeast coast** holds some of the island's prettiest scenery, its craggy coves, islets and headlands rarely rattled by the developers. This is not, however, an act of aesthetic discretion, but rather because the harsh prevailing wind – the Tramuntana – makes life a tad too uncomfortable for the sun-seeking packagers. There are developed coves for sure – and four of them contain substantial villa resorts of little immediate appeal – but these are the exception rather than the rule. For the most part, this stretch of coast remains delightfully unspoilt.

Apart from the good-looking village of **Sa Mesquida**, reached from **Port de Maó's northern shore**, most of the northeast coast is approached via the enjoyable 25km-long minor road linking Maó and Fornells. This runs alongside cultivated fields protected by great stands of trees, with the low hills that form the backbone of the interior bumping away into the distance. At regular intervals you can turn off towards the seashore. The first turning takes you to **Es Grau**, the starting point for a delightful two- to three-hour

Traditional farm gate

Talayot

Port d'Addaia

Lighthouse, Cap de Favàritz

Fornells

Maó

Cala Santa Galdana

Ciutadella

hike along the coast or a shorter stroll along the marshy shores of **S'Albufera**, a freshwater lake noted for its birdlife. The next turning to the north leads to the windy bleakness of the **Cap de Favàritx** and it's north again for the four big resorts hereabouts – **Port d'Addaia**, **Na Macaret**, **Arenal d'en Castell** and **Son Parc**. Much more rewarding than this quartet, however, is **Fornells**, which boasts a delightful bayside location, and is, with its measured development, one of the most appealing resorts on the island. Fornells is also renowned for the excellence of its restaurants, and none of its three *hostals* is block-booked by package-tour operators, so you've a reasonable chance of a room even in the height of the season. There's no **beach** at Fornells itself, but it makes a good base for visiting some of the more remote cove beaches nearby – **Cala Pregonda** and **Platja de Binimel-Là**, to name but two.

There's a real shortage of non-package **accommodation** on the northeast coast – only Fornells is likely to have anything, though of course Maó is within easy striking distance, too. Public transport is also limited: one **bus** service leaves Maó for Fornells and the four big resorts once or twice daily except on Sunday from May to October and once daily on four days a week from November to April.

PORT DE MAÓ'S NORTH SHORE AND SA MESQUIDA

Port de Maó is an extended inlet linking Maó with the Mediterranean. Nudging out into the ocean, the steep hills and ridges of the promontory that constitutes the inlet's **north shore** both protect the harbour from the Tramuntana and have deterred the islanders from settling here. Recent development has spawned a pair of ritzy suburbs – Sant Antoni and **Cala Llonga** – but the key features remain the handsome old colonial villa, called **Golden Farm**, and the out-of-bounds fortress of **La Mola** which sprawls over the headland at its very tip. Also of interest are the two dinky little fishing villages that snuggle around rocky coves just over the hills on the island's northeast shore – **Es Murtar** and **Sa Mesquida**, with its wide sandy beach.

In terms of **practicalities**, there's nowhere to stay and neither is there any public transport, but distances are small – it's only 4.5km from Maó to Sa Mesquida – so a day-trip from Maó by bike, car, moped or even on foot is easily undertaken.

Port de Maó's south shore is described on p.102,
in Chapter One. The inlet is best explored by boat;
see p.89 for details of boat trips.

Golden Farm

Map 4, H5.

From the traffic island at the west end of Maó's harbour, a narrow byroad soon leaves the city behind, twisting up past the ugly, modern power station to thread over grassy hills with old stone walls and whitewashed farmhouses. After 2.5km, the road slips past the turning for Sa Mesquida (see p.119) to reach – after another 700m – the **Golden Farm** (no entry), a fine old, pastel-painted mansion in the British colonial style, perched on the hillside overlooking the port de Maó. A large portico with two arcaded galleries dominates the south (Maó) side of the house, the upper gallery – the balcony – equipped with a delicate balustrade; up above, classical deities decorate the tympanum, a trio of languorous figures in vaguely erotic poses. Albeit briefly, this mansion may have been **Admiral Nelson**'s headquarters during the island's third British occupation (1798–1802) and all sorts of folkloric tittle-tattle have alluded to romantic trysts here between Nelson and his mistress, Emma Hamilton. In fact, Nelson was much too concerned with events in Naples, where the Hamiltons were ensconced and where he was involved in supporting the Neapolitan king, the Bourbon Ferdinand, against the incursions of the French. Indeed, Nelson did his best to avoid visiting Menorca at all – he only came here once or twice for a couple of days apiece – despite it being crucial for Britain's naval control of the Mediterranean. In July 1799, his superior, Lord Keith, mustered his fleet at Port de Maó to resist a possible French attack and ordered Nelson to join him. Nelson refused point blank, writing to the Admiralty "I am fully aware of the act I have committed, but, sensible of my loyal intentions, I am prepared for any fate which may await my disobedience." The Admiralty let it go – a good job considering Trafalgar was just round the historical corner – and Keith ranted and raved in vain.

The clearest view of Golden Farm is on the way back (west) from La Mola.

East to La Mola

Further on from Golden Farm, the road skirts the well-heeled suburb of **Cala Llonga**, where modern villas tumble down the hillside to the water's edge, and offers fine but fleeting panoramas of both the harbour and its smaller islands. First up, on the west side of Cala Llonga, is **Illa del Rei**, whose huddle of buildings once accommodated a military hospital, and then – further east – comes **Illa Quarentena**, a Spanish naval base.

**For a fuller description of Illa del Rei, Illa Quarentena
and Illa del Llatzeret, see p.89.**

Beyond, the road weaves over a stretch of wind-raked heathland to reach its conclusion at the truncated causeway leading over to the formidable fortress of **La Mola** (map 4, I5), at the end of the promontory, some 6.5km from Maó. Work began on the fortress in the 1830s, its tiers of complementary bastions and gun emplacements designed to resist the most intensive of artillery bombardments. An attempt to bolster Spain's military position in the Mediterranean, the stronghold failed to impress anyone – Spain's decline was too advanced for that – but it did provide work for hundreds of Menorcans at a time of high unemployment. Much less savoury is La Mola's connection with Franco, who used several of its barracks as a high-security political prison until 1968. The army is no longer in possession of the fortress and today you can walk across the causeway, past the battered old barrier, to explore the fort on Sunday mornings (only) in winter, and on most days from May to August, but it's a forlorn spot. In truth, with the army gone, no one is quite sure what should be done with it.

To the right of the road as it approaches the causeway is the **Illa del Llatzaret**, a former isolation hospital for infectious diseases, which was made more secure when it was cut off from the peninsula by a canal in 1900.

Es Murtar

Map 4, H5.

Returning from La Mola, you'll see a signposted turning – just to the west of Golden Farm. The road wriggles north over the hills for 1.2km to reach the short side road to **ES**

MURTAR, a tiny fishing village whose whitewashed houses are tucked in between the cliffs and a narrow cove. It's a pretty spot, though there's nothing specific to see or do.

Sa Mesquida

Map 4, H5.

Back on the road, a further 600m or so will take you to **SA MESQUIDA**, whose charming whitewashed houses flank a rough and rocky shoreline spiked by miniature pinnacles and bony islets, three of which guard the tiny harbour. Overlooking the scene is the prominent **Torre de Sa Mesquida** (no access), a watchtower of medieval provenance. The tower's battered stonework culminates in a machicolation (projecting parapet), from the apertures of which the defenders could dump boiling oil and water and whatever else came to hand on the heads of their attackers. There's nowhere to stay in Sa Mesquida, but there is a first-rate **restaurant**, the *Cap Roig* (℡971 188 383), which offers tasty seafood and fine views out to sea from the cliffs at the start of the village.

The road pushes on through the village, swinging up and over the hills to reach, after 800m, the **beach**, a wide arc of pale-brown sand overlooked by bare hills. It's not an especially appetizing spot, but it is the nearest beach to Maó.

ES GRAU

Map 4, H4.

The first right turn off the Maó–Fornells road threads its way up through wooded hills and clips past pastureland to **ES GRAU**. Es Grau is itself a neat and trim little village that overlooks a horseshoe-shaped bay, where pine trees and sand dunes fringe an unenticing arc of greyish sand. The shallow waters here, however, are ideal for children, and on weekends the handful of **bars** and **restaurants** that dot the main street are crowded with holidaying Mahonese. The most popular place is the *Bar Es Grau*, with a charming shaded terrace, located on the water's edge at the start of the village. Alternatively, you could head a few metres beyond to the *Tamarindos* (☏971 359 420), a café–restaurant noted for its inexpensive seafood.

ILLA D'EN COLOM

Map 4, H3.

Easily reached from Es Grau by boat is the **Illa d'en Colom** (Pigeon Island), a rocky, one-kilometre-square islet lying just offshore. It's now uninhabited, but in the eighteenth century, the British quarantined sick sailors here, and the Spanish followed suit until they built the hospital on the Illa del Llatzaret in Maó harbour (see p.89). The exposed east side of the Illa d'en Colom is bleak and bare, its vegetation stunted by the prevailing winds, but the sheltered west side is a bit more luxuriant and has a couple of **beaches**, the more scenic of which is **S'Arenal d'en Moro**. **Boats** to the island leave from the tiny jetty at the far end of Es Grau's main street. There's no sailing schedule as such, but boats leave every half-hour or so every day throughout the summer from 10am – just wait around at the jetty. You can get off the boat at either beach and the return fare will set you back about 800ptas/€4.82.

For a fine and gentle coastal hike
beginning at Es Grau, see p.123.

S'ALBUFERA PARC NATURAL

Map 4, G3.

The scrub-covered dunes behind Es Grau's beach form the

northeastern periphery of an expanse of dune that encircles the freshwater lagoon of **S'Albufera**. Only 2km from east to west and a couple of hundred metres wide, the lagoon has just one outlet, the faint stream – La Gola – that trickles out into the bay beside Es Grau. The lake was once fished for bass, grey mullet and eels – a real island delicacy – but fishing and hunting have been banned since the creation of the **Parc Natural S'Albufera d'es Grau** (☎971 431 782) in the 1990s. The park boasts a varied terrain, including dunes, which are glued together by a combination of Aleppo pine, marram grass and beach thistle, and wetland, concentrated at the west end of the lake and containing patches of saltworts and rushes. The lagoon and its surroundings are rich in birdlife, attracting thousands of migrant birds in spring and autumn.

The Parc Natural S'Albufera d'es Grau is one part of a larger Parc Natural that also protects the Illa d'en Colom (see opposite) and the coastline north to Cap de Favàritx (see p.124).

The access road into the park begins 2km back from Es Grau on the road to Maó. Just 1.5km long, it skims past the plush villas of the Shangril-Là development before terminating at a car park, from where clearly marked paths run (in either direction) along the lake's southern shore. It's easy walking and the scenery is gentle on the eye, the blue of the lake set against the rolling greens and yellows of the dunes. Birders – both casual and enthusiasts – should aim for **Es Prat**, the large patch of wetland at the west end of the lake, and be sure to pack your binoculars.

For information on Menorca's birdlife, see p.222.

S'ALBUFERA PARC NATURAL

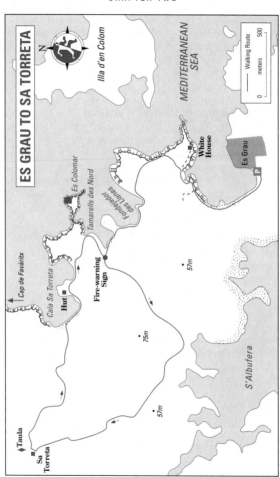

A COASTAL WALK FROM ES GRAU TO SA TORRETA

ES GRAU TO SA TORRETA

Illa d'en Colom

MEDITERRANEAN SEA

Walking Route

meters

0   500

White House

Es Grau

P

Cap de Favàritx

Es Colomar

Fondelador des Llanes

Tamarells des Nord

Cala Sa Torreta

Hut

Fire-warning Sign

57m

75m

57m

S'Albufera

Taula

Sa Torreta

A COASTAL WALK FROM ES GRAU TO SA TORRETA

9km; 100m ascent; 2hr–2hr 30min

This coastal walk takes you from the small resort of Es Grau (see p.119) along one of the wildest sections of the Menorcan seaboard, before detouring inland around the S'Albufera lagoon to visit the Talayotic site of Sa Torreta, one of the remotest prehistoric enclosures on the island. The going is easy throughout, along well-marked tracks, with only one modest ascent towards the highest point of the walk at Sa Torreta farm. There's also a small section of backtracking at the end of the walk, though this is no hardship given the splendour of the coastal scenery.

Starting at the car park at the entrance to Es Grau, walk round the long sandy beach and follow the path on the far side as it climbs up onto the low cliffs. At the top, ignore the well-defined track that heads off left and continue straight on, descending sharply, then follow the path as it bears right until you see a solitary white house ahead.

About 50m before you reach the house, a path branches off up to the left. Follow this to the top of the hill, where you'll see the craggy Illa d'en Colom (see p.120) off the coast directly ahead. The path goes straight on, then swings left, giving increasingly expansive views of the rugged coast to either side, without a single sign of human habitation in sight until the lighthouse on Cap de Favàritx hoves into view way ahead.

As soon as you see the lighthouse, look for the path that descends to your right. Go down this path, past a curious abandoned rock-dwelling built into the cliffside, then continue left along the coast, following any of the various paths which cross the scrub. The walk here takes you between low, convoluted clumps of mastic and wild olive dotted with spiky

Continues over

pin-cushions of *Launaea cervicornis* (try not to sit on them). Aim for the **Martello tower** at the tip of the headland of Es Colomar ahead, passing the trash-covered inlet of Fondejador des Llanes to reach the small sandy beach of **Tamarells des Nord**.

Cross the beach to the **fire-warning sign** on the far side (remember this point for later on), then go through the gap in the wall and head left to reach, after 25m, a major track. Turn left and follow this track inland as it climbs into a beautifully enclosed and secluded valley. After 750m, the track swings right and you have your first proper view of the **S'Albufera** lagoon ahead, one of Menorca's richest ornithological sites, although you're just too far away from the lake here to see much of its birdlife. (For more on the lagoon, see p.121.) The path gradually ascends through cow pasture before splitting into three. Take the middle track and climb to another fork at the top, then go right, up along a beautiful stonewalled lane, through a gate and across a field, making for the farmhouse of **Sa Torreta** ahead. Monte Toro (see p.146) begins to fill the view in the distance as you ascend, while to your left there's an overgrown and impassable walled track, typical of many of the island's abandoned donkey trails.

Reach a T-junction and turn left to arrive at the farm. At the first farm building continue straight ahead over the gate, cross

CAP DE FAVÀRITX

Map 4, G2.

Back on the Maó–Fornells road and heading northwest from the Es Grau turning, it's just over 5.5km to the right turn that weaves its way north to **Cap de Favàritx**. This side road cuts along a slender valley and slips through dumpy little hills to reach, after 6km, an unsigned fork where you veer the yard, then immediately go right to reach an old circular threshing floor after 25m. Stop here and look behind you to spot Sa Torreta **taula and talayot**. Now you can see it, turn round, retrace your steps for 10m and cross the fields through the gap in the wall on your right to reach the walled enclosure, one of the least-visited prehistoric sites on Menorca, and one of the few on the northern side of the island. The fine four-metre *taula* and partly collapsed *talayot* here are proof of the longevity of Menorca's megalithic culture, post-dating the earlier and more famous examples at Trepucó (see p.95) by as much as a thousand years.

You're now at the highest point of the walk, with grand views to the coast below. Rejoin the path by the threshing floor and follow it for 1.2km down to the sea at **Cala Sa Torreta**, a remote, sandy beach covered in dried seaweed and seaborne rubbish – not much good for swimming, though the clump of Aleppo pines behind the beach is a good spot for a picnic and some birdwatching. From the beach, take the wide track that climbs up to your right, past a small hut, and continue across the headland back towards Tamarells des Nord. As you rejoin the seafront the path swings right. Walk inland for 100m to a fork, then go left another 100m and you should see the fire-warning sign you passed earlier. Head for this, and then retrace your steps back to Es Grau.

right for the final leg of the journey. The further you go, the barer the landscape becomes – grass gives way to succulents, but even they can't survive on the wind-stripped headland where the solitary **lighthouse** shines out over a bare lunar-like landscape of tightly layered, crumbly slate. The light-house is closed to the public, but the views out over the coast are dramatic and you can pick your way along the adjacent rocks, though if the wind is up this isn't much fun.

CAP DE FAVÀRITX

In 1756, Cap de Favàritx witnessed one of the British Navy's more embarrassing moments when admiral **John Byng** (1704–57) anchored his fleet off here à propos of nothing in particular. The French had besieged the British garrison at Fort San Felipe (see p.105) at the start of the Seven Years' War and Byng had been dispatched to Menorca to relieve them. Instead, he dillied and he dallied, allegedly reading and re-reading the Admiralty's instruction book, and managed to get caught with his nautical trousers down when the French fleet turned up off Cap de Favàritx, too. The resulting battle was an inconclusive affair, but Byng faint-heartedly withdrew to Gibraltar, abandoning the British garrison to its fate. Back in London, the Prime Minister, the Duke of Newcastle, fumed: "He shall be tried immediately; he shall be hanged directly" – and proceeded to carry out his threat. On his return, Byng was court-martialled and shot by firing squad on his own flagship in Portsmouth harbour, an event which famously prompted **Voltaire** to remark in his *Candide* that the British needed to shoot an admiral now and again "pour encourager les autres".

PORT D'ADDAIA

Map 4, F2.

"I shall ever think of Adaia, and of the company I enjoyed at that charming little Retirement, with the utmost Complacency and Satisfaction," wrote John Armstrong, an engineer in the British army, in the 1740s. If he could only see it now. The old **PORT D'ADDAIA**, at the mouth of a long, wooded inlet, has mushroomed dreary holiday homes, supermarkets and a marina, and as if that weren't bad enough, the neighbouring headlands now heave with the villas and apartment buildings of two oversized resorts, low-key **NA MACARET** (map 4, F2) and the more bois-

PORT D'ADDAIA

terous **ARENAL D'EN CASTELL** (map 4, F2). A redeeming feature is the latter's wide and sandy beach, set within a circular, cliff-edged cove, but otherwise you'll probably be keen to move on – by returning along the access road that's shared by all three resorts.

SON PARC

Map 4, F2.

The next turning along the Maó–Fornells road leads to **SON PARC**, a workaday grid of holiday homes flanking a golf course. One of the more upmarket resorts, Son Parc is fringed by thick pine woods and has a wide, pink-tinged sandy beach, equipped with a seasonal restaurant and beach bar. For a tad more isolation, walk the 1km north to **Cala Pudent**, a peaceful sandy strip set beside a narrow inlet. A stony track connecting the two beaches runs just behind the seashore.

FORNELLS

Map 4, E1.

FORNELLS, a low-rise, classically pretty fishing village at the mouth of a long and chubby bay, has been popular with tourists for years, above all for its **seafood restaurants**, whose speciality, *caldereta de llagosta* (*langosta* in Castilian), is a fabulously tasty – and often wincingly expensive – lobster stew. Nevertheless, there's been comparatively little development, just a slim trail of holiday homes extending north from the old village in a suitably unobtrusive style. Behind the village and across the bay lie rockily austere headlands where winter storms and ocean spray keep vegetation to a minimum. This bleak terrain envelops a quartet of ruined **fortifications** – evidence of the harbour's past importance – of which two are easy to reach: an old **watchtower**

peering out over the coast on the headland beyond Fornells and a shattered **fort** in the village itself. Built to protect the inlet from Arab and Turkish corsairs in the late seventeenth century, the forts were refurbished by the British, who constructed another on an island in the middle of the bay and posted a garrison. In a controversial piece of early tourist development, one of the British commanders turned a local chapel into a tavern, incurring the disapproval of fellow officer John Armstrong: "In the Temple of Bacchus, no bounds are set to their [the soldiers'] Debauches and such a quantity of Wine is daily swallowed down, as would stagger Credulity itself." Quite, but there again, there wasn't much else for the squaddies to do.

Fornells has no **beach** to speak of, but there is a strip of sand 1.5km back down the access road beside the apartment complex of Ses Salines (more interesting beaches in the area are detailed below). The village's sweeping inlet also provides ideal conditions for **scuba diving** and **windsurfing**. The Menorca Diving Club, on the seafront at the south end of the village, rents out equipment and organizes diving courses (☎971 376 412), as does the Diving Center Fornells, just across the street (☎971 376 431). At both, advance reservations for courses and equipment are strongly advised. As for windsurfing, Windsurf Fornells (☎971 376 458), situated beside the main access road on the southern edge of the village, offers tuition to both novices and more experienced hands, and teaches sailing skills too. Lessons include the use of their wetsuits, boards or boats.

Fornells is just 8km from Es Mercadal (see p.145) at the centre of the island. It's a lovely journey, with the road zipping through a range of red-soiled, pine-dusted hills.

FORNELLS

●

PRACTICALITIES

Buses from Maó and Es Mercadal pull in beside the minuscule main square, Plaça S'Algaret; for an idea of frequency of buses and journey times from Maó and Es Mercadal, see box on p.34. There's no tourist office, but this is hardly a hindrance as almost all of the amenities are within a few metres of the square, beginning with two (of the village's three) reasonably priced and comfortable **hostals**. Perhaps surprisingly, there's a fair chance of a vacancy in one or other of them even in the high season – but it's best to book ahead just in case.

Hostal Fornells

c/Major 17 ⓣ 971 376 676,
ⓕ 971 376 688.
The smartest of the village's *hostals*, this pleasant three-star establishment occupies a well-kept, two-storey building by the bay at the mini-resort of Ses Salines, 1.5km south of Fornells. It has a swimming pool and attractive gardens, too. ❻.

Hostal-residencia La Palma

Plaça S'Algaret 3
ⓣ & ⓕ 971 376 634.

A straightforward, two-star establishment with 23 guest rooms, all en suite, decorated in brisk modern style.
April–Oct. ❹.

S'Algaret

Plaça S'Algaret 7
ⓣ 971 376 674, ⓕ 971 376 666.
Bang in the centre of Fornells, on the main square, this two-star *hostal* is a neat little place, with slightly old-fashioned furnishings and plain but cheerful rooms.
Open May–Oct. ❺.

ACCOMMODATION PRICE CODES

After each accommodation entry in this guide you'll find a symbol that corresponds to one of nine price categories. These categories represent the minimum you can expect to pay for a double room in high season; for a single room, expect to pay around two-thirds the price of a double. Note that in the more upmarket *hostals* and *pensions*, and in anything calling itself a hotel, you'll pay a tax (IVA) of seven percent on top of the room price.

❶ Under 3000ptas/€18
❷ 3000–4000ptas/€18–24
❸ 4000–6000ptas/€24–36
❹ 6000–8000ptas/€36–48
❺ 8000–10,000ptas/€48–60
❻ 10,000–14,000ptas/€60–84
❼ 14,000–20,000ptas/€84–120
❽ 20,000–25,000ptas/€120–150
❾ Over 25,000ptas/€150

EATING

With the British garrison long gone, nightlife in Fornells is confined to the expensive **restaurants** that edge the waterfront on either side of the main square. Such is their reputation, that King Juan Carlos has been known to drop by on his yacht, and many people phone up days in advance with their orders.

Es Cranc

c/Escoles 31 ☎ 971 376 442. A couple of minutes' walk north of Plaça S'Algaret, in the heart of the old village, this is a smooth and polished restaurant offering a wide variety of fish dishes.

Es Pla

Passeig Es Pla s/n ☎ 971 376 655. The royal favourite, this harbourside restaurant, metres from Plaça S'Algaret, with its sedately bourgeois dining room, offers a superb paella for two for around

7500ptas/€45.07, as well as the traditional lobster stew.

Es Port

c/Riera 5 ☏ 971 376 403.
On the waterfront, just off Plaça S'Algaret, a relaxed and easygoing restaurant which concentrates on a magnificent *caldereta de llagosta*.

Sibaris

Plaça S'Algaret 1
☏ 971 376 619.
Hard-to-beat seafood specialist with a superb *caldereta de llagosta*.

BEYOND FORNELLS

The wild and rocky coastline west of Fornells boasts several **cove beaches** of outstanding beauty. Getting to them, however, can be a problem: the developers have barely touched this portion of the island, so the remoter spots are sometimes poorly signposted and the access roads are of very variable quality. Some are gravel or dirt tracks, particularly slippery after rain, others are asphalted but extremely narrow, and others are a mixture of all three. These byroads branch off from the narrow but metalled country lane which crosses the lovely pastoral hinterland. Aside from the beaches, of which the **Platja de Binimel-Là** is possibly the best, the most dramatic scenery is on **Cap de Cavalleria**, whose louring seacliffs rise precipitously from the ocean.

   Public transport around here is, as you might expect, non-existent and there's nowhere to stay.

Cala Tirant

Map 4, E2.
From Fornells, the obvious starting point for a coastal excursion is the stepped crossroads about 3km south of the

village, where the roads from Maó and Es Mercadal meet. At the junction, a signposted turning leads west down a country lane to pass, after 1.9km, the clearly marked turning to **Cala Tirant**. This side road is unmade, so it's a rough and dusty two-kilometre drive down to the cove, where a thick arc of ochre-coloured sand lies trapped between bumpy headlands, with grassy dunes and marshland to the rear. It's an attractive spot, but not a perfect one – there are villa developments on both sides of the cove and the beach is exposed to the north wind. Facilities catering for the villa residents include a beach bar, loungers, pedaloes and windsurfing.

Cap de Cavalleria

Map 4, D1.

West of the Cala Tirant turn-off, the country lane continues through a charming landscape of old stone walls and scattered farmsteads. After about 1.1km, keep straight on at the intersection and proceed for another 1km or so to the signposted right turning that leads north (along an asphalted byroad) towards **Cap de Cavalleria**, named after the *cavalleries* – baronial estates – into which Menorca was divided after the *Reconquista*. This is easy driving, and 4km later, halfway to the cape, you stumble across the **Ecomuseu Cap de Cavalleria** (daily: April–June & Oct 10am–7pm; July–Sept 10am–8pm; 350ptas/€2.10), an odd little museum occupying an old farmstead perched on a hillock with wide views of the cape. The Romans settled on the sheltered side of this headland in 123 AD and it was here they built the town and port of Sanisera on the ruins of an earlier Phoenician settlement, though almost nothing survives from either period. This ancient history convinced the European Union to fund the Ecomuseu, though it's hard not to think it was more of a job creation scheme – an

THE MARTELLO TOWER

Popular with the British military in the late eighteenth and early nineteenth centuries, the design of the **Martello Tower**, a combined barracks, gun battery and storehouse, was copied from a Corsican tower (at Martello Point) that had proved particularly troublesome to the Royal Navy when they had tried to capture it. These self-contained, semi-self-sufficient defensive fortifications, equipped with thick walls and a protected entrance, proved so successful and easy to build that they were erected in every corner of the empire, only becoming obsolete in the 1870s with advances in artillery technology.

impression the museum's paltry if gallant collection of Roman and Talayotic bits and pieces does little to dispel. The long cove which the Romans colonized – the **Port de Sanitja** – lies some 700m north of the museum, just west of the road to the cape. Archeologists have explored the site, but the main historical artefact is the Martello Tower – the **Torre de Sanitja** – built at the mouth of the inlet by the British at the end of the eighteenth century.

North of the museum, the road becomes bumpy and narrow as it slices across a sparse plateau that rises abruptly as it reaches the Cap de Cavalleria. This is Menorca's northernmost point, a bleak and wind-buffeted hunk of rock with mighty seacliffs, 90m high, and a lonely lighthouse (no access).

Platja de Binimel-Là

Map 4, D2.

Back on the country lane, it's a further 1.6km west to the signposted turning for **Platja de Binimel-Là**. At first, the dirt access road is wide and fairly easy to negotiate, but, after 1.5km, you hang a left and the last bit of road deteriorates – 500m of bone-jangling motoring, so most people park short of the beach. Once you've arrived, you'll spy a tiny freshwater lake set behind a narrow band of dark-red dunes which in turn gives onto a beautiful sand-and-pebble beach. This is a popular spot, though there are several more secluded and much smaller beaches on the east side of the cove, reached by clambering along the seashore. In the summer, there's usually an ad-hoc beach bar, and it's possible to rent **pedaloes** and **windsurfing boards**. The beach lacks trees and shade, so you may be confronted with the odd sight of bathers protecting themselves from the sun by plastering themselves in mud from the stream running across the beach.

One significant problem at Binimel-Là is the seaweed and detritus that sometimes get driven onto the beach by a northerly wind. If this has happened, and if you've come equipped with reasonably stout shoes and a hiking map, move on to **Cala Pregonda** (map 4, D2), a splendid, sea-stack-studded bay, with a wide sandy beach, thirty minutes' walk away to the west. The terrain isn't difficult, though there's no clear route except at the start: climb the white-washed steps over the wall at the west end of Binimel-Là beach and follow the wide track beyond across the salt flats and round a pebble-strewn cove; then keep straight to clamber over a small headland and it is down below.

Returning to the country lane, travel 400m west from the Binimel-Là turning and hang a left for the gentle byroad that will bring you into Es Mercadal (see p.145).

Central Menorca

Central Menorca incorporates the agricultural heart of the island, its rippling hills and rolling plains dotted with scores of whitewashed farmsteads. It's true that the tourist boom has knocked some of the stuffing out of the island's agriculture – witness the many unkempt fields – but it's surprising, considering Menorca's package popularity, just how traditional things are here. The land still carries the myriad marks of past agrarian endeavours in its dry-stone walls, stone ziggurats – built to shelter cattle from wind and sun – and old twisted gates made from olive branches. In addition, the land is dotted with scores of prehistoric stone memorials – primarily *navetas*, *taulas* and *talayots* – left by its earliest inhabitants, and representing the island's most distinctive historical sights. None of the four little towns of the interior – Alaior, Es Mercadal, Ferreries and Es Migjorn Gran – has been much modernized, each containing a comely ensemble of old houses dating back to the eighteenth century, sometimes further. All four towns are either on or easily reached from the 45km-long C721 Maó–Ciutadella road which spines the island.

West from Maó, the **C721** begins by clipping across a flattish agricultural district on its way to the hilltop town of **Alaior**, which boasts a pretty little centre of mazy cobbled streets. Alaior is also host to a couple of cheese-making factories, where you can sample local brands, and is just 3km from one of the island's most extensive prehistoric sites, **Torralba d'en Salord**. Further west, the C721 soon slides into the antique village of **Es Mercadal**, overlooked by **Monte Toro**, the island's highest peak, its summit occupied by both a military lookout point and a convent. The road to the mountaintop is excellent and the views superb, revealing the geological make-up of the island: to the north, reddish sandstone hills bump down to a fretted coastline, while to the south the limestone plain is gashed by wooded gorges (*barrancs*). This is an essential detour – unlike the excursion south to the seaside resort of **Son Bou**, a grimly modern affair only redeemed by its long sandy beach.

From Es Mercadal, it's a short journey southwest to **Es Migjorn Gran**, a pleasant if unremarkable little town that is both the starting point for an excellent two- to two-and-a-half-hour hike down the **Barranc de Binigaus** and situated close to another sprawling resort, **Sant Tomàs**. Back on the C721, you'll soon reach the westernmost of the four towns of the interior, **Ferreries**, whose rural surroundings are good for hiking – this chapter's second recommended walk is detailed here. Ferreries is also near to the **Binisues** manor house and the shattered ruins of the hilltop **Castell Santa Agueda**, once an important Moorish stronghold. A short excursion south from Ferreries leads to **Cala Santa Galdana**, an attractive resort of manageable proportions that's within easy hiking distance of several superb and isolated cove beaches.

For part of the way at least, there is an alternative to the C721 – the **Camí d'en Kane**, named after Richard Kane, Menorca's first British governor (see box on p.138), who devoted much time and energy to improving the island's communications. His principal achievement was the construction of a highway between Maó and Ciutadella –

funded by a tax on alcohol – and although much of Kane's original road has disappeared beneath the C721, a healthy portion has survived, running north of the C721 between Maó and Es Mercadal. A lovely route, the old road follows the agricultural contours of the island, passing ancient haciendas, olive groves, pasture and mile after mile of drystone wall. To reach it, take the Fornells road out of Maó and, 1.2km after the Es Grau turning, watch for the Camí d'en Kane sign on the left.

The C721 is marked by green-and-white **kilometre posts,** which make it easy to plot your progress.

There's no public transport along the Camí d'en Kane, but **buses** plying the C721 are fast and frequent, with supplementary summertime services running from Maó to Sant Tomàs and Son Bou, and from Ferreries to Cala Santa Galdana. Es Migjorn Gran is readily reachable by bus from

ACCOMMODATION PRICE CODES

After each accommodation entry in this guide you'll find a symbol that corresponds to one of nine price categories. These categories represent the minimum you can expect to pay for a double room in high season; for a single room, expect to pay around two-thirds the price of a double. Note that in the more upmarket *hostals* and *pensions*, and in anything calling itself a hotel, you'll pay a tax (IVA) of seven percent on top of the room price.

❶ Under 3000ptas/€18
❷ 3000–4000ptas/€18–24
❸ 4000–6000ptas/€24–36
❹ 6000–8000ptas/€36–48

❺ 8000–10,000ptas/€48–60
❻ 10,000–14,000ptas/€60–84
❼ 14,000–20,000ptas/€84–120
❽ 20,000–25,000ptas/€120–150

❾ Over 25,000ptas/€150

CENTRAL MENORCA

RICHARD KANE

Born in Ulster in 1666, **Richard Kane** was the quintessential military man. His long career in the British army included service in Canada and campaigns with the Duke of Marlborough. In 1713, following the Treaty of Utrecht, Kane was appointed Lieutenant-Governor of Menorca. He was transferred in 1720, but returned a decade later for a second stint, staying until 1736, the year of his death.

When Kane arrived in Menorca, he found a dispirited and impoverished population, governed from Ciutadella by a reactionary oligarchy. Kane's initial preoccupation was with the island's **food supply**, which was woefully inadequate. He promptly set about draining swampland near Maó and introduced new and improved strains of seed corn. The governor also had livestock imported from England – hence the Friesian cattle that remain the mainstay of the island's cheese-making industry. Meanwhile, a tax on alcohol provided the cash to develop Menorca's infrastructure, resulting in improved port facilities at Maó and the construction of the first **road** right across the island.

These were innovations not at all to the taste of the Menorcan aristocracy, who, holed up in Ciutadella, were further offended when Kane arranged for the capital to be moved to Maó. They bombarded London with complaints, eventually inducing a formal governmental response in an open letter to the islanders entitled *A Vindication of Colonel Kane*. Most Menorcans, however, seem to have welcomed Kane's benevolent administration – though not in the matter of **religion**. Here, the governor created genuine offence by holding Protestant services for his troops in Catholic churches. That apart, there's little doubt that, by the time of his death, Kane was a widely respected figure, whose endeavours were ill served by the colonial indifference of some of his successors.

both Maó and Ciutadella. **Accommodation**, on the other hand, is difficult to come by for independent travellers. The resorts are dominated by the package-tourist industry, though you can, of course, try pot luck. Of the four inland towns, only Es Mercadal and Es Migjorn Gran have recommendable places – but muster just three in total.

ALAIOR AND AROUND

Map 4, F4.

Cheese is as good a reason as any to stop at **ALAIOR**, an old market town 12km from Maó which has long been the nucleus of the island's dairy industry. There are two major companies, La Payesa and Coinga, both of which have factory shops near to – and signposted from – the old main road as it cuts through the southern periphery of town. From the new bypass, which swings round the town to the south, the easiest option is to come off at the easternmost of the three Alaior exits. From this direction, the first – and rather more folksy – shop you reach is owned by **La Payesa**, c/Banyer 64 (Mon–Fri 9am–1pm & 5–8pm, Sat 9am–1pm; ☏971 371 072), while the second is the larger outlet of **Coinga**, c/Es Mercadal 8 (Mon–Fri 9am–1pm & 5–8pm, Sat 9am–1pm; ☏971 371 227). Both companies sell a similar product, known generically as *Queso Mahon*, after the port, Maó, from which it was traditionally exported. It's a richly textured, white, semi-fat cheese made from pasteurized cow's milk with a touch of ewe's milk added for extra flavour. The cheese is sold at four different stages of maturity, either *tierno* (young), *semi-curado* (semi-mature), *curado* (mature) or *añejo* (very mature). Both shops have the full range and, although quite expensive, their prices are the most competitive you'll see.

Both cheese shops are in the lower part of Alaior; the medieval centre, a tangle of narrow streets and bright white

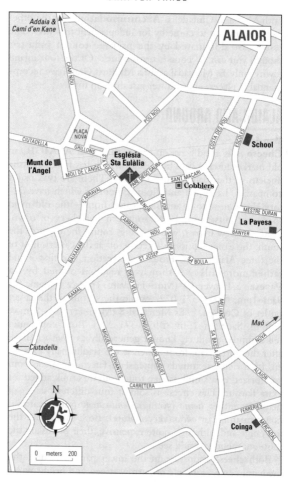

ALAIOR

Addaia &
Camí d'en Kane

CAMÍ NOU

POU NOU

PLAÇA
NOVA

CIUTADELLA

GRILLONS

Munt de
l'Angel

MOLÍ DE L'ANGEL

STA EULÀLIA

Església
Sta Eulàlia

PARE DIEGO SAURA

COSTA DES POU

ESCOLES

School

SANT MACARI

Cobblers

S-ARRAVAL

MENOR

MAJOR

MESTRE DURAN

La Payesa

BAIXAMAR

CARRARO

NOU

G SANJURJO

BANYER

S-DIEGO VEL

ST JOSEP

SA BOLLA

RAMAL

MIGUEL DE CERVANTES

AVINGUDA DEL PARE HUGUET

MELANS

Maó

SA BASSA ROJA

ALAIOR

Ciutadella

CARRETERA

NOVA

FERRERIES

MERCADAL

Coinga

N

0   meters   200

houses, climbs the steep hillside above. It's a quick two-minute drive or a strenuous one-kilometre walk up c/Bassa Roja to the top, where the imposing parish church of **Santa Eulàlia**, a magnificent edifice of fortress-like proportions built between 1674 and 1690, has recently been restored. The main doorway is a Baroque extravagance, its exuberant scrollwork dripping with fruits and fronds, while the facade above accommodates a rose window and a pair of balustrades. Beyond the church – just up the hill to the northwest along the L-shaped c/Moli de l'Angel – a mini-watchtower is plonked on top of the **Munt de l'Angel**, from where you can look out over the countryside. From the end of c/Moli de l'Angel, it's a few metres north to the old town's main square, **Plaça Nova**, an attractive piazza flanked by pastel-painted civic buildings of considerable age.

Practicalities

As for practicalities, **buses** to Alaior pull in beside the school to the east of – and about ten minutes' walk from – the old town. There's nowhere to stay, but for **food**, *The Cobblers Restaurant*, in an old mansion at c/Sant Macari 6 (daily late March to Nov, but call for hours before May and after Sept; ☎971 371 400), does excellent meat dishes – try the lamb – served in charming surroundings, either inside under the beamed ceiling or outside in the courtyard. The restaurant is just to the east of Santa Eulàlia: take c/Pare Diego Saura, turn right onto c/Verge Sa Muntanyeta and it is straight ahead.

Apart from a bite to eat and a quick gambol round the town, there's not too much reason to hang around – unless, that is, you happen to be here in the second weekend of August. This is when Alaior lets loose for the **Festa de Sant Llorenç**, a drunken celebration and display of horsemanship. As its highlight, with the town square packed, a

ALAIOR AND AROUND

procession of horses tears through the crowd, bucking and rearing, with their riders clinging on for dear life. Although no one seems to get hurt, you'd probably do best to witness the spectacle from the safety of a balcony.

Around Alaior: the Torralba d'en Salord

Map 4, F5. Mon–Sat 10am–1pm & 3–6pm; 400ptas/€2.41.

One of the more extensive Talayotic settlements, **Torralba d'en Salord** lies about 3km southeast of Alaior beside the road to Cala En Porter. The site is muddled by the old (and disused) Cala En Porter road, which slices right through the site, and by the modern stone walls built alongside both the old and new roads. Nevertheless, it doesn't take too long to figure things out. From the car park, signs direct you round the Talayotic remains, beginning with the *taula*, one of the best preserved on the island; the rectangular shrine surrounding it is also in good condition, and has been the subject of minute examination and much conjecture by archeologists. They discovered that several of the recesses contained large fire pits, which may well have been used for the ritual slaughter of animals. It was, however, the unearthing of a tiny bronze bull that really got the experts going, the suggestion being that, just as the bull was venerated by other prehistoric Mediterranean peoples, so it was worshipped here in Menorca, with the *taula* a stylized representation of a bull's head. The argument continues to this day. Beyond the *taula*, the signed trail circumnavigates the remainder of the site, which contains a confusion of stone remains, none of them especially revealing. The most noteworthy are the battered remains of a *talayot* just across from the *taula* and, about 30m further to the north, an underground chamber roofed with stone slabs.

From Torralba d'en Salord, it's just 3km to the
south coast resort of Cala en Porter (see p.112).

SOUTH TO TORRE D'EN GAUMÉS, SON BOU AND SANT JAUME MEDITERRANI

West of Alaior on the C721, take the Son Bou turning for
the beaches of the south coast and, if you still have the
enthusiasm, the rambling Talayotic settlement of **Torre
d'en Gaumés** (map 4, E5; free; open access). The drive to
both is easy enough – for the coast keep straight, for the
ruins go left at the signposted fork 2.5km south of the
C721 and follow the asphalted lane for another 2km. The
site possesses no fewer than three *talayots*, the largest of
which is next to a broken-down *taula* in the centre of a
badly ruined circular enclosure. Together, these remains
form what is presumed to have been the public part of the
village and it was here in the enclosure that archeologists
unearthed a little bronze figure of the Egyptian god of
knowledge, Imhotep, a discovery which reinforced the theory that these enclosures possessed religious significance. It's
impossible to interpret precisely the remains surrounding
the outside of the enclosure, as the site was inhabited – and
continually modified – well into Roman times. That said,
you can pick out the broadly circular outlines of a sequence
of private dwellings dating from as early as 1500 BC.

Son Bou and Sant Jaume Mediterrani

Map 4, E5.

At **SON BOU**, 8km south of Alaior, the antiquarian interest is maintained by an extensive **cave complex**, cut into
the cliff-face above the final part of the approach road, and

the foundations of an early Christian **basilica**, set behind the beach at the east end of the resort. They're hardly popular attractions, however, when compared with the **beach**, a whopping pale-gold strand some 3km long and 40m wide. This is Menorca's longest beach, and behind it has mushroomed a massive tourist complex of skyscraper hotels and villa-villages that spreads west into the twin resort of **SANT JAUME MEDITERRANI**. The sand shelves gently into the sea, but the bathing isn't quite as safe as it appears: ocean currents are hazardous, particularly when the wind picks up, and you should watch for the green or red flags. The beach accommodates several beach bars, and **watersports** equipment is widely available – everything from jet-skis, snorkels and windsurfing boards to sunbeds and pedaloes.

The development is at its crassest – and the crowds at their worst – towards the east end of the beach, where the foreshore is dominated by several huge sky-rise hotels, including the *Club Sol Milanos* (℡971 371 200, ℻971 371 226; ❾; May–Oct) and the *Club Sol Pinguinos* (same details). These two hotels, with their spruce, modern, balconied bedrooms, share facilities, including sun terraces, outside pools, bars and restaurants. A little to the west, a strip of dune-fringed, marshy scrubland runs behind the beach. This has provided the shoreline with some much needed protection, pushing the villa developments a kilometre or so inland. As a result, the bathing along this stretch of coast is far more secluded. In addition, one of Menorca's two **campsites** is here, the *Son Bou* (℡971 372 605, ⓦ*www.infotelecom.es/sonbou*; April to mid-Oct), just 3km inland from Sant Jaume Mediterrani on the road linking the resort and the Torre-solí Nou *urbanització* (but not Son Bou itself) with the C721. This well-equipped campsite has 430 pitches, as well as its own swimming pool, tennis courts, laundry, supermarket and restaurant. In high season (July &

Aug), campers pay 984ptas/€5.92 each, plus 545ptas/€3.28 to 1091ptas/€6.57/for a site, depending on size; cars (652ptas/€3.92) and IVA (7 percent) further add to the bill and there are small supplementary charges for electrical hook-ups and hot water. Shoulder-season rates are around 25 percent less.

> To get to the Son Bou campsite from the C721,
> do not take the Son Bou turning, but watch for the next
> turning just to the west; the campsite is signed.

ES MERCADAL AND AROUND

Map 4, E3.

Ten kilometres northwest of Alaior along the C721 you arrive at **ES MERCADAL**, squatting amongst the hills at the very centre of the island. Another old market town, it's an amiable little place of whitewashed houses and trim allotments whose antique centre straddles a quaint water-course. Tucked down c/Major, at no.16, is a Ruritanian **Ajuntament** (town hall), and the minuscule main square, a few paces away, has a couple of sleepy cafés. Furthermore, the town boasts one top-notch **restaurant**, popular with tourists, the *Can Aguedet*, metres from the C721 at c/Lepanto 30 (☎971 375 391; daily 1–4pm & 8–11.30pm), which serves up outstanding *Cocina Menorquína* – Menorcan cuisine. Prices are reasonable with, for instance, monkfish in leek sauce costing 2400ptas/€14.45 and grilled squid 1550ptas/€9.33. Es Mercadal also has a one-star **hostal-residencia**, the spick-and-span *Jeni*, in a modern building at c/Miranda del Toro 81 (☎971 375 059, ⓕ971 375 124; ❻). The 36 rooms here are comfortable, with attractive modern furnishings; there's a rooftop swimming pool, and the bar, though a little glum, is a pleasant enough spot to nurse a drink. To get there, leave the main square – Sa Plaça – along c/Nou and take the first left and then the first right.

Buses to Es Mercadal from Maó, Ciutadella and Sant Tomàs stop just off the C721 on Avinguda Metge Camps, which leads on to c/Nou. For information on frequency of buses and journey times see box on p.34.

Beside the C721 just before you reach Es Mercadal at the 20km post, is **Sa Farinera**, where an old manor house and small factory dating from 1905 have been turned into a tourist complex. There's a café, a restaurant and a museum, as well as wine, souvenir, toy and ceramic shops – plus an over-indulgence of cacti in the front garden.

Around Es Mercadal: Monte Toro

Map 4, E3.

From Es Mercadal you can set off on the ascent of **Monte Toro**, a steep 3.2km climb along a serpentine, but easily driveable, road. At 357m, the summit is the island's highest point and offers wonderful vistas: on a good day you can see almost the whole island, on a bad one, to Fornells, at least. From this lofty vantage point, Menorca's geological division becomes apparent: to the north, Devonian rock (mostly reddish sandstone) supports a rolling, sparsely populated landscape edged by a ragged coastline; to the south, limestone predominates in a rippling plain that boasts the island's best farmland and, as it approaches the south coast, its deepest valleys.

It's likely that the name of the hill is derived from the Moorish Al Thor ("high point"), but medieval Christians invented an alternative etymology. In predictable fashion, this involves villagers (or monks) spotting a mysterious light on the mountain and, on closer investigation, being confronted by a bull (*toro*) which, lo and behold, stops being nasty when he hears their prayers and obligingly leads them to a miracle-making statue of the Virgin. Whatever the truth, a statue of the Virgin – the Verge del Toro – was installed in a shrine in the thirteenth century and Monte Toro has been a place of pilgrimage ever since. The ceremonial highlight is May 8, when the **Festa de la Verge del Toro** (Festival of the Virgin of the Bull) begins with a special mass at the Monte Toro church and continues with a knees-up down in Es Mercadal.

The road signs say "Monte Toro," but in fact many locals (and some maps) assert that "El Toro" is more correct. The argument illustrates the difficulties involved in the renaming process undertaken since the death of Franco. In this case, "Toro" is derived from the Moorish for high point or mountain and thus, if this linguistic root is acknowledged, "Monte Toro" means, nonsensically, Mount Mountain. El Toro, allegedly the purer rendition, ignores, of course, the Spanish and Catalan "Toro" meaning bull.

The Augustinians plonked a monastery on the summit in the seventeenth century, but panicky islanders soon interrupted their reveries by building a small fortress here against an Ottoman invasion. Bits of both the monastery and the fort survive, the former incorporated within the present **convent**, the latter in a square stone **tower** that is now part of an army outpost bristling with all sorts of aerials and radar dishes. Overshadowing both is a monumentally ugly **statue** of Christ that, oddly enough, unites church and state: it was erected in honour of those Menorcans who died in a grubby colonial war launched by Spain in Morocco in the 1920s.

All of the army post and much of the convent is out of

bounds, but the public part, approached across a handsome courtyard with a dinky little well, encompasses a couple of gift shops, a delightful terrace café – from where there are more great views – a simple restaurant, where the *menú del día* costs 1800ptas/€10.84, and a charming church. Entry to the **church** is through a shallow porch, which is packed with bright flowers and deep-green shrubs. Inside, the barrel-vaulted nave is a modest, truncated affair dating from 1595, its gloominess partly dispelled by a central dome and racks of candles. The most prominent feature is the gaudy, 1940s high-altar piece, whose fancy woodwork swarms with cherubs and frames the much-venerated **Verge del Toro**, depicting the crowned Virgin holding Jesus in her arms with the enterprising bull of folklore fame at her feet. The statue is typical of the so-called black Catalan Madonnas – black after the staining of the wood.

Es Mercadal is an important crossroads: to the west along the C721 lies Ferreries (see p.154), while to the southwest are Es Migjorn Gran and Sant Tomàs (see below). North, the road meanders through red-soiled hills and fields to reach the coast, after 8km, at the delightful village of Fornells (see p.127).

SOUTHWEST TO ES MIGJORN GRAN AND SANT TOMÀS

Southwest from Es Mercadal, the road weaves a rustic route to **ES MIGJORN GRAN** (map 4, D4), a sleepy little town that trails along a gentle ridge overlooking intricate terraced fields. Of the several towns founded on the island in the eighteenth century, this is the only one not to have been laid out by foreigners. Consequently, the gridiron street plan of the likes of Es Castell (see p.103) and Sant Lluís (see p.108) is replaced here by a more organic lay-out, the houses of the old agricultural workers straggling along the elongated main street, c/Major, as it curves through town.

Es Migjorn Gran may be small and quiet, but it is linked by **bus** to Maó and Ferreries (see box on p.34 for more details) and is the starting point for an excellent hike (see box on p.151); furthermore, it has two **places to stay**. The cheaper is the fourteen-room *La Palmera*, a simple *casa de huéspedes* (guesthouse), which occupies an older three-storey house in the middle of town at c/Major 85 (☎971 370 023; ❹; May–Sept). The other is the *Fonda S'engolidor*, c/Major 3 (☎971 370 193; May–Sept; ❺), whose four spick-and-span guest rooms are upstairs in an attractively restored eighteenth-century house towards the south (Ferreries) end of town. Down below is the best **restaurant** in town, the reasonably priced *S'engolidor 58*, c/Major 3 (☎971 370 193), where the emphasis is on traditional Menorcan cuisine. The restaurant also possesses a delightful garden terrace (open summer only), with views over a wooded gorge. A good second choice is *Ca'n Pilar*, a café–restaurant at the north (Es Mercadal) end of town on c/Major.

**Heading northwest from Es Migjorn Gran,
it's just 7km to Ferreries (see p.154) along an
attractive country road which twists and turns its way
through shady gorges and past terraced hills.**

Sant Tomàs

Map 4, D5.

South of Es Migjorn Gran, the road shuttles along a wooded ravine that leads down to the south coast – and the

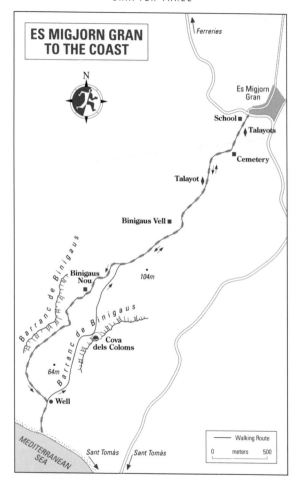

A WALK FROM ES MIGJORN GRAN TO THE COAST, VIA THE BARRANC DE BINIGAUS

Despite its modest dimensions, Menorca packs a surprising degree of diversity into its landscape. One of the island's most unexpected – and best hidden – topographical features is the series of dramatic limestone gorges, or *barrancs*, which score the southern coast, running from the inland hills down to the sea. Starting in the inland town of **Es Migjorn Gran**, this walk follows one of these, the **Barranc de Binigaus**, down to the coast near Sant Tomàs, passing through an area rich in Talayotic remains and impressive natural limestone formations.

The walk starts on the western edge of **Es Migjorn Gran**, where the main road from Ferreries reaches the first houses at the edge of the town. Approaching from Ferreries, look for the unsigned road off on the right, opposite house nos. 26 and 28 and the street sign for Avinguda Binicurdell.

Walk down this road, past a school and a fine old enclosure housing the substantial remains of two **talayots**. Beyond here, the road becomes rougher, running picturesquely between limestone walls flanked by handsome Aleppo pines. Some 200m further on you'll past another *talayot* on your right, followed by an attractive ensemble of white houses and Menorcan-style wooden gates. Continue, passing overgrown enclosures littered with limestone boulders, until you reach the farm of **Binigaus Vell** after 1km (the word *bini*, incidentally, is a Moorish legacy, meaning "sons" in Arabic, and a common component of many place names across the island).

Just past here you'll have your first sight of the sea, with views of Mallorca on a clear day. The path swings right, through an intricate but overgrown system of terraces and enclosures before climbing past a strangely eroded limestone outcrop to reach the brow of the hill. From here, the farmhouse

Continues over

of Binigaus Nou is visible ahead with the dramatic limestone gorge of the Barranc de Binigaus behind it, issuing into the sea via a narrow defile – your eventual goal – far ahead and below.

Two more *talayots* become visible to your left on the far side of gorge, part of a landscape which is hereabouts an incredible jumble of stone, with natural limestone formations and prehistoric remains mixed chaotically with more modern agricultural enclosures and terracing. Descend to the farmhouse of Binigaus Nou, a curiously baronial-looking – but now largely derelict – structure, and walk round to the left rear-hand side of the house. Here, there's an unusual Talayotic hypostyle chamber – a gloomy little semi-subterranean burrow supported by a few rudimentary pillars – and a terrific view of the stacked-up field terracing on the hillside behind.

Beyond here the path descends into the *barranc*. Go down to the bottom, passing more overgrown terracing to either side, until the track swings right and narrows at the bottom to reach a Menorcan gate and a well. Walk through the gate and head on 100m to reach the sea next to a gun emplacement buried in the dunes, surrounded – and virtually covered – by fantastically windswept vegetation. If you're in need of rest and

crass hotel and apartment buildings of **SANT TOMÀS**. The three-kilometre-long sandy **beach**, however, is superb, very similar to that of Son Bou, a couple of headlands away to the east – though all is not quite as it seems. A thunderous storm stripped the existing sand away in 1989, and what you see has been imported. The beach looks very inviting as it slopes gently into the ocean, but there are sometimes dangerous undercurrents so you should observe the green or red flags. The road reaches the shore halfway along the beach, which is called **Platja Sant Adeodat** to refreshment, head left and walk along the coast for 500m to reach the resort of Sant Tomàs (see below).

Return to the gate and well and now, instead of going left along the track, head straight ahead over the filled-in gap in the wall and contour round the hill to the right (there's no track here), keeping to the edge of the fields. After 200m you'll see a gap in the wall ahead. Head for this and pick up the trail on the far side, then follow this path for 500m as it runs along the top of a stone terrace until you reach a walled enclosure. Go right here, along the narrowing gorge, beneath increasingly impressive limestone cliffs, pockmarked with caves, until after a further 500m you reach a small T-junction. Go right 20m to the top of the path, then follow the zigzagging stone terrace up to reach the Cova dels Coloms – a huge, damp natural cave, impressive for its size if nothing else.

Return to the T-junction and go left. A few metres beyond, there's another insignificant-looking split in the path – take care to choose the upper trail, or you'll get stuck in the *barranc*. Follow the path as it climbs briskly out of the gorge, returning you to the original path you came down on between Binigaus Vell and Binigaus Nou, and retrace your steps to Es Migjorn Gran, a walk of about 25 minutes.

the west and **Platja Sant Tomàs** to the east. The latter is easily the more congested and it's here you'll find the high-rise hotels, among which the air-conditioned, ultra-modern *Santo Tomàs* is the most lavish (℡971 370 025, ℻971 370 204; ❾; April–Oct), while the marginally less expensive *Sol Cóndores* will do just as well (℡971 370 050, ℻971 370 348; ❾; May–Oct). Both have pools, restaurants, night-time entertainment and many types of sports facility. Windsurfing boards, jet-skis and pedaloes can all be rented on the beach nearby.

FERRERIES

Map 4, C4.

Tucked into a hollow beneath a steep hill, 8km from Es Mercadal on the C721 and 7km from Es Migjorn Gran, lies **FERRERIES**, with its narrow, sloping streets, framed by terraced fields. A surprise here is the pagoda-like piece of modern sculpture in the main square, the **Plaça Espanya**, while, just up the hill, the old town centre is marked by the neatly shuttered **Ajuntament**, primly facing the old parish church of **Sant Bartomeu**, a largely eighteenth-century edifice with a belfry of 1884 tacked on to the top. The liveliest time to be here is Saturday morning when a fresh produce **market** fills out the Plaça Espanya. Otherwise, there's not much to detain you unless you're after a country hike (see p.156) or keen to visit the Jaime Mascaró **factory shoe and leather shop**, 1km or so east of town along the C721.

Ferreries has a lively Saturday market 9am–1pm.

One definite plus here is the *Vimpi* **café-bar**, beside the C721 on Plaça Joan Carles, which serves some of the tastiest *tapas* on the island at 350–600ptas/€2.10–3.61. You wouldn't choose to stay in Ferreries – it's just too quiet – which is just as well because there's no recommendable accommodation. **Buses** to Ferreries stop in front of the *Vimpi*, which is a couple of minutes' walk from Plaça Espanya, straight up Avinguda Verge del Toro.

For information on frequency and times of buses to and from Ferreries see box on p.34.

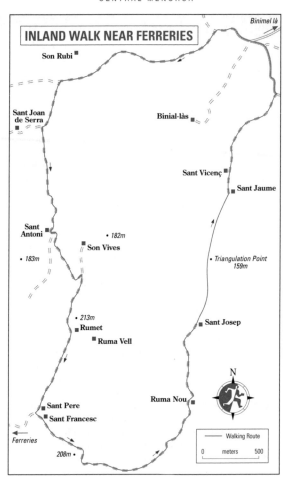

INLAND WALK NEAR FERRERIES

Binimel là

Son Rubi ■

Sant Joan
de Serra ■

Binial-làs ■

Sant Vicenç ■

Sant Jaume ■

Sant
Antoni ■

• 182m

Son Vives ■

• 183m

• Triangulation Point
159m

• 213m

Rumet ■

Ruma Vell ■

Sant Josep ■

Sant Pere ■

Sant Francesc ■

Ruma Nou ■

Ferreries

208m •

N

——— Walking Route

0   meters   500

AN INLAND WALK NEAR FERRERIES

This circular inland walk takes you through the miniature hills north of the small town of Ferreries, with fine views out over the interior of the island and down to either coast. Although most of the walk uses the access tracks of the many farms you'll pass en route, there are precious few signs of cultivation hereabouts. Indeed, apart from the occasional cow pasture, most of the land is given over to scrub and game enclosures, evidence of the declining state of Menorcan agriculture. If you have your own transport, it's best to start at the farm of Sant Francesc, though at a pinch you could do the walk from Ferreries itself, which is regularly connected by bus to both Ciutadella and Maó. Note, though, that this adds around 4km to the total distance, plus a steep climb up to Sant Francesc at the beginning of the route.

To reach the start of the walk, first find the roundabout on the eastern edge of Ferreries, by the Meubles allés store, where the Es Migjorn road meets the highway to Maó. Take the unsigned northern exit off this roundabout across the industrial estate (*polígon industrial*), past the Lamborghini showroom (displaying tractors, not sport cars), just beyond which the road becomes a country lane. Follow this lane for 1km to a fork at the Camí de Marcona sign, then go right and continue for a further 1km to the top of a steep hill, where you reach the farms of Sant Pere and Sant Francesc and the beginning of the walk.

Park considerately if you've driven here, then head through the gate to Sant Francesc and along the ridgetop track, from where there are marvellous views of both the north and south coasts, the heights of Monte Toro, Fornells, and, looking back, the neat white cluster of houses that comprises Ferreries. This is also a good place to spot Menorca's resident birds of prey, such as the booted eagle or red kite, circling on the thermals overhead or on the plains below.

Follow this track for 1km, passing the first of innumerable *Coto Privado de Caza* ("private game enclosure") signs, then swing left in front of a gate festooned with no-entry signs and past a clump of weirdly wind-shaped wild olive on the brow of the hill. Around 500m further on you pass through another set of gates, marked *propriedad privado* (private property) – act responsibly and it's extremely unlikely that anyone will object to your being there. Continue across an area of scrub full of small, elusive birds, following the track straight ahead through Ruma Nou farm and on for another 500m to reach Sant Josep.

Head round the left side of the farmhouse, crossing a muddy cow pasture then going carefully around the gate at the far end. Follow the track straight on along the ridgetop for 100m until it veers right through a gap in the wall and then disappears. Ahead you'll see the farms of Sant Jaume and Sant Vicenc – your next goal – though the lack of a clear path makes finding a route down to them slightly difficult. Follow the overgrown ridgetop wall for another 100m to reach a semi-ruined triangulation point at the highest point of the ridge. From here, you'll spy the ruined fortifications of the Castell Santa Agueda (see p.162) on the hilltop to your left, and the rocky finger of the Cap de Cavalleria (see p.132) stretching into the sea ahead. The next 500m is a bit of a scramble: climb over the wall by the triangulation point (there's a stepping stone to help you over), then follow the ridgetop wall down to Sant Jaume, climbing over a couple more small walls en route, until you emerge on the broad track in front of the farm.

The remainder of the walk is either on surfaced roads or well-defined paths. Follow the track in front of Sant Jaume farm for 500m to hit a metalled road and turn left, with the strange, fortress-like natural rock formation at the summit of El Pujol hill away to your right. Then continue along the road over

Continues over

AN INLAND WALK NEAR FERRERIES

a T-junction and past the following turn off to the right as the road swings left until the houses of Son Rubi appear on the bluff ahead. Carry on past the entrance to Son Rubi, after which the road reverts to dirt track.

At the fork 300m ahead go left, passing a line of small fig trees on your right followed by the entrance to Sant Joan de Serra. The path then swings left again, with Castell Santa Agueda, now closer to hand, rearing into view once more on your right. Some 250m past the Sant Joan de Serra turn-off, pass through the gates to San Antoni de Ruma. Climb up to the farmhouse and make a left turn at the fork just beyond onto a metalled road. Gird your loins here for a final climb back up to the ridgetop, ascending steeply into a narrow wooded valley. Reach the T-junction at the top and turn left for the final kilometre back to your starting point at Sant Francesc.

SOUTH OF FERRERIES: CALA SANTA GALDANA

Map 4, C5.

South from Ferreries, an excellent eight-kilometre road clips through a picturesque pastoral landscape down to **CALA SANTA GALDANA**. Once a much-loved beauty spot, the bay has experienced a rash of development since the building of the road and is now cluttered with high-rises. But, despite the concrete, there's no denying the beauty of the setting, the curving sandy **beach** framed by pine-studded, limestone cliffs and intercepted by a rocky promontory adjacent to a narrow river. Early in the morning or out of season is the best time to appreciate the scene – or you can escape the crowds by hiking round the headland beside the *Hotel Audax* at the west end of the bay. Alternatively, it's possible to hire out all sorts of **watersports** equipment – from pedaloes and water scooters to windsurfing boards and snorkelling tackle; and small boats ply regularly to other more secluded beaches (see below).

Among the resort's three high-rise **hotels**, you're most likely to find a vacant room at the luxurious, four-star *Audax* (☎971 154 646, ☎971 154 647; ❾; April–Oct), though if you're prepared to pay this much, make sure you get a sea-facing balcony. The comparable *Cala Galdana*, set just back from the beach (☎971 154 500, ☎971 154 526; ❾; April–Oct) and the massive, three-star *Sol Élite Gavilanes* (☎971 154 545, ☎971 154 546; ❾; April–Oct) both have spick-and-span modern rooms, but lack style or special interest. At the other end of the market, the simple *S'Atalaia* **campsite** is located about 4km back down the road towards Ferreries (☎971 373 095, ☎971 374 232; open all year). Pine trees shade much of the site, which has an outdoor swimming pool and a restaurant–bar. It can accommodate about a hundred guests and advance reservations are strongly advised. Charges range from 545ptas/€3.28 to 1091ptas/€6.57 for a site depending on size, plus 652ptas/€3.92 for a vehicle, and 984ptas/€5.91 per person.

Back in the resort, there's a good-quality seafood **restaurant**, *El Mirador* (☎971 154 503), built into the promontory that pokes out from the beach, though you do pay over the odds for the setting. If your budget doesn't stretch that far, other less expensive choices are stuck behind the *Hotel Audax* on c/Mirador. Additional facilities include **car rental** outlets – for instance Autosmenorsur (☎971 154 675), metres from the *Hotel Cala Galdana* – and Radio-Taxi Salord Ferrerías (☎971 1550 68). There are regular **buses** to Cala Santa Galdana from Ferreries from May to October.

Around Cala Santa Galdana

Several exquisite **cove beaches** (*calas*) lie within easy reach of Cala Santa Galdana, the most obvious choice being **Cala**

Mitjana, just 1km to the east, and further on, idyllic **Cala Trebalúger** and **Cala Macarella**.

Cala Mitjana
Map 4, C5.

The footpath to **Cala Mitjana** begins beside the *Hotel Sol Élite Gavilanes* at the Plaça Na Gran in Cala Santa Galdana. A gate at the back of the hotel's parking lot leads onto an easy-to-follow path through coastal pine woods. At the first fork veer right and after a few minutes you'll reach a clearing which you should cross diagonally to the left. Beyond the clearing, the path soon descends to the beach. Once you get there you'll be rewarded with a broad strip of sand set beneath wooded cliffs at the end of a beguiling bay – though sometimes there's an unpleasant smell from an accumulation of seaweed. A favourite sport here is jumping into the crystal-clear water from the surrounding cliffs.

Cala Trebalúger
Map 4, D5.

Equally beautiful, but also afflicted with periodic seaweed problems, is **Cala Trebalúger**, a further 2.5km east and best reached by boat from Cala Santa Galdana (summer 1–2 daily). Cala Trebalúger boasts a beautiful arc of sand flanked by steep cliffs and crossed by a stream which emerges from the gorge behind. There are no beach facilities, so you'll need to take your own food and drink.

Cala Macarella
Map 4, B5.

Walking west from Cala Santa Galdana on the footpath starting opposite the *Hotel Audax* (at the top of the small flight of steps beside the telephone boxes) it takes about forty minutes to reach **Cala Macarella**. Here, severe, partly wooded limestone cliffs surround a band of white sand that shelves gently into the Med. It's a beautiful spot, with ideal conditions for swimming – and, unlike the other beaches around Cala Santa Galdana, seaweed is never a problem. There's a touch of development in the form of a summertime beach bar, and sunbeds and pedaloes for rent, but it's nothing excessive.

WEST OF FERRERIES: BINISUES AND CASTELL SANTA AGUEDA

A lattice of rough country roads covers the sparsely inhabited hills and farmland in between Ferreries and the north coast. The district's main attractions are the rural manor house of **Binisues** and the nearby **Castell Santa Agueda**, whose modest remains perch atop the peak of the same name, Menorca's second highest at 268m. To get to both the mansion and the castle, take the C721 west out of Ferreries and watch for the (clearly signed) right turn after about 3km.

Binisues

Map 4, C3. May–Oct daily 11am–7pm; 500ptas/€3.
Turning right off the C721 just west of Ferreries, you'll soon spy the pastel-painted stonework of **Binisues** on a gentle ridge to the left. The house occupies a grand setting, overlooking the valleys and hills of central Menorca, and its elegant symmetries reflect the self-confidence of the island's nineteenth-century aristocracy. The interior, however, is a yawn. Presumably, the intention is to re-create the mansion's old aristocratic air, but the accumulated knick-knacks look as if they've been thrown in haphazardly. Even worse, if you persevere beyond the family rooms, you'll find an assortment of old agricultural implements on the second floor and a

collection of mounted butterflies above – you're much better off sipping coffee at the restaurant and admiring the view.

Castell Santa Agueda

Map 4, C3.

About 3km west of the Binisues turning, the C721 leaves the central hills for the flatlands surrounding Ciutadella (see p.165). Within easy striking distance of the main road in between Binisues and Ciutadella are a clutch of clearly signed prehistoric sites, principally Torrellafuda and the Naveta d'es Tudons (see p.187), 5km from Ciutadella – just after kilometre post 40 – and the island's best-preserved naveta. For more on Menorca's prehistory in general, see p.195.

Returning to the lane below Binisues, it's about 2km more to the deserted schoolhouse (and parking space) on the right-hand side which marks the start of the hour-long hike up the rocky and lightly wooded mountainside to the **Castell Santa Agueda**. The Romans were the first to recognize the hill's strategic value, fortifying the summit in the second century BC, but it was the Moors who developed the stronghold, and it was here that they made their final stand against Alfonso III's invasion in 1287. Fresh from their defeat at Maó, the demoralized Moors didn't put up much of a fight – though they would certainly have been more determined if they had known of their ultimate fate. After the surrender, the Catalans demanded a heavy ransom for every captive. Those who couldn't pay were enslaved and those who weren't fit to work as slaves were shoved onto ships, taken out to sea and thrown overboard. Nowadays, little remains of the Moorish castle bar a few crumbling turrets and walls, but the views are spectacular.

Ciutadella and
the west

Like Maó, **CIUTADELLA** sits high above its harbour, but here navigation is far more difficult, up a narrow channel too slender for all but the smallest of cargo ships. Nonetheless, despite this nautical inconvenience, Ciutadella was the island's capital up until fairly recently: the Romans chose it, the Moors adopted it as Medina Minurka, and the Catalans of the *Reconquista* flattened the place and began all over again. In the event, the medieval Catalan town didn't last either – in 1558, Turkish corsairs razed the place and carted off three thousand captives (around eighty percent of the population) to the slave markets of Istanbul. As news spread of the disaster, the Pope organized a European whip-round, and, with the money in the bag, an intrepid Menorcan doctor, one Marcos Marti, ventured east to Istanbul to buy the slaves back. Marti was remarkably successful – but there again, the Turks were raiding for the money, not to fight a religious war – and the returning hostages, together with the survivors of the assault, determinedly rebuilt Ciutadella in grand style. They re-fortified the town's compact centre and then, reassured, set about adorning it with fine stone churches and sweeping mansions.

**The background to the Turkish raid
of 1558 is explained on p.172.**

Throughout the seventeenth century, Menorca's leading landowners hung out in Ciutadella, confident of their position and power. They were, however, in for a shock: for the colonial powers of the eighteenth century, the town's feeble port had no appeal when compared with Maó's magnificent inlet, and the British simply – and abruptly – moved the capital to Maó in 1722. Thereafter, Maó flourished as a trading centre, while Ciutadella stagnated – a long-lasting economic reverie that has, by coincidence, preserved the town's old and beautiful centre as if in aspic.

Despite the fact that Ciutadella had lost its capital status, the bulk of the Menorcan aristocracy decided to remain. The island's foreign rulers pretty much left them to stew in their own juice – an increasingly redundant, landowning class far from the wheels of mercantile power. Consequently, there's very little British or French influence in Ciutadella's **architecture**: instead, the narrow, cobbled streets boast fine old palaces, hidden away behind high walls, and a set of Baroque and Gothic churches very much in the Spanish tradition. Essentially, it's the whole ensemble, centred on stately **Plaça d'es Born**, that gives Ciutadella its appeal rather than any specific sight, though the mostly Gothic **cathedral** is a delight, as is the eclectic **Museu Diocesà de Menorca**. An ambitious renovation programme has further enhanced the town, restoring most of the old stone facades to their honey-coloured best. Added to this are some excellent **restaurants**, especially on the harbourfront, and a reasonably adequate supply of *hostals* and **hotels**. It's a lovely place to stay, and nothing else on

Menorca rivals the evening *passeig* (promenade), when the townsfolk amble the narrow streets of the centre, dropping in on pavement cafés as the sun sets. Allow at least a couple of days, more if you seek out one of the beguiling cove **beaches** within easy striking distance of town. There are several wonderful spots to choose from, but **Cala Turqueta** and **Cala d'Algairens** are probably the pick of the bunch. Spare time also for the prehistoric sites hereabouts, most notably the **Naveta d'es Tudons** and **Son Catlar**.

Ciutadella

Map 5, C4.

All of Ciutadella's key attractions are clustered in the compact **town centre**, a rabbit warren of lanes, fringed by fine old mansions and handsome churches. Most of the centre is pedestrianized, but it only takes a few minutes to walk from one side to the other, and keeping your bearings is fairly straightforward – the main square and harbour are on the west side of the centre, the ring road to the east.

ARRIVAL

Buses from Maó and points east arrive at the station on c/Barcelona, just south off the end of the Camí de Maó, an extension of the main island highway, the C721. **Catamarans** from Cala Rajada, on Mallorca, dock in the harbour right below the Plaça d'es Born, as do **car ferries** from Mallorca's Port d'Alcúdia. For more information on ferry services see p.18 in *Basics*.

If you're **driving** in, there's no missing the ring road, which, under various names – principally Avinguda Jaume I

El Conqueridor and Avinguda Capità Negrete – encircles the old town. Approaching from the east, turn left when you hit it and keep going until you reach its conclusion beside the Plaça dels Pins; if you can't find a **parking** spot actually on this square, turn left at the top near the bus stops and drive down Passeig Sant Nicolau, where there's always space.

Avinguda Capità Negrete is named in honour of the Spanish captain, who, with just forty full-time soldiers and six hundred members of the local militia, bravely resisted the Turkish attack of 1558 for as long as he possibly could.

INFORMATION AND SERVICES

The **Oficina d'Informació Turistica** (May–Oct Mon–Fri 9am–1.30pm & 6–8pm, Sat 9am–1pm; Nov–April Mon–Fri 9am–1.30pm & 5–7pm, Sat 9am–1pm; ℡971 382 693) has a good range of information on Menorca as a whole and Ciutadella in particular. This includes bus timetables, ferry schedules, lists of *hostals* and hotels, and free maps. They will not, however, help you find accommodation. The tourist office is directly opposite the Cathedral on Plaça Catedral, bang in the middle of the old town.

The town's main **banks** are Banca March, at Plaça d'es Born 10 and Plaça Alfons III, 5; and Sa Nostra, c/Maó 2, on Plaça Nova. The **post office** is handily located at Plaça d'es Born 8 (Mon–Fri 8.30am–2.30pm, Sat 9.30am–1pm), while **internet** access is available at *Café Internet*, Plaça dels Pins 37 (200ptas/€1.20 per hour). Basic medical needs are catered for by several **pharmacies** in town; there's one at Plaça Nova 2.

GETTING AROUND

Ciutadella's compact centre is easily seen on foot. Handy for exploring other parts of the west coast is the network of **local buses** that leaves from Plaça dels Pins, on the west side of the town centre next to the main square, Plaça d'es Born. **Taxis** leave from Plaça dels Pins and Avinguda Constitució, round the corner from Plaça Alfons III. You've also the choice of half-a-dozen **car-rental** companies. Among them, there's an Avis outlet on the ring road at Avinguda Jaume I El Conqueridor 81 (℡971 381 174) and a Betacar along the street at no. 59 (℡971 382 998). **Bicycles** and **mopeds** can be rented from Bicicletas Tolo, c/Sant Isidre 32, off Plaça Artrutx (℡971 381 576).

For information on journey times and frequency of
buses to and from Ciutadella, see box on p.34.

ACCOMMODATION

There's hardly a plethora of **accommodation** in Ciutadella, but the town does have four quality hotels that aren't booked up by package-tour operators – the *Geminis*, *Patricia*, *Playa Grande* and *Sant Ignasi* – and a handful of fairly comfortable and reasonably priced *hostals* dotted in and around the centre. The establishments listed below are open all year, unless otherwise specified.

INEXPENSIVE

Hotel Madrid
c/Madrid s/n ℡971 380 328.
Fourteen quite comfortable rooms in a run-of-the-mill, villa-style building with its own ground-floor café–bar. Located near the waterfront, a fifteen-minute walk west of

PRICE CODES

After each accommodation entry in this guide you'll find a symbol that corresponds to one of nine price categories. These categories represent the minimum you can expect to pay for a double room in high season; for a single room, expect to pay around two-thirds the price of a double. Note that in the more upmarket *hostals* and *pensions*, and in anything calling itself a hotel, you'll pay a tax (IVA) of seven percent on top of the room price.

① Under 3000ptas/€18
② 3000–4000ptas/€18–24
③ 4000–6000ptas/€24–36
④ 6000–8000ptas/€36–48
⑤ 8000–10,000ptas/€48–60
⑥ 10,000–14,000ptas/€60–84
⑦ 14,000–20,000ptas/€84–120
⑧ 20,000–25,000ptas/€120–150
⑨ Over 25,000ptas/€150

the town centre. To get there, follow Passeig Sant Nicolau from the Plaça dels Pins, take the third turning on the left (e/Saragossa) and you'll hit c/Madrid just east of the *hostal* at the first major intersection. ④.

Hostal-residencia Oasis

c/Sant Isidre 33 ☎971 382 197.
Footsteps away from Plaça Artrutx, an attractive one-star with nine simple rooms set around a gaudily decorated courtyard-restaurant. ❸.

Hostal Sa Prensa

c/Madrid s/n ☎971 382 698.
Recently refurbished, villa-like, one-star *hostal* with six spartan bedrooms above a café–bar. It's a fifteen-minute walk west of the centre, close to the rocky seashore at the end of c/Madrid. To get there, follow Passeig Sant Nicolau from the Plaça dels Pins, take the fourth turning on the left (c/Joan Ramis i Ramis) and you'll hit c/Madrid just beside the *hostal* at the first major intersection. ❸.

MODERATE

Hotel-residencia Alfonso III

Camí de Maó 53 ⓣ 971 380 150, ⓕ 971 481 529.
Located beside the main road from Maó, a couple of minutes' walk from the ring road, a brashly modern, but reasonably well-maintained hotel with fifty simple one-star rooms. Try to get a room at the back away from the noisy road. ❺.

Hotel Balear

Camí de Maó 178 ⓣ 971 482 341, ⓕ 971 482 557.
A modern, three-storey hotel in an unappetizing location, beside – and some 500m east of the end of – the main Maó–Ciutadella road. The rooms are OK, nothing more, but they are all en suite and there's a good chance of a vacancy here when everywhere else is full. ❺.

Hostal-residencia Ciutadella

c/Sant Eloi 10

ⓣ & ⓕ 971 383 462.
Unassuming yet comfortable two-star, in an old terraced house down a narrow side street off Plaça Alfons III. ❺.

Hotel-residencia Geminis

c/Josepa Rossinyol 4 ⓣ 971 384 644, ⓕ 971 383 683.
Distinctively painted in pink and white with blue awnings, this well tended, very comfortable two-star has thirty rooms, each decorated in bright modern style. The rooms at the front have Art Deco-style balconies and overlook a quiet and prosperous suburban street. To get there on foot, walk a few paces down c/Mossèn J. Salord i Farnés from the ring road and watch for the archway on the right; go through the arch and the hotel's on the right. Closed Jan. ❺.

Hostal-residencia Menurka

c/Domingo Savio 6 ⓣ 971 381 415, ⓕ 971 381 282.
A tidy two-star establishment of 21 rooms, some with

balconies, though they overlook a mundane side street. C/Domingo Savio is just east of the town centre, one block up from Camí de Maó. ❻.

All Ciutadella hotels and restaurants recommended in this chapter are shown on map 6 at the back of the *Guide*.

EXPENSIVE

Hotel Esmeralda
Passeig Sant Nicolau 171
☎971 380 250, ℹ971 380 258.
Located at the west end of the street, a fifteen-minute walk from the centre. The sweeping curves of this four-storey hotel are a classic example of 1960s design, with a swimming pool and private gardens out front. Most of the bedrooms have wide and expansive balconies and face out to sea, but the bulk are booked up by package-tour operators. Open April–Oct. ❼.

Hotel-residencia Patricia
Passeig Sant Nicolau 90 ☎971 385 511, ℹ971 481 120.
The smartest hotel in town, popular with business folk and handy for the centre.

Extremely comfortable, ultra-modern rooms with all facilities, the only downer being the lack of a sea view – though the best rooms have rooftop balconies with wide vistas over the town centre. The hotel also has a swimming pool. ❼.

Hotel Playa Grande
c/Bisbe Juano 2 ☎971 382 445, ℹ971 381 536.
This pleasant hotel with its brisk modern interior is located about ten minutes' walk south of Plaça dels Pins, at the foot of c/Mallorca. At the front, its balconied rooms overlook a narrow cove and a busy road, so if you're a light sleeper you're probably better off asking for a room at the back. Closed Jan. ❼.

Hotel Sant Ignasi
Carretera Cala Morell s/n ☎971

385 575, Ⓕ 971 480 537. This elegant nineteenth-century manor house has been tastefully converted into an immaculate, excellent-value hotel. Each of the twenty bedrooms is individually decorated in a style that blends with the original building, and there are gardens and an outside pool too. It's in the middle of the countryside, though the surrounding farmland is flat and dull. The hotel is about 4km northeast of the centre of Ciutadella, clearly signposted (down a very narrow 1.5km-long lane) from the road to Cala Morell. ❼.

THE TOWN

Flanked by handsome stone buildings, the mazy lanes and alleys of Ciutadella's charming **centre** crowd around the fortified cliff that shadows the south side of the harbour. The main plazas and points of interest are within a few strides of each other, on and around the expansive Plaça d'es Born. Much to its advantage, most of the old centre is pedestrianized.

Plaça d'es Born

Map 6, H5.
Primarily a nineteenth-century creation, **Plaça d'es Born** is easily the finest main square in the Balearic Islands. In the middle soars an **obelisk** commemorating the futile defence against the Turks in 1558, a brutal episode that was actually something of an accident. The Ottomans had dispatched 15,000 soldiers and 150 warships west to assist their French allies against the Habsburgs. With no particular place to go, the Turks rolled around the Mediterranean for a few weeks and, after deciding Maó wasn't worth the candle, they hap-

pened on Ciutadella, where the garrison numbered just forty. For the Menorcans, the results were cataclysmic. The one-sided siege ended with the destruction of the town and the enslavement of its population – there was so much damage that when the new Spanish governor arrived, he was forced to live in a cave. The obelisk's Latin inscription, penned by the mid-nineteenth-century politician and historian Josep Quadrado, reads, "Here we fought until death for our religion and our country in the year 1558." Such grandiose nationalism was typical of Quadrodo, then the region's most prominent politician and leader of the reactionary Catholic Union, which bombarded Madrid with complaints and petitions whenever central government did anything progressive.

Just to the north of Plaça d'es Born along c/Sa Muradeta, a wide flight of steps leads down to the harbour, where yachts and fishing smacks bob up and down in front of a series of waterside restaurants (see p.184), with the old town walls forming a scenic background.

The Ajuntament and the Teatre d'es Born

On the western side of the Plaça d'es Born stands the **Ajuntament** (town hall), whose early nineteenth-century arches and crenellations mimic Moorish style, purposely recalling the time when the site was occupied by the Wali's *alcázar* (palace). From here, it's a few paces along the north side of the square to the **Teatre d'es Born**, a neat, late nineteenth-century structure built to salvage some municipal pride. The merchants of Maó had just built an opera house and, pricked into cultural action, the oligarchs of Ciutadella promptly followed suit – though they weren't quite as energetic when it came to actually getting people to perform here. After years of neglect, the theatre has now been restored and is in use as both a theatre and cinema.

The Palau Torresaura, Palau Salord and Església de St Francesc

The northeast corner of the Plaça d'es Born is marked by the sweeping lines of the **Palau Torresaura**, built in the nineteenth century, but looking far older, and the grandest of several aristocratic mansions edging the plaza. Embellished by a handsome loggia, its frontage proclaims the family coat of arms above a large wooden door leading into a spacious coutryard. The antique interior, however, is off limits – like most of its neighbours, the house is still owner-occupied. An exception is the adjacent **Palau Salord** (May–Oct Mon–Sat 10am–2pm; 400ptas/€2.40), which is entered round the corner on c/Major d'es Born, the narrow cobbled street that leads to the Cathedral (see p.174). Dating from 1813, this rambling mansion has seen more illustrious days, but it's still of some mild interest for its sequence of high-ceilinged rooms redolent of nine-teenth-century aristocratic life.

Tucked away in the southeast corner of the square, the **Església de St Francesc** is a clean-lined, airy structure, whose hybrid architecture reflects the island's ups and downs. The original church was constructed shortly after the *Reconquista* and it was here in 1301 that King Jaume II met his nobles to parcel up the island into the feudal estates – the *Cavalleries* (from *cavaller*, the Catalan for knight) – that cemented his kingdom. In 1558, the Turks fired the church, but it was rebuilt to the original specifications in the 1590s, with further embellishments added later – the Baroque side door in the eighteenth century, the dome in the nineteenth. Like most of Ciutadella's churches, the interior was ransacked by Republicans in the Civil War, but bits and pieces did survive, notably several chintzy carved wood altars and a motley crew of polychromatic saints.

The Cathedral

Map 6, J4. Mon–Sat 8am–1pm & 6.30–9pm.

From beside Palau Salord, c/Major d'es Born leads to the **Cathedral**, a handsome structure built by Jaume II at the beginning of the fourteenth century on the site of the chief mosque, but remodelled after the Turkish onslaught of 1558. During the rebuilding, the flying buttresses of the original were partly encased within a thick stone wall to guard against future attack and this gives the Cathedral its distinctive appearance. The Gothic side door – on the south side of the church – was, however, left intact, its arching columns decorated with strange-looking beasts and the coats of arms of Aragon and Ciutadella, all surmounted by a delicate carving of the Magi honouring the infant Christ. Another survivor was the set of fierce-looking gargoyles that decorates the buttresses at roof level. The principal (west) entrance was added much later, in 1813, its flashy Neoclassical portico in contrast with the rest of the church and the intricate rose window immediately above.

Inside, light filters through the stained glass of the narrow, lofty windows to bathe the high altar in an ethereal glow. There's also a sequence of glitzy Baroque side chapels and a wonderfully kitschy, pointed high-altar canopy – or baldachin. The wall behind the high altar carries a medieval panel painting, the *Purification of the Virgin*, but most of the church's old furnishings and fittings were destroyed in a frenzy of anticlericalism when the Republicans took control of Menorca during the Civil War. Although the British had made Maó the island's capital in 1722, Ciutadella remained Menorca's ecclesiastical centre and, almost without exception, its resident Catholic hierarchy were rich and reactionary in equal measure. They enthusiastically proclaimed their support for the officers of Maó garrison when the latter declared for Franco in July 1936, but this turned out to be a major gaffe. The bulk of the garrison stayed loyal to the Republic, and, allied with local left-wing groups, they captured the rebels, shot their leaders and ransacked Ciutadella's main churches as retribution.

The Palau Olivar

Map 6, I4.

Directly opposite the Cathedral's west entrance is the **Palau Olivar** (no access), whose stern, eighteenth-century facade is partly relieved by a pair of miniature balconies fronted by wrought-iron grilles. In 1707, the house witnessed one of the town's crueller episodes, when a reclusive mother and daughter who worked and lived here were accused of witchcraft. Found guilty on palpably potty charges, the older woman was sent to prison for life, and the younger was executed – by any standard, a heavy price to pay for not joining in the town's social life.

Església del Roser

Map 6, J5.

From Plaça Catedral, the stone-flagged piazza beside the church, cut south down c/Roser and you'll soon pass the tiny **Església del Roser**, whose striking Churrigueresque facade, dating from the seventeenth century, boasts a quartet of pillars festooned with intricate tracery. The church was the subject of bitter controversy when the British commandeered it for Church of England services – which was not at all to the liking of the Dominican friars who owned the place.

The Museu Diocesà de Menorca

Map 6, J5. Tues–Sat 10.30am–1.30pm, plus May–Sept Sun 10.30am–1.30pm; 300ptas/€1.80.

At the far end of c/Roser, turn left past the palatial, seventeenth-century mansion of **Can Saura**, which is distinguished by its elegant stonework and overhanging eaves, and then left again for c/Seminari and the **Museu Diocesà de Menorca** (Diocesan Museum). Housed in an old and dignified convent and its church – the Església dels Socors – the museum is a delight. Before you go in, take a look at the elongated perimeter wall, a sober affair cheered by the delicate flutings of a Neoclassical portal that once served as the main entrance to the church. On top of the doorway, a bizarre sculpted cameo is the town's most unusual sight, depicting the Virgin Mary, armed with a cudgel, standing menacingly over a cringing, cat-like dragon–devil. Inside, the conventual buildings surround an immaculately preserved Baroque **cloister**, whose vaulted aisles sport coats of arms and religious motifs. The museum's collection is distributed chronologically among the tiny rooms edging the cloister; the labelling – where it exists – is in Spanish. The first three rooms hold a hotchpotch of Talayotic and early classical archeological finds, notably a superbly crafted, miniature bull and a similarly exquisite little mermaid (*sirena*), almost certainly Greek bronzes dating from the fifth century BC. Room 4 is devoted to the workaday paintings of a local artist, Pere Daura, and Room 5 has scale models of old Menorcan buildings made by one of the priests. Rooms 6–8 occupy parts of the old refectory and display some dreadful religious paintings, as well as all sorts of ecclesiastical tackle. There are elaborate monstrances, communion cups, reliquaries, croziers and such like, but it's the general glitter that impresses, rather than any individual piece. The adjoining **church** is often used for temporary exhibitions featuring local – or at least Catalan – artists.

The market

Map 6, K5. Mornings Mon–Sat.

Immediately north of the museum along c/Seminari, turn right down c/Socors to make the quick detour east to the **market** (*mercat*), which rambles over two miniature squares, Plaça Francesc Netto and Plaça Llibertat. This is another delightful corner of the old town, where fresh fruit, vegetable, meat and fish stalls mingle with lively and inexpensive cafés selling the freshest of *ensaimadas*. The fish stalls occupy a dinky little structure of 1895, the rest fill out a slender arcaded gallery that was constructed thirty years before as part of a municipal drive to clean up the town's food supply.

Café–bar Ulises, in the market on Plaça Llibertat, sells some of the tastiest *ensaimadas* in town.

The Capella del Sant Crist

Map 6, J5.

Doubling back to c/Seminari along c/Socors, turn right to pass the savings bank which occupies the **Palau Saura**, built in grand style by the British for a Menorcan aristocrat, one Joan Miquel Saura, in return for his help in planning their successful invasion of 1708. Just north along the street is the flamboyant facade of the **Capella del Sant Crist**, a Baroque extravaganza with garlands of fruit and a pair of gargoyle-like faces. Inside, the intimate, candle-lit nave supports an octagonal stone dome and is also home to an unattributed medieval panel painting depicting three saints of local significance. The skeletal crucified Christ above the high altar is supposed to have dripped with sweat in 1661 and remains a popular object of devotion.

The Estatua des Be

Map 6, J4.

From the chapel, it's a few metres north to the narrow, pedestrianized main street that runs through the old town – here c/J. M. Quadrado. Look to the left and you'll spy a perky bronze lamb – the **Estatua des Be** – stuck on a column. The lamb, symbolizing the Lamb of God and carrying a flag bearing the cross of St John the Baptist, is a reminder of Ciutadella's biggest shindig, the Festa de Sant Joan, held from June 23 to 25.

For more on the Festa de Sant Joan, see p.64.

Santa Clara

Map 6, K3.

Directly opposite the top of c/Seminari, a long, straight street – c/Santa Clara – shoots off north, hemmed in by the walls of old aristocratic palaces. At the top is the convent of **Santa Clara**, a mundanely modern incarnation of a centuries-old foundation. In 1749, this was the site of a scandal that had tongues clacking from Ciutadella to Maó. During the night, three young women hopped over the convent wall and placed themselves under the protection of their British boyfriends. Even worse, as far as the local clergy were concerned, they wanted to turn Protestant and marry their men. In this delicate situation, Governor Blakeney had the room where the women were staying sealed up by a priest every night. But he refused to send them back to the convent and allowed the weddings to go ahead, thereby compounding a religious animosity – Catholic subject against Protestant master – which had begun in the days of Richard Kane.

- -

Ses Industries, at c/Santa Clara 6, has the town's widest selection of wines, gins, cognacs and liqueurs.

- -

The Museu Municipal

Map 6, J2. Mid-April to Oct Tues–Sat 11am–2pm & 7–10pm, Sun 7–10pm; Nov–April Tues–Sat 10am–2pm; 300ptas/€1.80. Note that opening times change frequently.

Beyond Santa Clara, at the end of c/Portal de Sa Font, the **Museu Municipal** occupies part of the old municipal fortifications, a massive honeysuckle-clad bastion overlooking a slender ravine that once had, until it was redirected, a river running along its base and into the harbour. Inside the museum, a long vaulted chamber is given over to a wide range of archeological artefacts, among which there's a substantial collection of Talayotic remains, featuring finds garnered from all over the island and covering the several phases of Talayotic civilization. The earlier pieces, dating from around 1400 to 700 BC, include many examples of crudely crafted beakers and tumblers. Later work – from around 120 BC – reveals a far greater degree of sophistication, both in terms of kitchenware, with bowls and tumblers particularly common, and bronze weaponry, notably several finely chiselled arrow-heads. From this later period comes most of the (imported) jewellery, whose fine detail and miniature size suggests a Carthaginian origin. A leaflet detailing the exhibits in English is available free at reception. Temporary exhibitions take place downstairs.

THE RISSAGA

Almost all of the time, Ciutadella's long and slender harbour is as flat as a mill-pond, but every so often, for reasons that remain obscure, it is subjected to a violent disturbance, the Rissaga. This begins with sudden changes to the water level and is followed by a dramatic rush of water into the harbour before normality returns. The last great Rissaga of 1984 submerged the harbourside beneath two metres of water.

From the Museu Municipal, it's a five-minute walk back to Plaça d'es Born along c/Sa Muradeta with pleasant views down the ravine to the harbour.

East from c/Seminari to Plaça Alfons III

From the top of c/Seminari, the pedestrianized main street of the old town runs east as c/J. M. Quadrado. The first stretch is crimped by a block of whitewashed, vaulted arches, **Ses Voltes**, distinctly Moorish in inspiration and a suitable setting for a string of busy shops and cafés. Just beyond is **Plaça Nova** (map 6, K4), an attractive little square edged by some of the most popular pavement cafés in town. Just off the square along c/Sant Antoni, a narrow archway cuts through what was once the town wall, which explains the name of the alley beyond, Qui no Passa (The one that doesn't go through). Returning to Plaça Nova, c/Maó leads east to leave the cramped alleys of the old town at **Plaça Alfons III**, a traffic-choked square that was once the site of Ciutadella's east gate. The big old windmill here, the **Molí d'es Comte**, looks as if it should be in the countryside, its forlorn appearance not helped by its partial conversion into a bar.

The Castell de Sant Nicolau

Map 6, A6. Mon–Sat 7.30–9.30pm; free.

West from Plaça d'es Born, Passeig Sant Nicolau runs along the northern edge of Plaça S'Esplanada and reaches, after about 800m, the headland **Castell de Sant Nicolau**. This seventeenth-century watchtower is a dinky little thing, equipped with a drawbridge, oil holes and turrets, all stuck on unwelcoming rocks. The interior, however, is disappointingly bare and is, indeed, only open in the evening, when people come here to watch the sun set out beyond Mallorca.

Beside the castle is a statue honouring **David Glasgow Farragut**, who is shown with telescope in hand and wind in his hair. The son of a Ciutadellan who emigrated to America in 1776, Farragut entered the US navy in 1810, the start of a long naval career distinguished by several audacious attacks on Confederate strongholds in the Civil War. Most famously, Farragut forced the surrender of New Orleans in 1862 and as a result of this and other actions was made an admiral of the US fleet four years later. He visited Menorca in 1867 and was greeted by cheering crowds everywhere he went – in Ciutadella, the throng was so dense that he had to abandon his carriage and walk to his lodgings near the Cathedral. At church the next day, his secretary wrote approvingly that "hundreds of eyes were riveted upon the pleasant countenance of the unappalled admiral".

EATING, DRINKING AND NIGHTLIFE

For an early **breakfast** the best place to go is the market (*mercat*) on Plaça Llibertat, where a couple of simple cafés serve coffee and fresh pastries. Later in the day, around **lunch time**, aim for c/J. M. Quadrado, Plaça Nova and

Plaça Alfons III, which together hold a good selection of inexpensive café–bars, offering *tapas* and light meals. In the **evening**, more ambitious and expensive food is available at a string of excellent restaurants down by the harbourside, or at a couple of good establishments tucked away near Plaça d'es Born. Almost all the harbourside places have the advantage of an outside terrace, but note that – unlike those restaurants near the Plaça d'es Born – they usually close down in winter. Most places open daily during high season, though restaurants usually take a siesta between 4pm and 7pm or 8pm.

People don't come to Ciutadella for the **nightlife**, but there are a couple of late-night bars dotted round the old town and these are a good deal more authentic than the cluster of places down at the harbourside tourist zone. If you want to savour the flavour of the old town, your best bet is the pavement cafés of Plaça Nova, where you can nurse a drink and watch the early evening crowds amble by.

Ciutadella has several patisseries, but easily the best is the Pastisseria Mol, c/Roser 2, which sells excellent takeaway pizza slices, filled bread rolls and mouthwatering cakes from Monday to Saturday.
The shop is located across the square from the Cathedral.

CAFÉS AND CAFÉ–BARS

Café–bar Aurora
Plaça Alfons III, 3.
Next to the ring road on the eastern edge of the old town.

Open all day for both *tapas* and full meals, with the emphasis on Menorcan standbys. *Tapas* 400–900ptas/€2.40–5.42, *racions* about twenty percent more.

Café–bar Ca'n Nito
Plaça d'es Born 12.
Brisk, modern café of little
distinction, but it does serve
tapas right through the day,
seven days a week.

Café Central
c/Bisbe 2.
Busy little place next to the
Cathedral's main entrance,
serving traditional Menorcan
tapas, including various
sausages and cheeses. Open
summer only.

Pa amb oli
c/Nou de Julio s/n.
Just off Plaça d'es Born,
kitted out in vaguely rustic
style, this excellent café–bar
specializes in all things
Menorcan, with bowls of
peppers and olives liberally
distributed on the counter
and smoked sausages hanging
from the ceiling. The food is
filling, delicious and
traditional – and inexpensive,
too. Highly recommended.

Cafeteria Sa Barreta
c/J. M. Quadrado 16.
In the vaulted arches – Ses
Voltes – bang in the middle

of the old town, this
unassuming family-run café is
great for fresh *pa amb oli* and
other traditional Menorcan
snacks – sausage and so forth.

Café–bar Sa Llesca
Plaça Nova 4.
One of several pleasant, and
largely indistinguishable,
café–bars on this tiny square.
The ground-floor terrace café
is one of the more popular
spots in the old town and
there's a first-floor dining
room inside too.

La Torre de Papel
Camí de Maó 46.
The most urbane coffee
house in town, all polished
wood floors, with a
bookshop at the front, and a
tiny terrace café at the back.
Open Mon–Fri 10am–1pm
& 5–8pm.

Café–bar Ulises
Plaça Llibertat.
Amenable, low-key café–bar
next to the market. A locals'
favourite, their *ensaimadas*, a
snip at 200ptas/€1.20 each,
are probably the best in town.

CIUTADELLA: EATING, DRINKING AND NIGHTLIFE

For a Menorcan food glossary see pp.50–57.

RESTAURANTS

Café Balear

c/Marina s/n.
Justifiably popular, this attractively decorated café–restaurant sits at the back of the harbour by the bridge. Its pint-sized terrace is the best place to eat, but there are tables inside too. The food is first-rate – delicious shellfish, pasta and *tapas* all at reasonable prices.

El Bribón

c/Marina 107 ℡ 971 385 050.
Next door to *Casa Manolo*, a superb harbourside restaurant specializing in seafood, often prepared in traditional Menorcan style. Reckon on around 1800ptas/€10.84 for the *menú del día*, 2000–2500ptas/€12.04–15.06 for a main course.

La Guitarra

c/Dolors 1 ℡ 971 381 355.
Located a short walk from the Cathedral, this is arguably the best restaurant in town. This superb spot features the very best of Menorcan cuisine with main courses – anything from seafood to lamb – averaging a very reasonable 1500ptas/€9.03. The restaurant occupies an old cellar, whose stone walls sport a scattering of agricultural antiques. Highly recommended. Open Mon–Sat 12.30–3.30pm & 7.30–11pm; closed Sun.

El Horno

c/Forn 12 ℡ 971 380 767.
Near the northeast corner of Plaça d'es Born, a French-style basement restaurant, with good and reasonably priced food. Open evenings only.

Casa Manolo

c/Marina 109 ℡ 971 380 003.
At the end of the long line of restaurants flanking the south side of the harbour, *Casa Manolo* does fabulous seafood, with main courses averaging around 2500ptas/€15.06.

La Payesa

c/Marina 65 ☎ 971 380 021.
Popular tourist restaurant with a wide-ranging menu, featuring everything from pizzas through omelettes to seafood. Very child-friendly.

All Ciutadella hotels, restaurants and bars are recommended in this chapter are shown on map 6 at the back of the *Guide*.

BARS

Asere

c/Pere Capllonch s/n.
Ciutadella's busiest nightspot, this late-night tourist bar tunnels into the cliffside beside the harbour – at the foot of the steps near the bridge. Don't be surprised if it changes its name: until recently it was called the *Aladdino*.

Bar Es Moli

Camí de Maó 1.
Housed in the Moli d'es Comte, the old windmill across the street from Plaça Alfons III, this is a noisy and gritty café–bar, with a (very) young Menorcan crowd. Open till 1am.

Bar Sa Placeta

Plaça Artrutx s/n.
A tiny, modern neighbourhood bar just off the ring road. In a pleasantly revamped old building – hence the stone walls.

Unger Madison

c/Sant Joan 8.
Near Plaça Artrutx, the chicest bar in town with angular wooden tables, soft lighting and modern paintings on the wall. First-rate selection of domestic and imported wines. Open Mon–Fri from 6pm till early in the morning, Sat from 8pm; closed Sun.

CIUTADELLA: EATING, DRINKING AND NIGHTLIFE

West Menorca

Within easy striking distance of Ciutadella are the diverse attractions of **west Menorca**, beginning with one of the island's finest prehistoric remains, the **Naveta d'es Tudons**, located beside the C721 just east of town. Alternatively, it's southeast across the island's rural interior to the pristine cove **beaches** that notch the southern shore. There are several delightful spots to choose from, but two of the most appealing are **Cala des Talaier** and beautiful **Cala Turqueta**. As is common hereabouts, each of these coves is on private land, which means that there's a modest charge to get onto the beach, and the landowner prohibits access during the winter. There's no such restriction to the northeast of Ciutadella at the smart villa-village of **Cala Morell**, which occupies a singularly bleak and barren cove northeast of town, though here the sand of the south coast is left behind for brownish grit.

Entirely different is the intensively developed **west coast**, where long lines of villas carpet the flat and treeless seashore on either side of Ciutadella, from **Cala en Forcat** and **Els Delfins** in the north to the **Cap d'Artrutx**, 14km away to the south. By and large, this is all pretty dreadful, a remorseless suburban sprawl that is ugly and dull in equal measure. Here and there, however, the villas bunch round a narrow cove to form reasonably pleasant resorts. The pick of these is **Cala Blanca**, which also possesses a recommendable hotel with a reasonable chance of a room in high season.

From May to October, **buses** leave Ciutadella's Plaça dels Pins for the tourist settlements of the west coast hourly and there's a reasonably regular winter service too; see box on p.34 for more details. There are, however, no buses northeast from town towards Cala Morell or southeast towards

Cala Turqueta; buses to Maó pass by the Naveta d'es Tudons regularly, but check the driver is prepared to stop nearby before you depart.

EAST OF CIUTADELLA – THE NAVETA D'ES TUDONS AND TORRELLAFUDA

The best-preserved *naveta* on the island, the **Naveta d'es Tudons** (map 5, F4), can be found in a field to the east of Ciutadella, approximately 5km along the C721, then five minutes' walk from the roadside car park – but be aware that the sign is easy to miss. Seven metres high and fourteen long, the *naveta* is made of massive stone blocks slotted together using a sophisticated dry-stone technique. The narrow entrance on the west side leads into a small antechamber, which was once sealed off by a stone slab; beyond, lies the main chamber where the bones of the dead were stashed away after the flesh had been removed. Folkloric memories of the *navetas'* original purpose survived into modern times, for the Menorcans were loathe to go near these odd-looking and solitary monuments until well into the nineteenth century.

If your enthusiasm for prehistory has been fired, you should also take in **Torrellafuda** (map 5, G4), where a broken *taula* stands in the shadow of olive trees abutting a particularly well-preserved *talayot*. There are Cyclopean walls here too, but it's the setting that appeals as much as the remains, with the site encircled by fertile farmland – a perfect spot for a picnic. To get here, look out for the sign on the C721 about 2.5km east of Naveta d'es Tudons. Turn down the lane, bump the 800m to the car park, and it's a couple of minutes' walk.

Back on the C721, it's another 600m or so to the signed turning that leads to a third (vaguely) noteworthy Talayotic site, **Torretrencada** (map 5, G5), where a wind-scoured *taula* stands surrounded by drystone walls and the scant remains of a prehistoric stone circle.

For more on Menorca's prehistoric remains, see p.195.

SOUTHEAST OF CIUTADELLA

Beginning at the traffic island on c/Alfons V, the cross-country **Camí de Sant Joan de Missa** runs southeast from Ciutadella to the remote coves of the south coast. After about 3km, you reach the clearly marked farmhouse of **Son Vivó**, where the road branches into two with each (signposted) **fork** leading to several south-coast beaches, the nearest of which are about 8km away from town. Both roads are in (fairly) good condition and the signs are (usually) easy to follow, but the beaches mentioned below are all on private land and access is only permitted in the summer at a cost of about 700ptas/€4.21 per person. In all cases, the last stretch of the journey is a walk down to the beach from a parking lot, though this is hardly a hardship: the coastal scenery is delightful and anyway you're only dealing with a five- to ten-minute walk, if that. Incidentally, if you've rented a moped be prepared for a bumpy ride and watch out for the dust and muck churned up by passing cars.

South to Cala des Talaier and Cala Turqueta

Taking the more easterly road from the Son Vivó fork, you arrive after about 1.5km at the **Ermita de St Joan de Missa**, a squat, brightly whitewashed church with a dinky little bell tower. There's a fork here too, but the signs are easy to follow and you keep straight, with the road slicing across the countryside, before swerving round the **Marjal Vella farmhouse**. Shortly afterwards, about 3.7km from the church, the road passes the metal gate that marks the start of the two-kilometre-long, privately owned lane leading to the **Cala des Talaier** (map 5, F9), where a tiny strip of pale sand is backed by pine trees and overlooked by a ruined watchtower.

Back on the road, it's a further 600m or so to the start of the one-kilometre-long private lane that leads down to the little dell behind **Cala Turqueta** (map 5, G8), a lovely cove flanked by wooded limestone cliffs. The beach, a sheltered horseshoe of white sand, slopes gently into the sea, making ideal conditions for bathing, and because there are no facilities it's most unusual to find a crowd.

Son Catlar

Map 5, E7.
Back at the Son Vivó fork, it's 3km along the more westerly road to **Son Catlar**, the largest prehistoric settlement on Menorca and one which was still expanding when the Romans arrived in force in 123 BC. The most impressive feature of this Talayotic village is its extraordinary stone wall, originally three metres high and made of massive blocks – the square towers were added later. Inside the walls, however, all is confusion. The widely scattered remains are largely incomprehensible and only the *taula* compound and the five battered *talayots* make any sense.

Platges Son Saura

Map 5, F9.
Pushing on south from Son Catlar, you'll find the asphalt peters out around 1.5km further down the road, just before

you reach the ornate gateway that bars the entrance to the **Torre Saura farmhouse**. At the farmhouse, there's a privately owned parking lot on the left and from here a two-kilometre-long trail leads down to a wide horseshoe-shaped cove that shelters two beaches, the **Platges Son Saura**. Sometimes visitors are allowed to drive down the trail, sometimes not, but it is difficult going, especially after rain. The west side of the cove is more exposed and is often sticky with seaweed, so aim for the more sheltered eastern side where a wide arc of white sand is fringed by pines.

NORTHEAST OF CIUTADELLA – CALA MORELL AND CALA D'ALGAIARENS

Signposted from the C721 on the outskirts of Ciutadella, a well-surfaced country lane carves across a pastoral landscape on its way to **Cala Morell**, known for its prehistoric caves, and the attractive beaches of **Cala d'Algaiarens**.

Cala Morell

Map 5, F2.

The small tourist settlement of **CALA MORELL**, just 8km from Ciutadella, is one of the more refined *urbanitzacions*, its streets – named in Latin after the constellations – hugging a narrow and rocky bay. Besides swimming off the gritty beach, you can visit some of the man-made caves for which Cala Morell is noted, visible beside the road as you approach the village. Dating from the late Bronze and Iron Ages, the caves form one of the largest prehistoric necropolises known in Europe, and are surprisingly sophisticated, with central pillars supporting the roofs, and, in some instances, windows cut into the rock and classical designs carved in relief. No one owns the caves, so there's unlimited access – just scramble up from the road. The sight of one or two is sufficient for most visitors, but if you're after more than a glimpse, bring a torch.

Cala d'Algaiarens

Map 5, G2.

Backtracking along the country lane from Cala Morell, it's about 3km to the signed intersection. A narrow side road forks east from here across farmland to reach – after 2.5km – a guarded gate, where the landowner levies 700ptas/€4.21 for the one-kilometre onward drive down to **Cala d'Algaiarens**. Backed by attractive dunes and pine forests, the two sandy cove beaches here offer excellent swimming in sheltered waters.

SOUTH ALONG THE COAST FROM CIUTADELLA TO CAP D'ARTRUTX

Heading south from Ciutadella along the main coastal road, you're soon amongst the interminable villa complexes that extend almost without interruption as far as **Cap d'Artrutx**, at the southwest tip of the island. This is all rather depressing, but, amidst the aesthetic gloom, the resort of **CALA BLANCA** (map 5, C6) does at least possess a modicum of charm, its low limestone seacliffs framing a narrow cove and a small sandy beach. The swimming is safe and the beach has all the usual resort facilities, including a bar and water-ski-, lounger- and pedalo-rental. For somewhere to stay, there's little to choose between several sky-rise **hotels**, but the package-dominated *Mediterrani* probably has the edge, with spacious balconied and air-conditioned rooms just footsteps away from the beach (℡971 384 203, ℻971 386 162; ❼; May–Oct).

CONTEXTS

CONTEXTS

A brief history of Menorca

The earliest inhabitants of the Balearics seem to have reached the islands from the Iberian peninsula, and carbon dating of remains indicates that human occupation was well established by 4000 BC. The discovery of pottery, flints and animal horns fashioned into tools suggests that these early people were **Neolithic pastoralists**, who supplemented their food supplies by hunting. They hunted in particular the now-extinct *Myotragus balearicus*, a species of goat. Hundreds of these animals' skulls have been discovered and several are exhibited in Ciutadella's Museu Municipal (see p.179). The frequency of these finds together with the discovery of what look like remains of crude corrals on the north coast of Mallorca has encouraged some experts to assert that *Myotragus* was domesticated; this assertion is, however, strongly contested.

Why, or how, these Neolithic peoples moved to the Balearic Islands is unknown. Indeed, the first landfall may have been accidental, made by early seafarers travelling along the shores of the Mediterranean – part of a great wave of migration that is known to have taken place in the

Neolithic period. Many of the oldest archeological finds have been discovered in natural **caves**, where it seems likely these early settlers first sought shelter and protection. Later, cave complexes were dug out of the soft limestone that is found on both Mallorca and Menorca. These complexes comprised living quarters, usually circular and sometimes with a domed ceiling, as well as longer, straighter funerary chambers. The best examples are at **Cales Coves** (see p.111), near Cala en Porter, a complex which contains no fewer than 145 excavated chambers, and at (the more readily accessible) resort of **Cala Morell** (see p.190). These complexes represent the flourishing of what is commonly called the **Balearic Cave Culture**.

The Balearic cave dwellers soon came into regular contact with other cultures; the Mediterranean Sea, with its relatively calm and tide-free waters, has always acted as a conduit of civilization. The discovery of Beaker ware at Deià, in Mallorca, indicates one of the earliest of these outside influences. The **Beaker People**, whose artefacts have been found right across Western Europe, are named after their practice of burying their dead with pottery beakers. They had knowledge of the use of bronze, an alloy of copper and tin, and they exported their bronze-working skills into the Balearics in around 1400 BC. This technological revolution marked the end of the cave culture and the beginning of the Talayotic period.

The Talayotic period

The megalithic remains of the **Talayotic period**, which extended almost to the Christian era, are strewn all over Mallorca and Menorca – though, surprisingly, there's no evidence of them on Ibiza. The structure that gives its name to the period is the **talayot** (from *atalaya*, Arabic for "watchtower"), a cone-shaped tower with a circular base, between five and ten metres in height, built without mortar or cement. There are literally dozens of ruined *talayots* on Menorca and the detail of their original design varies from site to site: some are solid, others contain one or more chambers; most are found in settlements, but there are solitary examples too. This diversity has helped to generate considerable debate about their original purpose, with scholars suggesting variously that they were built for defence, as dwellings for chieftains, as burial sites or as storehouses. The mystery of the *talayots* is compounded by their unusualness. The only Mediterranean structures they resemble are the Nuragh towers found on Sardinia. A Sardinian connection would support the view that this phase in the Balearics' development resulted from contact with other cultures, though Sardinia is but one of several options, with Egypt, Crete and Greece also touted as possible influences. Whatever the truth, it is clear that by 1000 BC a relatively sophisticated, largely pastoral society had developed on both Mallorca and Menorca, with at least some of the islanders occupying the walled settlements that still dot the islands' interiors. On Menorca, the best illustration is **Son Catlar** (see p.189), not far from Ciutadella. Like other Menorcan settlements of the period, Son Catlar was occupied well into the Roman period.

There's no doubt that the Talayotic culture reached its highest level of development on Menorca, and it's here you'll find the most enigmatic remains of the period. These are the **taulas** ("tables" in Catalan), T-shaped structures standing as high as four metres and consisting of two massive dressed stones. Their purpose is unknown, though many theories have been advanced. One early nineteenth-century writer suggested that they were altars used for human sacrifice, but unfortunately for this lurid theory, the height of most *taulas* makes it very unlikely. Other writers have noted that many *taulas* are surrounded by

THE TALAYOTIC PERIOD

Phoenicians, Greeks and Carthaginians

Fearful of attack from the sea, the island's Talayotic peoples built their walled settlements a few kilometres inland. This pattern was, however, modified during the first millennium BC, when the Balearics became a staging post for the **Phoenicians**, maritime traders from the eastern Mediterranean whose long voyages reached as far as Cornwall. According to the Roman historian Pliny, the Phoenicians established a large settlement at **Sanisera** on Menorca's north coast and archeologists have also discovered Phoenician artefacts at Alcúdia on Mallorca. In general, however, very few Phoenician remains have been found on the Balearics – just a handful of bronze items, jewellery and pieces of coloured glass.

The Phoenicians were displaced by **Greeks** from around 800 BC, as several city-states explored the western Mediterranean in search of trade and potential colonies. Like the Phoenicians, the Greeks appear to have used the Balearics primarily as a staging post, for no Greek buildings have survived on either Mallorca or Menorca. The absence of metal apparently made the islands unsuitable for long-term colonization, and the belligerence of the native population may have played a part, too: the Greeks coined another name for the islands, the "**Balearics**", which they derived from *ballein*, meaning "to throw from a sling". The islanders were adept at this form of warfare, and many early visitors were repelled with showers of polished sling-stones. Some historians dispute this theory, claiming rather that the name comes from the Baleri tribe of Sardinia.

The Greeks were also discouraged from colonization by the growth of the **Carthaginian** empire across the western Mediterranean. The Phoenicians had established Carthage, on the North African coast, under the leadership of the princess Elissa, better known as Dido, the tragic heroine of Virgil's

Aeneid. According to the Greek historian Diodorus Siculus, the Carthaginians began to colonize the Balearics in the early seventh century BC, and the islands were firmly under their control by the beginning of the third century BC, if not earlier. Little is known of the Carthaginian occupation except that the Carthaginians established several new settlements, including Jamma (Ciutadella) and Maghen (Maó), after Magon a Carthaginian commander. It is also claimed that the famous Carthaginian general, Hannibal, was born on Mallorca, though Ibiza and Malta claim this honour too.

In the third century BC, the expansion of the Carthaginian empire across the Mediterranean and up into the Iberian Peninsula triggered two **Punic Wars** with Rome. In both of these wars the Balearics proved extremely valuable, first as stepping stones from the North African coast to the European mainland, and second, as a source of mercenaries. Balearic slingers were highly valued and accompanied Hannibal and his elephants across the Alps in the Second Punic War, when (for reasons that remain obscure) the islanders refused gold and demanded payment in wine and women instead. After Hannibal's defeat by the Romans at the battle of Zama in 202 BC, Carthaginian power began to wane and they withdrew from Mallorca and Menorca, although they continued to have some influence over Ibiza for at least another seventy years.

Romans, Vandals and Byzantines

As the Carthaginians retreated, so the **Romans** advanced, incorporating Ibiza within their empire after the final victory over Carthage in 146 BC. On Mallorca and Menorca, the islanders took advantage of the prolonged military chaos to profit from piracy, until finally, in 123 BC, the Romans, led by the consul Quintus Metellus, restored maritime order by occupying both islands. These victories earned

Metellus the title "Balearico" from the Roman senate and two of the islands were given new names, Balearis Major (Mallorca) and Balearis Minor (Menorca).

For the next five hundred years, all of the Balearic Islands were part of the **Roman Empire**. Among many developments, Roman colonists introduced viticulture, turning the Balearics into a wine-exporting area, and initiated olive-oil production from newly planted groves. As was their custom, the Romans consolidated their control of the islands by building roads and establishing towns. On Menorca, they developed Port Magonum (Maó) as an administrative centre, while Sanisera – previously the site of a Phoenician trading post – became an important port. Initially, the Balearics were part of the Roman province of Tarraconensis (Tarragona), but in 404 AD the islands became a province in their own right with the name Balearica.

By this time, however, the Roman Empire was in decline, its defences unable to resist the westward-moving tribes of central Asia. One of these tribes, the **Vandals**, swept across the Balearics in around 425 AD, thereby ending Roman rule. So thoroughgoing was the destruction they wrought that very few signs of the Romans have survived, the only significant remains being those of Pollentia at Alcúdia, on Mallorca.

The Vandals had been Christianized long before they reached the Mediterranean, but they were followers of the **Arian** sect. This interpretation of Christianity, founded by Arius, an Alexandrian priest, insisted that Christ the Son and God the Father were two distinct figures, not elements of the Trinity. To orthodox Christians, this seemed dangerously close to the pagan belief in a multiplicity of gods, and, by the end of the fourth century AD, Arianism had been forcibly extirpated within the Roman Empire. However, the sect continued to flourish amongst the Germanic peoples of the Rhine, including the Vandals, who, armed with

ROMANS, VANDALS AND BYZANTINES

their "heretical" beliefs, had no religious truck with their new Balearic subjects, persecuting them and destroying their churches. As a consequence, only a handful of Christian remains from this period have survived, primarily the ruins of the basilica at **Son Bou** (see p.143).

In 533, the Vandals were defeated in North Africa by the Byzantine general, Count Belisarius. This brought the Balearics under **Byzantine** rule, and, for a time, restored prosperity and stability. However, the islands were too far removed from Constantinople to be of much imperial importance, and, when the empire was threatened from the east at the end of the seventh century, they were abandoned in all but name.

The Moors

As the influence of Byzantium receded, so militant Islam moved in from the south and east to fill the vacuum. In 707–8, the **Moors** of North Africa conducted an extended raid against Mallorca, destroying its entire fleet and carrying away slaves and booty. By 716, the Balearics' position had become even more vulnerable with the completion of the Moorish conquest of Spain. In 798, the Balearics were again sacked by the Moors – who were still more interested in plunder than settlement – and in desperation the islanders appealed for help to **Charlemagne**, the Frankish Holy Roman Emperor. As emperor, Charlemagne was the military – the Pope the spiritual – leader of Western Christendom, so the appeal signified the final severance of the Balearics' links with Byzantium.

Charlemagne's attempt to protect the islands from the Moors met with some success, but the respite was only temporary. By the middle of the ninth century, the Christian position had deteriorated so badly that the Balearics were compelled to enter a non-aggression pact

with the Moors, and, to add to the islanders' woes, the
Balearics suffered a full-scale Viking raid in 859. Finally, at
the beginning of the tenth century, the **Emir of Cordoba**
conquered both Menorca and Mallorca. Moorish rule lasted
over three hundred years, though internal political divisions
among the Muslims meant that the islands experienced several different regimes. In the early eleventh century, the
emirate of Cordoba collapsed and control passed to the *wali*
(governor) of Denia, on the Spanish mainland. This administration allowed the Christians – who were known as
Mozarabs – to practise their faith, and the islands prospered from their position at the heart of the trade routes
between North Africa and Islamic Spain.

In 1085, the Balearics became an independent emirate
with a new dynasty of *walis*, from **Amortadha** in North
Africa. They pursued a more aggressive foreign and domestic policy, raiding the towns of the mainland and persecuting their Christian citizens. These actions blighted trade
and thereby enraged the emergent city-states of Italy at a
time when Christendom was fired by crusading zeal.
Anticipating retaliation, the Amortadhas fortified Palma,
which was known at this time as Medina Mayurka, and several mountain strongholds on both islands, including
Menorca's Santa Agueda. The Christian attack came in
1114 when a grand Italian fleet – led by the ships of Pisa
and supported by the pope as a mini-crusade – landed an
army of 70,000 Catalan and Italian soldiers on Ibiza. The
island was soon captured, but Mallorca, the crusaders' next
target, proved a much more difficult proposition. Medina
Mayurka's coastal defences proved impregnable, so the
Christians assaulted the landward defences instead, the con-
centric lines of the fortifications forcing them into a long
series of bloody engagements. When the city finally fell, the
invaders took a bitter revenge, slaughtering most of the sur-
viving Muslim population. However, despite their victory,

THE MOORS

203

the Christians had neither the will nor the resources to consolidate their position and, loading their vessels with freed slaves and loot, they returned home.

It took the Moors just two years to re-establish themselves on the islands, this time under the leadership of the **Almoravids**, a North African Berber tribe who had previously controlled southern Spain. The Almoravids proved to be tolerant and progressive rulers, and the Balearics prospered under them: agriculture improved, particularly through the development of irrigation, and trade expanded as commercial agreements were struck with the Italian cities of Genoa and Pisa. The Pisans, Crusaders earlier in the century, defied a papal ban on trade with Muslims to finalize the deal – consciences could, it seems, be flexible even in the "devout" Middle Ages when access to the precious goods of the east (silks, carpets and spices) was the prize.

Jaume I and the Reconquista

In 1203, the Almoravids were supplanted by the **Almohad** dynasty, who forcibly converted the islands' Christian population to Islam and started raiding the mainland. This was an extraordinary miscalculation, as the kingdoms of Aragón and Catalunya had recently been united, thereby strengthening the Christian position in this part of Spain. The unification was a major step in the changing balance of power – with their forces combined, the Christians were able to launch the *Reconquista* (Reconquest), which was eventually to drive the Moors from the entire peninsula. Part of the Christian jigsaw was the Balearics and, in 1228, the Emir of Mallorca imprudently antagonized the young **King Jaume I** of Aragón and Catalunya by seizing a couple of his ships. The king's advisers, with their eyes firmly fixed on the islands' wealth, determined to capitalize on the offence. They organized the first Balearic publicity evening, a feast at which the king was presented with a multitude of island delicacies and Catalan sailors told of the archipelago's prosperity. And so, insulted by the emir and persuaded by his nobility, Jaume I committed himself to a full-scale invasion.

Jaume's expedition of 150 ships, 16,000 men and 1500 horses set sail for Mallorca in September 1229. The king had originally planned to land at Pollença, in the northeast, but adverse weather conditions forced the fleet further south, and it eventually anchored off Sant Elm. The following day, the Catalans defeated the Moorish forces sent to oppose the landing and Jaume promptly pushed east, laying siege to Medina Mayurka. It took three months to breach the walls, but on December 31 the city finally fell and Jaume was hailed as **"El Conqueridor"**.

The cost of launching an invasion on this scale placed an enormous strain on the resources of a medieval monarch. With this in mind, Jaume subcontracted the capture of Ibiza, entering into an agreement, in 1231, with the Crown Prince of Portugal, Don Pedro, and the Count of Roussillon. In return for the capture of the island, the count and the prince were to be allowed to divide Ibiza between themselves, provided they acknowledged the suzerainty of Jaume. This project initially faltered, but revived with the addition of the Archbishop of Tarragona. The three allies captured Ibiza in 1235 and divided the spoils, although Don Pedro waived his rights and his share passed to Jaume.

In the meantime, Jaume had acquired the overlordship of Menorca. Unable to afford another full-scale invasion, the king devised a cunning ruse. In 1232, he returned to Mallorca with just three galleys, which he dispatched to Menorca carrying envoys, while he camped out in the mountains above Capdepera, on Mallorca. As night fell and his envoys negotiated with the enemy, Jaume ordered the lighting of as many bonfires as possible to illuminate the sky and give the impression of a vast army. The strategem worked and the next day, mindful of the bloodbath following the invasion of Mallorca, the Menorcan Moors capitulated. According to the king's own account, they informed his envoys that "they gave great thanks to God and to me for the message I had sent them for they knew well they could not long defend themselves against me". The terms of submission were generous: the Moors handed over Ciutadella, their principal settlement, and a number of other strongpoints, but Jaume acknowledged the Muslims as his subjects and appointed one of their leaders as his *rais* (governor).

The retention of Moorish government in Menorca, albeit under the suzerainty of the king, was in marked contrast to events on Mallorca. Here, the land was divided into eight blocks, with four passing to the king and the rest to his most trusted followers, who leased their holdings in the feudal fashion, granting land to tenants in return for military service. In 1230, Jaume consolidated his position by issuing the **Carta de Població** (People's Charter), guaranteeing equality before the law, an extremely progressive precept for the period. Furthermore, Mallorca was exempted from taxation to encourage Catalan immigration, and special rights were given to Jews resident on the island, a measure designed to stimulate trade. Twenty years later, Jaume also initiated a distinctive form of government for Mallorca, with a governing body of six **jurats** (adjudicators) – one from the nobility, two knights, two merchants and one peasant. At the end of each year the *jurats* elected their successors. This form of government remained in place until the sixteenth century.

From a modern perspective, the downside of the *Reconquista* of Mallorca was the wholesale demolition of almost all Moorish buildings, with mosques systematically replaced by churches – and at a later date, the same policy was to be followed on Menorca. Jaume I died at Valencia in 1276. In his will he divided his kingdom between his two sons: Pedro received Catalunya, Aragón and Valencia, whilst Jaume II was bequeathed Montpellier, Roussillon and the Balearics. Jaume II was crowned in Mallorca on September 12.

The Balearic Kingdom

Jaume I's division of his kingdom infuriated **Pedro**, as the Balearics stood astride the shipping route between Barcelona and Sicily, where his wife was queen. He forced his brother to become his vassal, but in response Jaume II secretly schemed with the French. Pedro soon discovered his brother's treachery and promptly set about planning a full-blooded invasion, but he died before the assault could begin and it was left to his son, **Alfonso III**, to carry out his father's plans. Late in 1285, Alfonso's army captured Palma without too much trouble, which was just as well for its inhabitants: wherever Alfonso met with resistance – as he did later in the campaign at the castle of Alaró – he extracted a brutal revenge. Indeed, even by the standards of thirteenth-century Spain, Alfonso was considered excessively violent, and for his atrocities the pope excommunicated him – though not for long.

With Mallorca secured and Jaume deposed, Alfonso turned his attention to Menorca where he suspected the loyalty of the Moorish governor – the *rais* was allegedly in conspiratorial contact with the Moors of North Africa. Alfonso's army landed on Menorca in January 1287 and decisively defeated the Moors just outside Maó. The Moors retreated to the hilltop fortress of Santa Agueda (see p.162), but their resistance didn't amount to much and the whole island was Alfonso's within a few days. The king's treatment of the vanquished islanders was savage: those Muslims who were unable to buy their freedom were enslaved, and those who couldn't work as slaves – the old, the sick and the very young – were taken to sea and thrown overboard. Alfonso rewarded the nobles who had accompanied him with grants of land – parcelled out at the Església de St Francesc (see p.173) – and brought in hundreds of Catalan settlers. The capital, Medina Minurka, was renamed Ciutadella, and the island's mosques were converted to Christian usage, before being demolished and replaced.

Alfonso's violent career was cut short by his death in 1291 at the age of 25. His successor was his brother, Jaume, also the king of Sicily. A more temperate man, Jaume conducted negotiations through the papacy, which eventually led, in 1298, to the restoration of the partition envisaged by Jaume I: he himself presided over Catalunya, Aragón and Valencia, while his exiled uncle, **Jaume II**, ruled as king of Mallorca and Menorca. Restored to the crown, Jaume II devoted a great deal of time to improving the commerce and administration of the Balearics. To stimulate trade, he reissued the currency in gold and silver, and founded a string of inland towns across his kingdom, including Alaior and Es Mercadal. He also divided Menorca into seven parishes, ordering the construction of churches for each of them. Perhaps his most important act, though, was to grant Menorca its own **Carta de Població**, which bestowed the same legal rights as the Mallorcans enjoyed.

On his death in 1311, Jaume was succeeded by his asthmatic son, **Sancho**, who spent most of his time in his palace at the mountain village of Valldemossa, in Mallorca, where the mountain air was to his liking. Nonetheless, he did his job well, continuing the successful economic policies of his father and strengthening his fleet to protect his territories from North African pirates. Mallorca and Menorca boomed. Mallorca in particular had long served as the entrepôt between North Africa and Europe, its warehouses crammed with iron, figs, salt, oil and slaves, but in the early fourteenth century its industries flourished too, primarily shipbuilding and textiles.

Internationally, Sancho worked hard to avoid entanglement in the growing antagonism between Aragón and France, but the islanders' future still looked decidedly shaky when he died without issue in 1324. Theoretically, the Balearics should have passed to Aragón, but the local nobility moved fast to crown Sancho's ten-year-old nephew as **Jaume III**. Hoping to forestall Aragonese hostility, they then had him betrothed to the king of Aragón's five-year-old daughter, though in the long term this marriage did the new king little good. After he came of age, Jaume III's relations with his brother-in-law, Pedro IV of Aragón, quickly deteriorated, and Pedro successfully invaded the Balearics in response to an alleged plot against him. Jaume fled to his mainland possessions and sold Montpellier to the French to raise money for an invasion. He landed on Mallorca in 1349, but was no match for Pedro and was defeated and killed on the outskirts of Llucmajor. His son, the uncrowned **Jaume IV**, was also captured and although he eventually escaped, he was never able to drum up sufficient support to threaten the Aragonese.

Unification with Spain

For a variety of reasons the **unification** of the Balearics with Aragón – and their subsequent incorporation into Spain – proved a disaster. In particular, the mainland connection meant that the islands' nobility soon gravitated towards the Aragonese court, regarding their local estates as little more than sources of income to sustain their expensive lifestyles. More fundamentally, general economic trends moved firmly against the islands. After the fall of Constantinople to the Islamic Turks in 1453, the lucrative overland trade routes from the eastern Mediterranean to the Far East were blocked, and, just as bad, the Portuguese discovered the way around the Cape of Good Hope to the Indies. In 1479, **Fernando V of Aragón** married **Isabella I of Castile**, thereby uniting the two largest kingdoms in Spain, but yet again this was bad news for the islanders. The union brought mainland preoccupations and a centralized bureaucracy, which rendered the Balearics a provincial backwater – even more so when, following Columbus reaching the Americas in 1492, the focus of European trade moved from the Mediterranean to the Atlantic seaboard almost at a stroke. The last commercial straw was the royal decree that forbade Catalunya and the Balearics from trading with the New World. By the start of the sixteenth century, the Balearics were starved of foreign currency, and the islands' merchants had begun to leave, signalling a period of long-term economic decline.

Sixteenth-century decline

The islands' political and economic difficulties destabilized their social structures. The aristocracy was divided into warring factions, the rural districts were set against the towns, and, perhaps most unsettling of all, there were high taxes and an unreliable grain supply. In Mallorca, this turbulence coalesced in an armed uprising of peasants and artisans in 1521. Organized in a *Germania*, or armed brotherhood, the insurrectionists seized control of Palma, whose nobles beat a hasty retreat to the safety of Palma's castle – those who didn't move fast enough were slaughtered on the streets. The rebels held sway for two years, but finally royal authority was restored across the Balearics with the arrival of a large army led by the grandson of Fernando and Isabella, the **Emperor Charles V**, king of Spain and Habsburg Holy Roman Emperor.

The Balearics witnessed other sixteenth-century horrors with the renewal of large-scale maritime raids from North Africa. This upsurge of piratical activity was partly stimulated by the final expulsion of the Moors from Spain in 1492, and partly by the emergence of the Ottoman Turks as a Mediterranean superpower. Muslim raiders ransacked a string of Mallorcan towns between 1530 and 1570, whilst the Ottoman admiral Khair-ed-din, better known as **Barbarossa**, ravaged Maó after a three-day siege in 1535. Hundreds of Menorcans were enslaved and carted off, prompting Charles V to construct the fort of Sant Felip to guard Maó harbour. Two decades later, the Turks returned and sacked Ciutadella, taking a further three thousand prisoners, representing about eighty percent of the city's population. Muslim incursions continued until the seventeenth century, but declined in frequency and intensity after a combined Italian and Spanish force destroyed the Turkish fleet at Lepanto in 1571.

British and French occupation

The Balearics' woes continued throughout much of the seventeenth century. Trade remained stagnant and the population declined, a sorry state of affairs that was exacerbated by continued internal tensions. The aristocratic families who dominated island society engaged in endless feuding, whilst the (often absentee) landowners failed to invest in their estates. By the 1630s, the population problem had become so critical that Philip IV exempted the islands from the levies that raised men for Spain's armies – though this gain was offset by the loss of 15,000 Mallorcans to the plague in 1652.

A new development was the regular appearance of **British** vessels in the Mediterranean, a corollary of Britain's increasing share of the region's seaborne trade and the

Royal Navy's commitment to protect its merchantmen from Algerian pirates. The British didn't have much use for Mallorca, and largely ignored it, but they were impressed by Maó's splendid harbour, a secure and sheltered deep-water anchorage where they first put in to take on water in 1621. In 1664, Charles II of England formalized matters by instructing his ambassador to Spain to "request immediate permission for British ships to use Balearic ports and particularly Port Mahon". The Spanish king granted the request, and the advantages were noted by a poetic British seaman, a certain John Baltharpe:

> Good this same is upon Minork
> For shipping very useful 'gainst the Turk.
> The King of Spain doth to our King it lend,
> As in the line above to that same end.

For a time the British were simply content to "borrow" Maó, but their expanding commercial interests prompted a yearning for a more permanent arrangement. It was the dynastic **War of the Spanish Succession** (1701–14), fought over the vacant throne of Spain, which gave them their opportunity. A British force invaded Menorca in 1708 and, meeting tepid resistance, captured the island in a fortnight. Apart from the benefits of Maó harbour, Menorca was also an ideal spot from which to blockade the French naval base at Toulon, thereby preventing the union of the French Atlantic and Mediterranean fleets. Indeed, so useful was Menorca to the British that they negotiated its retention at the **Treaty of Utrecht**, which rounded off the war.

The island's first British governor, **Sir Richard Kane**, was an energetic and capable man who strengthened Menorca as a military base, and worked hard at improving the administration of the island, its civilian facilities and economy. He built the first road across the island from Maó to Ciutadella and introduced improved strains of seed and livestock. During the first forty years of British occupation, the production of wine, vegetables and chickens increased by 500 percent. Relations between the occupying power and the islanders were generally good – though the Catholic clergy no doubt found it difficult to stomach the instruction to "pray for His Britannic Majesty".

The first phase of British domination ended when the **French** captured the island in 1756 at the start of the **Seven Years War**. Admiral Byng was dispatched to assist the beleaguered British force, but, after a lacklustre encounter with a French squadron, he withdrew, leaving the British garrison with no option but to surrender. Byng's indifferent performance cost him his life: he was court-martialled and executed for cowardice, prompting Voltaire's famous aphorism that the English shoot their admirals "pour encourager les autres". The new French governor built the township of **Sant Lluís** (see p.108) to house his Breton sailors and, once again, the Menorcans adjusted to the occupying power without too much difficulty. In 1763, Britain regained Menorca in exchange for the Philippines and Cuba, which it had captured from France during the Seven Years War.

The **second period of British occupation** proved far less successful than the first. The governor from 1763 to 1782, General Johnston, was an authoritarian and unpopular figure who undermined the Menorcans' trust in the British. The crunch came in 1781, when, with Britain at war with both Spain and France, the Duc de Crillon landed on the island with 8000 soldiers. In command of a much smaller force, the new British governor, General John Murray, withdrew to the fort of Sant Felip, where he was besieged for eight months. Succoured by the Menorcans, the Franco–Spanish army finally starved the British into submission; Murray's men were badly stricken with scurvy, and only 1120 survived. With the British vanquished, Menorca temporarily reverted to Spain.

The **third and final period of British rule** ran from 1798 to 1802, when the island was occupied for its value as a naval base in the Napoleonic Wars. Landing at Port d'Addaia, the British took just nine days – and suffered no casualties – in recapturing the island, helped in no small measure by the destruction of fort Sant Felip by the Spaniards in the mid-1780s. It seems that the Spanish high command did not believe they could defend the fortress, so they simply flattened it, thereby denying it to any colonial power – and, of course, making the island vulnerable in the process. The British finally relinquished all claims to Menorca in favour of Spain under the terms of the Treaty of Amiens in 1802.

The nineteenth century

With the British fleet – and its hundreds of sailors – gone, Menorca's economy took a nose-dive and remained in the doldrums for most of the nineteenth century, though the use of Maó as a training base by the American navy between 1815 and 1826 brought some measure of economic relief. Americans or no, the island remained a neglected outpost, extremely poor and subject to droughts, famines and epidemics of cholera. Consequently, the islanders were preoccupied with the art of survival rather than politics, and generally stayed out of the Carlist wars between the liberals and the conservatives which so bitterly divided the Spanish mainland. Many islanders emigrated, some to Algeria after it was acquired by the French in 1830, others to Florida and California. The leading political figure of the period was the historian **Josep Quadrodo**, who led the reactionary Catholic Union, which bombarded Madrid with petitions and greeted every conservative success with enthusiastic demonstrations.

Matters began to improve towards the end of the nineteenth century, when agriculture revived. Modern services, like gas and electricity, began to be installed and the island developed a thriving export industry in footwear. This was largely as a result of the efforts of a certain Don Jeronimo Cabrisas, a Menorcan who had made his fortune in Cuba, and later supplied many of the boots worn by troops in World War I. Around this time too, a **revival of Catalan culture**, led by the middle class of Barcelona, inspired sections of the Menorcan bourgeoisie. Catalan political groupings were formed and there were stirrings of discontent surrounding Madrid's edict pronouncing Castilian as the official language of the Balearics in place of the local dialect of Catalan. More ominously, the islanders were politically divided between conservatives and liberals, a bitter polarization that left Menorcan society unstable. This failure to create a political discourse between rival factions mirrored developments in the rest of Spain, and both here and on the mainland, instability was to be the harbinger of the military coup that ushered in the right-wing dictatorship of General Primo de Rivera in 1923.

The Spanish Civil War

During the **Spanish Civil War** (1936–39), Mallorca and Menorca supported opposing sides. General Goded made Mallorca an important base for the Fascists, but when General Bosch attempted to do the same on Menorca, his NCOs and men mutinied and, with the support of the civilian population, declared their support for the Republic. In the event – apart from a few bombing raids and an attempted Republican landing at Mallorca's Porto Cristo – the Balearics saw very little actual fighting. Nevertheless, the Menorcans were dangerously exposed towards the end of the war, when they were marooned as the last Republican stronghold. A peaceful conclusion was reached largely through the intervention of the British, who

THE SPANISH CIVIL WAR

brokered the surrender of the island aboard *HMS Devonshire*. Franco's troops occupied Menorca in April 1939 and the *Devonshire* left with 450 Menorcan refugees.

Recent times

Since World War II, the most significant development has been the emergence of **mass tourism** as the principal economic activity. From the 1950s onwards, tourism expanded at an extraordinary rate with, for example, the number of visitors to the island rising from 1500 in 1961 to half a million in 1973. The prodigious pace of development accelerated after the death of Franco in 1975, thereby further strengthening the local economy. One twist, however, was the relative price of real estate: traditionally, Menorcan landowners with coastal estates had given their younger children the poorer agricultural land near the seashore, but it was this land the developers wanted – and were prepared to pay fortunes for. Inevitably, this disrupted many a household, but the repercussions were hardly extreme, as the island's economy continued to grow at a prodigious rate. Indeed, the archipelago now has one of the highest per capita incomes in Spain, four times that of Extremadura for instance, and well above the EU average.

The Balearics also benefited from the political restructuring of Spain following the death of Franco. In 1978, just three years after the dictator's death, the Spanish parliament, the Cortes, passed a new **constitution**, which reorganized the country on a more federal basis and allowed for the establishment of regional Autonomous Communities. In practice, the demarcation of responsibilities between central and regional governments has proved problematic, leading to interminable wrangling, not least because the Socialists, who were in power from 1983 to 1996, waivered in their commitment to decentralization. Nonetheless, the

Balearics, constituted as the **Comunidad Autónoma de las Islas Baleares** in 1983, have used their new-found independence to assert the primacy of their native Catalan language – now the main language of education – and to exercise much more local control of their economy.

From 1996 to 2000, this trend towards **decentralization** continued under a Conservative government which was only able to secure a majority in the Cortes with the support of several regionally based nationalist parties, including Basque, Catalan and Balearic groupings. As a result, these regional groups were in a more powerful position than their numbers would otherwise justify, and were able to keep the momentum of decentralization going despite the innate centralist tendencies of Madrid Conservatives. In particular, most government expenditure came under the control of the regions and the Balearic administration used these resources to upgrade a string of holiday resorts and modernize much of the archipelago's infrastructure. In part, this reflected a particular concern with the somewhat tacky image of Ibiza and Mallorca and was accompanied by the imposition of stricter building controls across all the islands. On Menorca, the money also paid for a number of environmental schemes and the creation of a Parc Natural protecting the wetlands of S'Albufera d'es Grau and the adjacent coastline (see Chapter 2).

In addition, the Conservative-led Balearic administration made moves to curb tourist development, but in this they failed to keep pace with public sentiment as exemplified by a string of large-scale demonstrations during 1998 and 1999. The demonstrations focused on four primary and inter-related concerns – the spiralling cost of real estate, foreign ownership of land, untrammelled development and loutish behaviour in the cheaper resorts. This failure to keep abreast of popular feeling resulted in the defeat of the Conservatives in the **regional elections of 1999** and their

Flora and fauna

Despite its reputation as an over-developed, package-holiday destination, Menorca has much to offer **birders** and **botanists** alike. Separated from the Iberian Peninsula some fifty million years ago, the Balearic archipelago has evolved (at least in part) its own distinctive flora and fauna, with further variations between Menorca and the other islands. Among Menorca's **wildlife**, pride of place goes to the migratory birds which gather on the island's wetlands in April and May and from mid-September to early October. The island is also noted for its wide range of wild **flowers** and flowering **shrubs**.

Some of the islands' most important habitats have, however, been threatened by the developers. This has spawned an influential conservation group, **GOB** (Grup Balear d'Ornitologia i Defensa de la Naturalesa), which has launched several successful campaigns. It helped save Menorca's S'Albufera wetlands from further development, played a leading role in Mallorca's black vulture re-establishment programme, and successfully lobbied to increase the penalties for shooting protected birds. GOB has offices in Palma, Mallorca, at c/Can Verí 1 (☎971 721 105).

The account of the island's flora and fauna given below serves as a general introduction and includes mention of several important birding sites, cross-referenced to the descriptions given in the *Guide*. There's also a list of birds of specialist interest combined with potted descriptions, but for more specialist information (and illustrations) consult the **field guides** recommended on p.234.

Habitats

The Balearic Islands are a continuation of the Andalucian mountains of the Iberian Peninsula, from which they are separated by a submarine trench never less than 80km wide and up to 1500m deep. Unlike Mallorca, which is far more diverse, Menorca divides into two distinct but not dramatically different zones. The **northern half** of the island comprises rolling sandstone uplands punctuated by wide, shallow valleys and occasional peaks, the highest of which is Monte Toro at 357m. To the **south** lie undulating limestone lowlands and deeper valleys. Dramatic seacliffs and scores of rocky coves trim both north and south.

Menorca has a temperate Mediterranean **climate**, with winter frosts and snow a rarity, but has no mountain barrier to protect it from the cold dry wind (the Tramuntana) which regularly buffets the island from the north. This prevailing wind gives much of the island's vegetation a windblown look and has obliged its farmers to protect their crops with stone walls.

Menorcan flora

Menorca's indigenous vegetation is almost all **garigue**, partly forested open scrubland where the island's native trees – primarily Aleppo pines, wild olives, holm oaks and carobs – intermingle with imported species like ash, elm and poplar. However, intensive cultivation has reduced the original forest cover to a fraction of its former size, and nowadays only fifteen percent of the island is wooded.

The commonest of the island's native trees is the **Aleppo pine**, which has bright green spines, silvery twigs and ruddy-brown cones. Also common is the evergreen **holm oak** – which traditionally supplied acorns for pigs, wood for charcoal and bark for tanning – and the **carob tree**, which prefers the hottest and driest parts of the island. Arguably the island's most handsome tree, the carob boasts leaves of varying greenness and conspicuous fruits – large pods which start green, but ripen to black–brown. The **wild olive** is comparatively rare (and may not be indigenous), but the cultivated variety – which boasts silver-grey foliage and can grow up to 10m in height – is endemic and has long been a mainstay of the local economy. It also dramatically illustrates the effects of the Tramuntana, with grove upon grove bent almost double under the weight of the wind.

Menorca's soils nourish a superb range of **flowering shrubs**. There are too many to list in any detail, but look out for the deep-blue flowers of the **rosemary**, the reddish bloom of the **lentisk** (or mastic tree), the bright yellow **broom**, which begins blossoming in March, and the autumn-flowering **strawberry tree**. **Rockroses** are also widely distributed, the commonest members of the group being the spring-flowering, grey-leafed cistus, with its velvety leaves and pink flowers, and the narrow-leafed cistus whose bloom is white.

In spring and autumn, the fields, verges, woods and cliffs of Menorca brim with **wild flowers**. There are several hundred species and only in the depths of winter – from November to January – are all of them dormant. Well-known species include marigolds and daisies, violets and yellow primroses, as well as the resinous St John's wort, with its crinkled deep-green leaves, and several types of orchid. There's also the distinctive **asphodel**, whose tall spikes sport clusters of pink or white flowers from April to

June. The asphodel grows on overgrazed or infertile land and its starch-rich tubers were once used by shoemakers to make glue. Another common sight is the **prickly pear**, traditionally grown behind peasants' houses as a windbreak and toilet wall. A versatile plant, the smell of the prickly pear deflects insects (hence its use round toilets) and its fruit is easy to make into pig food or jam.

Menorca also boasts a handful of species entirely to itself, the most distinguished of them being the dwarf shrub **daphne rodriquezii**, a purple-flowering evergreen, present on the cliffs of the northeast coast. In addition, the cliffs of much of the coast have a flora uniquely adapted to the combination of limestone yet saline soils. Here, **aromatic inula**, a shrubby perennial with clusters of yellow flowers, grows beside the **common caper**, with its red pods and purple seeds, and the **sea aster**.

Finally, many islanders maintain splendid **gardens** containing species that flourish throughout the Mediterranean, most famously bougainvilleas, oleanders, geraniums and hibiscus.

Menorcan birds

The varied **birdlife** of Menorca includes birds of prey, wetland specialists, seabirds, waders and characteristic Mediterranean warblers, larks and pipits, but perhaps the most striking feature is the tameness of many of the birds – presumably because there is less shooting here than in almost any other part of the Mediterranean.

There are several hot-spots for birds, but wherever you are birds of prey should be evident. Of these, the Egyptian vulture is the most impressive; there are around a hundred of them and they make up Europe's only resident population. Red kites, booted eagles and ospreys can also be enjoyed all year and they are joined by marsh and hen harriers in winter. Peregrines, kestrels and, in winter, sparrowhawks complete the more reliable raptors, although in spring and autumn several others – such as the honey buzzard and black kite – may turn up. **Monte Toro** (see p.146), the highest point on Menorca, is as good a vantage point for birds of prey as any.

The island's best birdwatching spot is the marshland, reeds and garigue (partly forested scrubland) fringing the lake of **S'Albufera**, near Es Grau (see p.120), a nature reserve which is itself part of a larger Parc Naturel that extends north to Cap de Favaritx. The lake and its environs are popular with herons and egrets, the most elegant wetland birds. Over a year, little and cattle egrets, purple, grey, night and squacco herons will all be seen, too. Booted eagles are also common, flying over the area, and the muddy parts of the marsh attract many smaller waders in spring, the leggy black-winged stilt in summer. The lake itself hosts several thousand ducks in winter. The nearby pine woodland, next to the beach at Es Grau, is used by night herons that rest high in the trees by day and then move onto the marsh at dusk. Also at dusk, listen out for the plaintive single note of the scops owl against a backdrop of warblers, crakes, crickets and, most strikingly, the unforgettably rich-toned song of the nightingale. The tiny firecrest is common in the woodland and in the spring this whole area can be alive with hundreds of migrants.

There are smaller marshes elsewhere on the island and those at Cala Tirant in the north and Son Bou in the south are very good. The wetland at **Son Bou** (see p.143) holds the island's largest reedbed and the characteristic species of such a rich habitat are the noisy great reed warblers, moustached warbler and Cetti's warbler. The wetland at **Cala Tirant** (see p.131) can be just as good and the sandy area just inland of the beach is a good place to see the spectacular bee-eater, which breeds in several small colonies on the

SELECTED BIRDS OF MENORCA

The list below describes many of Menorca's most distinctive birds. We have given the English name, followed by the Latin, a useful cross-reference for those without a British field guide. We have used italics and capital for genus (first) name only. The description aims to capture the character of the bird and indicates preferred habitat.

Serin *Serinus serinus* (winter visitor). Tiny, green-and-yellow canary-like bird of the finch family, with characteristically buoyant flight. Appears in virtually any habitat.

Fan-tailed Warbler *Cisticola juncidis* (very common breeding resident). Typical small brown bird, but with very distinctive "zit-zit-zit" song, usually uttered in flight. Prefers wetland areas.

Nightingale *Luscinia megarhynchos* (common breeding summer visitor). Rich-brown coloured Robin-like bird with astonishingly rich, vigorous and varied song. Prefers to sing from small bushes, often deep inside and out of sight.

Wryneck *Jynx torquilla* (spring, autumn and winter visitor). Medium-sized bird with a complex pattern of brown, grey and lilac plumage. A member of the woodpecker family. Favours olive groves.

Hoopoe *Upupa epops* (common breeding resident). Pigeon-sized, pinky-brown bird with punkish black head-crest. It is named after its distinctive call "upupu upupu". Its wings sport a complex black-and-white barring, creating a striking sight when in flight. Favours open areas with some trees nearby for nesting.

Booted Eagle *Hieraaetus pennatus* (resident breeder). A small and incredibly agile eagle, similar in size to a Buzzard. Prefers the mountains of Mallorca, but happily hunts over Menorca's scrub and grasslands.

Eleonora's Falcon *Falco eleonorae* (spring and autumn migrant). One of the specialities of the western Mediterranean.

Dark, slim, elegant falcon. Hunts small birds and large insects with fantastic speed and agility. Often seen hunting insects near water.

Rock Thrush *Monticola saxatilis* (spring and autumn migrant). Beautifully coloured rock- and quarry-loving thrush. Males have a pale-blue head and orangey-red breast and tail. Females are a less distinctive brown and cream.

Blue Rock Thrush *Monticola solitariusc* (common breeding resident). Blue-coloured thrush, recalling a deep-blue starling. Can be found in any rugged, rocky areas at any time of year.

Firecrest *Regulus ignicapillus* (common breeding resident). The smallest bird on the island. This tiny, pale-green bird is named after its vivid orange and yellow crown. Abundant in any woodland.

Little Egret *Egretta garzetta* (spring and autumn migrant). Long-legged, elegant white wading bird. In summer has beautiful long white plumes trailing from the back of its head. Breeds at S'Albufera only. A wetland specialist, though well adapted to treetop life.

Little Bittern *Ixobrychus minutes* (spring and autumn visitor). Secretive wetland specialist. This is the smallest member of the heron family breeding in Europe, measuring little more than 30cm tall. The male is an attractive pink–cream colour with contrasting black wings and cap. Males advertise themselves with a far-carrying gruff basal note, repeated regularly.

Purple Heron *Ardea purpurea* (uncommon summer visitor). Large, slender heron of reed beds. The male plumage has beautiful purple and rich-brown tones. Despite its size it can be rather elusive, hiding in the dense cover of reeds.

Black-winged Stilt *Himantopus himantopus* (summer visitor). Incredibly long-legged black-and-white wader. Its medium size is somewhat extended by its long, straight, fine, red bill. Can appear anywhere there is mud, but particularly common on saltpans.

SELECTED BIRDS OF MENORCA

Kentish Plover *Charadrius alexandrinus* (spring and autumn visitor). Small, delicate wader of saltpans and marshes. Its pale brown upperbody contrasts with its gleaming-white head-collar and underparts.

Cetti's Warbler *Cettia cetti* (common breeding resident). This rather nondescript, chunky, wren-like warbler prefers dense thickets close to water. It possesses an astonishingly loud explosive song: "chet-chet-chet-chetchetchet".

Great Reed Warbler *Acrocephalus arundinaceus* (breeding summer visitor). This large, unstreaked, brown warbler can be found in significant numbers where there is reed and marsh vegetation. Its song is a loud and harsh mixture of unusual grating, croaking and creaking noises.

Scops Owl *Otus scops* (common breeding resident). This tiny owl (only 20cm tall) is stubbornly nocturnal. However, you will know it's there because at night its plaintive "tyoo" note is repeated every few seconds, monotonously, for long periods. Groves, plantations, small clumps of trees, conifer woodland and even gardens can host this bird.

Greater Flamingo *Phoenicopterus ruber* (spring visitor in small numbers). The unmistakable silhouette of this leggy wader with roseate wings, bill and legs can be seen on any wetland in spring, but in winter the southern areas and S'Albufera are best.

Great White Egret *Egretta alba* (winter visitor). This marshland specialist is really just a large version of the commoner Little Egret: an all-white, tall, elegant heron.

Audouin's Gull *Larus audouinii* (resident breeder). This rare gull favours the rocky coastline. It's the size and light-grey colour of a typical "seagull" but boasts a rather splendid red bill. Unfortunately, it takes three years for birds to reach this adult plumage and prior to this they are much less distinctive.

Bee-eater *Merops apiaster* (breeding summer visitor). A brightly coloured, medium-sized bird, with a slim body, long pointed wings and slightly de-curved bill. If the iridescent greens, orange, yellow and blue of this bird weren't distinctive enough, its bubbling "pruuk" call is almost as recognizable.

Egyptian Vulture *Neophron percnopterus* (breeding resident). Medium-sized raptor with small rather pointed protruding head and featherless face. Wings held flat when soaring. .

Cattle Egret *Bubulcus ibis* (mainly winter visitor). This small, heron-like wader is a regular winter visitor to the larger Balearic marshes. In winter, it is white, but is distinguished from the Little Egret by its stubby all-yellow bill and stockier gait.

Night Heron *Nycticorax nycticorax* (spring and autumn migrant). Adults of this medium-sized stocky heron are an attractive combination of black, grey and white. In contrast, younger birds up to three years old are a rather nondescript brown with cream speckling. This water bird is most active at night or dawn and dusk. By day, they roost in the tree canopy or large bushes.

Stone Curlew *Burhinus oedicnemus* (resident breeder, commoner in summer). Thickset wader that prefers dry, rolling countryside to mud. Has a large, yellow, almost reptilian eye. Largely dull brown with some darker streaking, but with relatively distinctive long, yellow legs. When in flight, its strikingly black-and-white wings become apparent.

Cory's Shearwater *Calonectris diomedia* (common breeder on offshore islands, but seen regularly all along the coast from March to August). Fairly large seabird. Like all the shearwaters, this bird flies close to the sea's surface with stiff outstretched wings. This pattern of flight as well as its size (nearly half a metre long with a wing span of more than a metre) are its most distinctive features, as its plumage is rather boring. At sea, it appears dark-backed and dirty-white below. Thousands breed on offshore islands across the Balearics and at sea they will often mix with the smaller pale brown **Mediterranean Shearwater**.

island. Nearby, the **Cap de Cavalleria** (see p.132), at the northern tip of the island, attracts the curious-looking stone curlew, several larks and pipits; ospreys can often be seen fishing in the cape's **Port de Sanitja** (see p.133). Another special Balearic bird is the distinctive red-billed Audouin's gull, one of the world's rarest gulls. A good place to see these is just off the coast by the lighthouse at the end of the cape, where Mediterranean shags and shearwaters are also regularly seen. Audouin's gulls are also viewable at Maó.

The lush vegetation in the bottom of the Algendar Gorge, just inland of **Cala Santa Galdana** (see p.158), is a magnet for small birds and a perfect setting to hear nightingales and the short explosive song of the Cetti's warbler. Above the gorge, booted eagles, Egyptian vultures and Alpine swifts nest. The ravine also attracts a wonderful array of butterflies.

Finally, although the barren, stony landscape of the northwest coast may seem an unpromising environment, **Punta de S'Escullar** is the site of one of the largest western Mediterranean colonies of Cory's shearwaters. Thousands return to their cliffside burrows in the late afternoon in summer. This rugged terrain also hosts the attractive blue rock thrush and migrant chats, wheatears and black redstarts. Pallid swifts and crag martins also breed on the cliffs.

Other Menorcan fauna

Menorca's **mammals** are an uninspiring bunch, a motley crew that includes weasels, feral cats, hedgehogs, rabbits, hares, mice and shrews, but the island does excel in its **reptiles**. Of the four species of lizard which inhabit the Balearics, Menorca has populations of three. There are two types of wall lizard – Lilfords, a green, black and blue version, and the olive-green and black-striped Italian lizard –

as well as the Moroccan rock lizard, with olive skin or reticulated blue–green coloration.

Common **insects** include grasshoppers and cicadas, whose summertime chirping is so evocative of warm Mediterranean nights, as well as over a hundred species of moth and around thirty types of **butterfly**. Two of the more striking butterflies are red admirals, which are seen in winter, and the clouded yellow and painted ladies, seen in spring.

OTHER MENORCAN FAUNA

Books

Most of the following **books** should be readily available in the UK, US or Canada. We have given UK and US publishers for each title wherever possible; o/p means out of print.

In the UK, Books on Spain (PO Box 207, Twickenham, London TW2 5BQ ☏020/8898 7789, ℱ8898 8812, Ⓦ*www.books-on-spain.com*) can supply all manner of rare and in- and out-of-print books about Spain. Their comprehensive catalogue, available free from the above address, includes sections on topics such as travel, the arts, history and culture, and there's also a separate brochure on the Balearic Islands.

History

Raymond Carr, *Spain 1808–1975* (Oxford University Press, UK) and *Modern Spain 1875–1980* (Oxford University Press, UK & US). Two of the best books available on modern Spanish history – concise and well-considered narratives. Of equal standing are Carr's (short-er) 300-page *Spain: a History* (Oxford University Press, UK & US); and *The Spanish Tragedy: the Civil War in Perspective* (Phoenix in UK).

J. H. Elliott, *Imperial Spain 1469–1716* (Penguin, UK & US). The best introduction to Spain's "golden age" – academically respected as well as being a gripping yarn. Also his erudite

The Revolt of the Catalans: a Study in the Decline of Spain 1598–1640 (o/p).

Desmond Gregory, *Minorca, the Illusory Prize: History of the British Occupation of Minorca between 1708 and 1802* (Fairleigh Dickinson University Press, UK & US). Exhaustive, scholarly and well-composed narrative detailing the British colonial involvement with Menorca. It's only published in hardback, however, and is expensive.

Bruce Laurie, *Life of Richard Kane: Britain's First Lieutenant Governor of Minorca* (Fairleigh Dickinson University Press, UK & US). Detailed historical biography providing an intriguing insight into eighteenth-century Menorca. Published only in hardback.

Hugh Thomas, *The Spanish Civil War* (Penguin, UK; Touchstone, US). Exhaustively researched, brilliantly detailed account of the war and the complex political manoeuvrings surrounding it, with sections on Mallorca and Menorca. First published in 1961, it remains easily the best book on the subject.

General background

Mossèn Antoni Alcover, *Folk Tales of Mallorca* (Editorial Moll in UK & US). The nineteenth-century priest and academic Mossèn Alcover spent decades collecting Mallorcan folk tales and this is a wide selection – almost 400 pages – of them. They range from the intensely religious through parable and proverb, but many reveal an unpleasant edge to rural island life, both vindictive and mean-spirited. There's no similar publication for Menorca, but the two islands have similar folkloric traditions, which makes this book intriguing background material.

Carrie B. Douglass, *Bulls, Bullfighting and Spanish Identities* (Arizona UP, in US). Anthropologist Douglass delves into the symbolism of the bull in the Spanish national psyche, and then goes on to examine the role of the bullfight in some of the many fiestas that encourage it.

John Hooper, *The New Spaniards: a Portrait of the New Spain* (Penguin in UK). Well-constructed and extremely perceptive portrait of post-Franco Spain; an excellent general introduction. Highly recommended.

George Orwell, *Homage to Catalonia* (Penguin in UK, Harcourt Brace in US). Stirring account of Orwell's participation in, and early enthusiasm for, leftist revolution in Barcelona, followed by his growing disillusionment with the factional fighting that divided the Republican forces during the ensuing Civil War.

Fiction

Arturo Barea, *The Forging of a Rebel* (o/p). A superb autobiographical trilogy, taking in the Spanish war in Morocco in the 1920s and Barea's own part in the civil war. It's sometimes reprinted in its component titles – *The Forge*, *The Track* and *The Clash*.

Juan Goytisolo, *Marks of Identity* (Serpent's Tail, UK &

US), *Count Julian* (Serpent's Tail, UK & US), *Juan the Landless* (Serpent's Tail, UK & US); also *The Virtues of the Solitary Bird* (Serpent's Tail, UK & US) and *Makbara* (Serpent's Tail, UK & US). Born in Barcelona in 1931, Goytisolo became a bitter enemy of the Franco regime and has spent most of his life in exile in Paris and Morocco. Widely acclaimed as one of Spain's leading modern novelists, his most celebrated works (the first three titles listed above) confront the ambivalent idea of Spain and Spanishness. The fourth of the five titles above (from 1988) is a deep and powerful study of pain and repression, the fifth (from 1980) explores the Arab culture of North Africa in sharp and perceptive style.

Juan Masoliver (ed), *The Origins of Desire: Modern Spanish Short Stories* (Serpent's Tail, UK & US). An enjoyable selection of short stories from some of Spain's leading contemporary writers, including Mallorca's own Valentí Puig and Carme Riera.

Ana María Matute, *School of the Sun* (Columbia University Press, US). The loss of childhood innocence on the Balearics, where old enmities are redefined during the Civil War.

Manuel Vazquez Montalban, *Murder in the Central Committee*; *The Angst-ridden Executive*; and *Off Side* (Serpent's Tail, UK & US). Riveting tales by Spain's most popular crime thriller writer, a long-time member of the Communist Party and now a well-known journalist resident in Barcelona. Montalban's great creation is the gourmand private detective Pepe Carvalho. Original and wonderfully entertaining. If this trio of titles whet your appetite, move on to *Southern Seas* (Serpent's Tail, UK & US) and a world of disillusioned communists, tawdry sex and nouvelle cuisine – key ingredients of post-Franco Spain.

Arturo Pérez-Reverte, *The Fencing Master* (Harvill in UK). Subtle, heavily symbolic novel set in 1860s Madrid and tracing the demise of the fencing master, a man in search of the perfect sword thrust. A journalist by profession, Pérez-Reverte is one of Spain's best-selling contemporary authors.

Maruja Torres, *Desperately Seeking Julio* (Fourth Estate, in US). The Julio is of course Iglesias (the original Spanish title – "It's Him!" – had no need for names) in this enjoyable romp of a novel. Torres is quite a name in Spain and writes for gossip columns.

Specialist guidebooks

David & Rosamund Brawn, *Menorca Walking Guide* (Discovery Walking Guides in UK). The Brawns have produced a number of inexpensive walking booklets that explore the nooks and crannies of the Balearics and the Canaries. This particular publication, one of the less inspired of the series, features fourteen walks in the vicinity of Maó. The longest takes three hours, the shortest thirty minutes. The directions are almost always easy to follow and the text clear, if a little twee. The twin booklets detailing the hikes come with a map (1:25,000). It is available in some Maó bookshops, but supplies are not reliable. The Brawns have also published a 1:40,000 *Touring & Walking Map of Menorca* (Discovery Walking Guides in UK). This is quite useful as a reference – and it is cheap – but, irritatingly, the spelling is mostly Castilian.

Flora and fauna

Christopher Grey-Wilson et al, *Collins Field Guide: Mediterranean Wild Flowers* (Harper Collins in UK). Excellent, comprehensive field guide.

Lars Jonsson, *Birds of Europe* (Helm in UK & US). As good a field guide as the Collins below, but more specialized.

Killian Mullarney et al, *Collins Bird Guide* (Harper Collins in UK, Princeton in US). It's hard to better this excellent field guide.

Oleg Polunin et al, *Flowers of Europe: a Field Guide* (Oxford in UK). First-rate field guide.

Enric Ramos, *The Birds of Menorca* (Editorial Moll in UK; o/p in US). Specialist handbook describing all the species of birds recorded in Menorca – in 170 pages. It's well illustrated, but you'll still need a field guide.

Language

Most Menorcans are bilingual, speaking **Castilian** (ie Spanish) and their local dialect of the **Catalan** language (Menorquín) with equal facility. Català (Catalan) has been the islanders' everyday language since the Reconquest and the subsequent absorption of the island into the medieval Kingdom of Aragón and Catalunya; Castilian, on the other hand, was imposed much later from the mainland as the language of government – and with especial rigour by Franco. As a result, Spain's recent move towards regional autonomy has been accompanied by the islanders' assertion of Catalan as their official language. The most obvious sign of this has been the change of all the old Castilian town and street names into Catalan versions. On paper, Catalan looks like a cross between French and Spanish and is generally easy to understand if you know those two, although when spoken it has a very harsh sound and is far harder to come to grips with.

Some background

When **Franco** came to power in 1939, publishing houses, bookshops and libraries were raided and Català books destroyed. There was some relaxation in the mid-1940s, but Franco excluded Catalan from the radio, TV, daily press and, most importantly, the schools throughout his dictatorship, which is why many older people cannot read or write Català, even if they speak it all the time.

Català is spoken by over six million people in total in the Balearics, Catalunya, part of Aragón, most of Valencia, Andorra and parts of the French Pyrenees; it is thus much more widely spoken than several better-known languages such as Danish, Finnish and Norwegian. It is a Romance language, stemming from Latin and more directly from medieval Provençal. Spaniards in the rest of the country belittle it by saying that to get a Català word you just cut a Castilian one in half (which is often true!), but in fact the grammar is much more complicated than Castilian and there are eight vowel sounds, three more than in Castilian.

Getting by in Menorca

Although Catalan is the preferred **language** of most islanders, you'll almost always get by perfectly well if you speak Castilian (Spanish) as long as you're aware of the use of Catalan in timetables and so forth. Once you get into it, Castilian is one of the easiest languages there is, the rules of pronunciation pretty straightforward and strictly observed. You'll find some basic pronunciation rules below for both Català and Castilian, and a selection of words and phrases in both languages. Castilian is certainly easier to pronounce, but don't be afraid to try Català, especially in the more out-of-the-way places – you'll generally get a good reception if you at least try communicating in the local language.

Castilian/Spanish: a few rules

Unless there's an accent, words ending in d, l, r, and z are **stressed** on the last syllable, all others on the second last.

All **vowels** are pure and short; combinations have predictable results.

A somewhere between the A sound of back and that of father.

E as in get.

I as in police.

O as in hot.

U as in rule.

C is lisped before E and I, hard otherwise: *cerca* is pronounced "thairka".

CH is pronounced as in English.

G works the same way, a guttural H sound (like the *ch* in loch) before E or I, a hard G elsewhere – *gigante* becomes "higante".

H is always silent.

J the same sound as a guttural G: *jamón* is pronounced "hamon".

LL sounds like an English Y: *tortilla* is pronounced "torteeya".

N as in English unless it has a tilde (accent) over it, when it becomes NY: *mañana* sounds like "man-yarna".

QU is pronounced like an English K.

R is rolled, RR doubly so.

V sounds more like B, *vino* becoming "beano".

X has an S sound before consonants, normal X before vowels.

Z is the same as a soft C, so *cerveza* becomes "thairvaitha".

Catalan: a few rules

With Català, don't be tempted to use the few rules of Spanish pronunciation you may know – in particular the soft Spanish Z and C don't apply, so unlike in the rest of Spain it's not "Barthelona" but "Barcelona", as in English.

A as in hat if stressed, as in alone when unstressed.

PHRASEBOOKS, DICTIONARIES AND TEACHING YOURSELF

Spanish

Numerous Spanish phrasebooks are available in Britain, the most user-friendly being the *Spanish Rough Guide Phrasebook*, laid out dictionary-style for instant access. Both Collins and Cassells publish dictionaries. For teaching yourself the language, the BBC tape series *España Viva* and *Digame* are excellent, as is their two-week crash course *Get By in Spanish*. Macmillan's *Breakthrough Spanish* is probably the best of the tape and book home study courses.

Catalan

The best book for learning Catalan is a total immersion course called *Digui Digui* (published by the Generalitat de Catalunya), a series of books and tapes that is presented entirely in Catalan; you will, however, need to speak Spanish to take this on. In Britain, the best place to find it is Grant & Cutler, 55 Great Marlborough Street, London W1 (☎020/7734 2012, *www.grant-c.demon.co.uk*). *Teach Yourself Catalan* (Hodder & Stoughton) is less ambitious, but perfectly adequate for most visitors – and it's presented in English. As for English–Catalan phrasebooks, the only one currently in print is *Parla Català* (Pia), whilst for a dictionary you're limited to the version published by Routledge.

E varies, but usually as in get.

I as in police.

IG sounds like the "tch" in the English scratch; *lleig* (ugly) is pronounced "yeah-tch".

O varies, but usually as in hot.

U somewhere between the U sound of put and rule.

Ç sounds like an English S; *plaça* is pronounced "plassa".

C followed by an E or I is soft; otherwise hard.

WORDS AND PHRASES

Basics

English	Spanish	Catalan
Yes, No, OK	*Sí, No, Vale*	*Si, No, Val*
Please, Thank you	*Por favor, Gracias*	*Per favor, Gràcies*
Where, When	*Dónde, Cuando*	*On, Quan*
What, How much	*Qué, Cuánto*	*Què, Quant*
Here, There	*Aquí, Allí, Allá*	*Aquí, Allí, Allà*
This, That	*Esto, Eso*	*Això, Allò*
Now, Later	*Ahora, Más tarde*	*Ara, Més tard*
Open, Closed	*Abierto/a, Cerrado/a*	*Obert, Tancat*
With, Without	*Con, Sin*	*Amb, Sense*
Good, Bad	*Buen(o)/a, Mal(o)/a*	*Bo(na), Dolent(a)*
Big, Small	*Gran(de), Pequeño/a*	*Gran, Petit(a)*
Cheap, Expensive	*Barato/a, Caro/a*	*Barat(a), Car(a)*
Hot, Cold	*Caliente, Frío/a*	*Calent(a), Fred(a)*
More, Less	*Más, Menos*	*Més, Menys*
Today, Tomorrow	*Hoy, Mañana*	*Avui, Demà*
Yesterday	*Ayer*	*Ahir*
Day before yesterday	*Anteayer*	*Abans-d'ahir*
Next week	*La semana que viene*	*La setmana que ve*
Next month	*El mes que viene*	*El mes que ve*

Greetings and responses

English	Spanish	Catalan
Hello, Goodbye	*Hola, Adiós*	*Hola, Adéu*
Good morning	*Buenos días*	*Bon dia*
Good afternoon/ night	*Buenas tardes/noches*	*Bona tarda/nit*
See you later	*Hasta luego*	*Fins després*
Sorry	*Lo siento/disculpéme*	*Ho sento*
Excuse me	*Con permiso/perdón*	*Perdoni*

Continues over

English	Spanish	Catalan
How are you?	¿Cómo está (usted)?	Com va?
I (don't) understand	(No) Entiendo	(No) Ho entenc
Not at all/ You're welcome	De nada	De res
Do you speak English?	¿Habla (usted) inglés?	Parla anglès?
I (don't) speak Spanish/Catalan	(No) Hablo Español	(No) Parlo Català
My name is . . .	Me llamo . . .	Em dic . . .
What's your name?	¿Como se llama usted?	Com es diu?
I am English	Soy inglés(a)	Sóc anglès(a)
Scottish	escocés(a)	escocès(a)
Australian	australiano/a	australià/ana
Canadian	canadiense/a	canadenc(a)
American	americano/a	americà/ana
Irish	irlandés(a)	irlandès(a)
Welsh	galés(a)	gallès(a)

	Hotels and transport	
English	Spanish	Catalan
I want	Quiero	Vull (pronounced "fwee")
I'd like	Quisiera	Voldria
Do you know . . . ?	¿Sabe . . . ?	Vostès saben . . . ?
I don't know	No sé	No sé
There is (is there?)	(¿)Hay(?)	Hi ha(?)
Give me . . .	Deme . . .	Doneu-me . . .
Do you have . . . ?	¿Tiene . . . ?	Té . . . ?
. . . the time	. . . la hora	. . . l'hora
. . . a room	. . . una habitación	. . . alguna habitació

. . . with two beds/ double bed	. . . con dos camas/ cama matrimonial	. . . amb dos llits/ llit per dues persones
. . . with shower/ bath	. . . con ducha/baño	. . . amb dutxa/bany
for one person (two people)	para una persona (dos personas)	per a una persona (dues persones)
for one night (one week)	para una noche (una semana)	per una nit (una setmana)
It's fine, how much is it?	Está bien, ¿cuánto es?	Esta bé, quant és?
It's too expensive	Es demasiado caro	És massa car
Don't you have anything cheaper?	¿No tiene algo más barato?	En té de més bon preu?
Can one . . . ?	¿Se puede . . . ?	Es pot . . . ?
. . . camp (near) here?	¿ . . . acampar aqui (cerca)?	. . . acampar a la vora?
Is there a hostel nearby?	¿Hay un hostal aquí cerca?	Hi ha un hostal a la vora?
It's not very far	No es muy lejos	No és gaire lluny
How do I get to . . . ?	¿Por donde se va a . . . ?	Per anar a . . . ?
Left, right, straight on	Izquierda, derecha, todo recto	A l'esquerra, a la dreta, tot recte
Where is . . . ?	¿Dónde está . . . ?	On és . . . ?
. . . the bus station	. . . la estación de autobuses	. . . l'estació de autobuses
. . . the bus stop	. . . la parada	. . . la parada
. . . the railway station	. . . la estación de ferrocarril	. . . l'estació
. . . the nearest bank	. . . el banco más cercano	. . . el banc més a prop

Continues over

English	Spanish	Catalan
. . . the post office	. . . el correo/ la oficina de correos	. . . l'oficina de correus correus
. . . the toilet	. . . el baño/aseo/ servicio	. . . la toaleta
Where does the bus to . . . leave from?	¿De dónde sale el autobús para . . . ?	De on surt el autobús a . . .?
Is this the train for Barcelona?	¿Es este el tren para Barcelona?	Aquest tren va a Barcelona?
I'd like a (return) ticket to . . .	Quisiera un billete (de ida y vuelta) para . . .	Voldria un bitllet (d'anar i tornar) a . . .
What time does it leave (arrive in . . .)?	¿A qué hora sale (llega a . . .)?	A quina hora surt (arriba a . . .)?
What is there to eat?	¿Qué hay para comer?	Què hi ha per menjar?
What's that?	¿Qué es eso?	Què és això?

Days of the week

English	Spanish	Catalan
Monday	lunes	dilluns
Tuesday	martes	dimarts
Wednesday	miércoles	dimecres
Thursday	jueves	dijous
Friday	viernes	divendres
Saturday	sábado	dissabte
Sunday	domingo	diumenge

Numbers

English	Spanish	Catalan
1	un/uno/una	un(a)
2	dos	dos (dues)

English	Spanish	Catalan
3	*tres*	*tres*
4	*cuatro*	*quatre*
5	*cinco*	*cinc*
6	*seis*	*sis*
7	*siete*	*set*
8	*ocho*	*vuit*
9	*nueve*	*nou*
10	*diez*	*deu*
11	*once*	*onze*
12	*doce*	*dotze*
13	*trece*	*tretze*
14	*catorce*	*catorze*
15	*quince*	*quinze*
16	*dieciseis*	*setze*
17	*diecisiete*	*disset*
18	*dieciocho*	*divuit*
19	*diecinueve*	*dinou*
20	*veinte*	*vint*
21	*veintiuno*	*vint-i-un*
30	*treinta*	*trenta*
40	*cuarenta*	*quaranta*
50	*cincuenta*	*cinquanta*
60	*sesenta*	*seixanta*
70	*setenta*	*setanta*
80	*ochenta*	*vuitanta*
90	*noventa*	*novanta*
100	*cien(to)*	*cent*
101	*ciento uno*	*cent un*
102	*ciento dos*	*cent dos (dues)*
200	*doscientos*	*dos-cents (dues-centes)*
500	*quinientos*	*cinc-cents*
1000	*mil*	*mil*
2000	*dos mil*	*dos mil*

WORDS AND PHRASES

G followed by E or I is like the "zh" in Zhivago; otherwise hard. H is always silent.

J as in the French "Jean".

LL sounds like an English Y or LY, like the "yuh" sound in million.

N as in English, though before F or V it sometimes sounds like an M.

NY replaces the Castilian Ñ.

QU before E or I sounds like K; before A or O as in "quit".

R is rolled, but only at the start of a word; at the end it's often silent.

T is pronounced as in English, though sometimes it sounds like a D, as in *viatge* or *dotze*.

TX is pronounced like English CH.

V at the start of a word sounds like B; in all other positions it's a soft "F" sound.

W is pronounced like a B/V.

X is like SH in most words, though in some, like *exit*, it sounds like an X.

Z is like the English Z in zoo.

Glossaries

Catalan terms

Albufera Lagoon (and surrounding wetlands).

Altar major High altar.

Ajuntament Town Hall.

Aparcament Parking.

Avinguda (Avgda) Avenue.

Badia Bay.

Barranc Ravine.

Barroc Baroque.

Basílica Catholic church with honorific privileges.

Cala Small bay, cove.

Camí Way or road.

Ca'n At the house of (contraction of *casa + en*).

Capella Chapel.

Carrer (c/) Street.

Carretera Road, highway.

Castell Castle.

Celler Cellar or a bar in a cellar.

Claustre Cloister.

Convent Convent or monastery.

Correu Post office.

Coves Caves.

Església Church.

Festa Festival.

Finca Estate or farmhouse.

Font Water fountain or spring.

Gòtic Gothic.

Illa Island.

Jardí Garden.

Llac Lake.

Mercat Market.

Mirador Watchtower or viewpoint.

Modernisme (Modernista) Literally "modernism" ("modernist"), the Catalan form of Art Nouveau, whose most famous exponent was Antoni Gaudí.

Monestir Monastery.

Museu Museum.

Naveta Prehistoric ossuary.

Nostra Senyora The Virgin Mary (lit. "Our Lady").

Oficina d'Informació Turística Tourist office.

Palau Palace, mansion or manor house.

Parc Park.

Passeig Boulevard; the evening stroll along it.

Plaça Square.

Platja Beach.

Pont Bridge.

Port Harbour, port.

Porta Door, gate.

Rei King.

Reial Royal.

Reina Queen.

Reixa Iron screen or grille, usually in front of a window.

Renaixença Rebirth, often used to describe the Catalan cultural revival at the end of the nineteenth and beginning of the twentieth centuries. Architecturally, this was expressed as *Modernisme*.

Retaule Retable or reredos, a wooden, ornamental panel behind an altar.

Riu River.

Romeria Pilgrimage or gathering at a shrine.

Santuari Sanctuary.

Sant/a Saint.

Serra Mountain range.

Talayot Cone-shaped prehistoric watchtower.

Taula Prehistoric, T-shaped stone monolith.

Torrent Stream or river (usually dry in summer).

Urbanització Modern urbanization or estate development.

Vall Valley.

Art and architectural terms

Ambulatory Covered passage around the outer edge of the choir in the chancel (see entry) of a church.

Apse Semicircular protrusion at (usually) the east end of a church.

Art Deco Geometrical style of art and architecture popular in the 1930s.

Art Nouveau Style of art, architecture and design based on highly stylized vegetal forms. Popular in the early part of the twentieth century. See also Modernisme above.

Baroque The art and architecture of the Counter Reformation, dating from around 1600 onwards. Distinguished by its ornate exuberance and (at its best) complex but harmonious spatial arrangement of interiors. Elements – particularly its gaudiness – remained popular in the Balearics well into the twentieth century.

Chancel The eastern part of a church, often separated from the nave by a screen or by the choir.

Churrigueresque Fancifully ornate form of Baroque art named after the Spaniard José Churriguera (1650–1723) and his extended family, its leading exponents.

Classical Architectural style incorporating Greek and Roman elements – pillars, domes, colonnades etc – at its height in the seventeenth century and revived, as Neoclassical, in the nineteenth.

Cyclopean Prehistoric style of dry-stone masonry comprising boulders of irregular form.

Gothic Gothic architectural style of the thirteenth to sixteenth centuries, characterized by pointed arches, rib vaulting, flying buttresses and a general emphasis on verticality.

Majolica In the fifteenth century, there was a vigorous trade in decorative pottery from Spain to Italy via Mallorca. The Italians coined the term "Majolica" to describe this imported Spanish pottery after the medieval name for the island through which it was traded, but thereafter it was applied to all tin-glazed pottery. The process of making "Majolica" began with the mixing and cleaning of clay, after which it was fired and retrieved at the biscuit (earthenware) stage. The biscuit was then cooled and dipped in a liquid glaze that contained tin and water. The water in the glaze was absorbed, leaving a dry surface ready for decoration. After painting, the pottery was returned to the kiln for a final firing, which fused the glaze and fixed the painting.

Additional glazings and firings added extra lustre. Initially, "Majolica" was dominated by greens and purples, but technological advances added blue, yellow and ochre in the fifteenth century. "Majolica" (of one sort or another) was produced in Mallorca up until the early twentieth century.

Plateresque Elaborately decorative Renaissance architectural style, named for its resemblance to silversmiths' work (*platería*).

Nave Main body of a church.

Neoclassical Architectural style derived from Greek and Roman elements – pillars, domes, colonnades, etc – and popular in the nineteenth century.

Presbytery The part of the church to the east of the choir and the site of the high altar.

Renaissance Movement in art and architecture developed in fifteenth-century Italy.

Retable Altarpiece.

Romanesque Early medieval architecture distinguished by squat forms, rounded arches and naïve sculpture.

Transept Arms of a cross-shaped church, placed at ninety degrees to nave and chancel.

Tympanum Sculpted, usually recessed, panel above a door.

Vault An arched ceiling or roof.

ART AND ARCHITECTURAL TERMS

INDEX

T

V

W

X

Stay in touch with us!

ROUGHNEWS is Rough Guides'
free newsletter.
In three issues a year we give you
news, travel issues, music reviews,
readers' letters and the latest
dispatches from authors on the road.

I would like to receive ROUGHNEWS: please put me on your free mailing list.

NAME ....

ADDRESS ....

Please clip or photocopy and send to: Rough Guides, 62-70 Shorts Gardens,
London WC2H 9AH, England

or Rough Guides, 375 Hudson Street, New York, NY 10014, USA.

ROUGH GUIDES: Travel

ROUGH GUIDES: Mini Guides, Travel Specials and Phrasebooks

MINI GUIDES

Antigua
Bangkok
Barbados
Big Island of Hawaii
Boston
Brussels
Budapest
Dublin
Edinburgh
Florence
Honolulu
Lisbon
London Restaurants
Madrid
Maui
Melbourne
New Orleans
St Lucia

Seattle
Sydney
Tokyo
Toronto

TRAVEL SPECIALS

First-Time Asia
First-Time Europe
More Women Travel

PHRASEBOOKS

Czech
Dutch
Egyptian Arabic
European
French

German
Greek
Hindi & Urdu
Hungarian
Indonesian
Italian
Japanese
Mandarin
  Chinese
Mexican
  Spanish
Polish
Portuguese
Russian
Spanish
Swahili
Thai
Turkish
Vietnamese

AVAILABLE AT ALL GOOD BOOKSHOPS

ROUGH GUIDES:
Reference and Music CDs

REFERENCE
Classical Music
Classical:
  100 Essential CDs
Drum'n'bass
House Music

World Music:
  100 Essential CDs
English Football
European Football
Internet
Millennium

**ROUGH GUIDE
  MUSIC CDs**
Music of the Andes
Australian
  Aboriginal
Brazilian Music
Cajun & Zydeco
Classic Jazz
Music of Colombia
Cuban Music
Eastern Europe
Music of Egypt
English Roots
  Music
Flamenco
India & Pakistan
Irish Music
Music of Japan
Kenya & Tanzania
Native American
North African
Music of Portugal

Reggae
Salsa
Scottish Music
South African
  Music
Music of Spain
Tango
Tex-Mex
West African Music
World Music
World Music Vol 2
Music of Zimbabwe

Jazz
Music USA
Opera
Opera:
  100 Essential CDs
Reggae
Rock
Rock:
  100 Essential CDs
Techno
World Music

AVAILABLE AT ALL GOOD BOOKSHOPS

Sorted

ROUGH GUIDES

100

Essentia

CDs

Eight titles,
one name

ROUGH GUIDES

Will you have enough stories to tell your grandchildren

Yahoo! Travel

Rough Guides
on the Web

www.travel.roughguides.com

We keep getting bigger and better! The Rough Guide to Travel Online
now covers more than 14,000 searchable locations. You're just a click
away from access to the most in-depth travel content, weekly
destination features, online reservation services, and an outspoken
community of fellow travelers. Whether you're looking for ideas for
your next holiday or you know exactly where you're going, join us online.

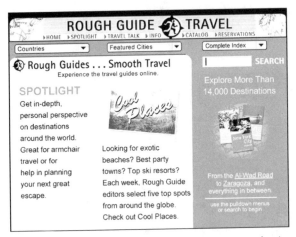

You can also find us on Yahoo!® Travel (http://travel.yahoo.com) and
Microsoft Expedia® UK (http://www.expediauk.com).

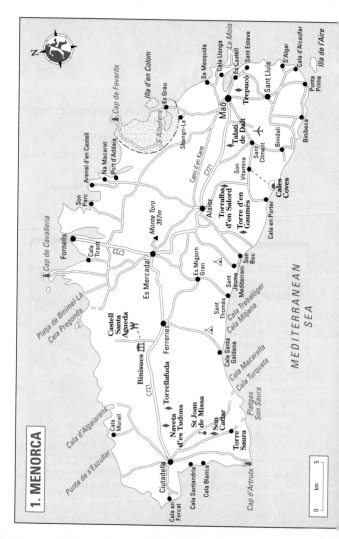

1. MENORCA

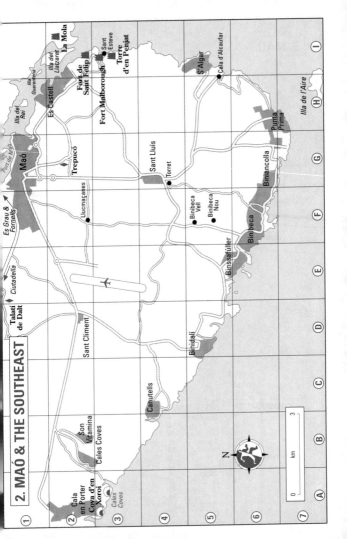

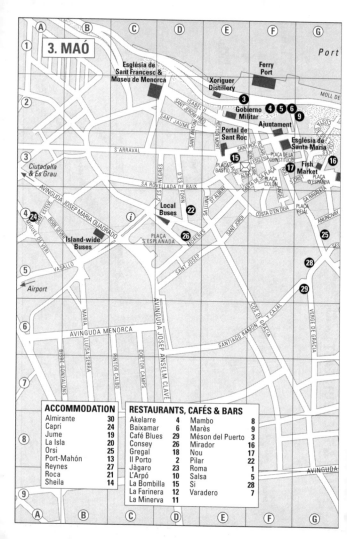

3. MAÓ

Port

A1

B1

Esglèsia de Sant Francesc & Museu de Menorca

Xoriguer Distillery

Ferry Port

MOLL DE

Gobierno Militar **3**

4 5 6
9

Ajuntament

Portal de Sant Roc

Esglèsia de Santa María

15

Fish Market **16**

17

Ciutadella & Es Grau

S'ARRAVAL

Local Buses **22**

26

Island-wide Buses

24

Airport

25

28

29

AVINGUDA MENORCA

ACCOMMODATION	
Almirante	30
Capri	24
Jume	19
La Isla	20
Orsi	25
Port-Mahón	13
Reynes	27
Roca	21
Sheila	14

RESTAURANTS, CAFÉS & BARS			
Akelarre	4	Mambo	8
Baixamar	6	Marès	9
Café Blues	29	Méson del Puerto	3
Consey	26	Mirador	16
Gregal	18	Nou	17
Il Porto	2	Pilar	22
Jàgaro	23	Roma	1
L'Arpó	10	Salsa	5
La Bombilla	15	Si	28
La Farinera	12	Varadero	7
La Minerva	11		

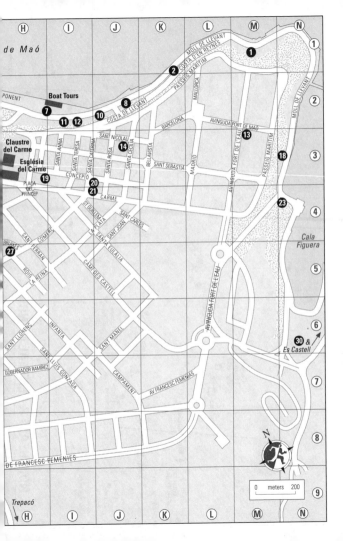

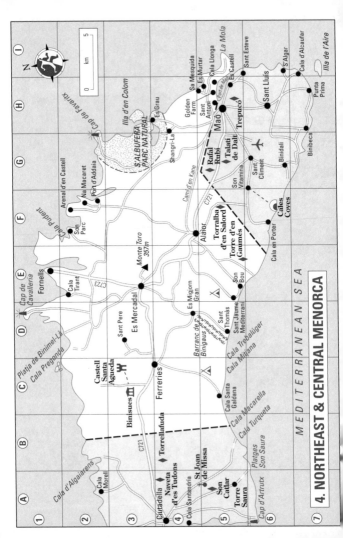

4. NORTHEAST & CENTRAL MENORCA

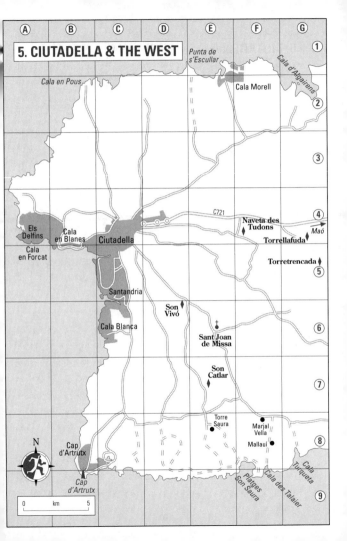

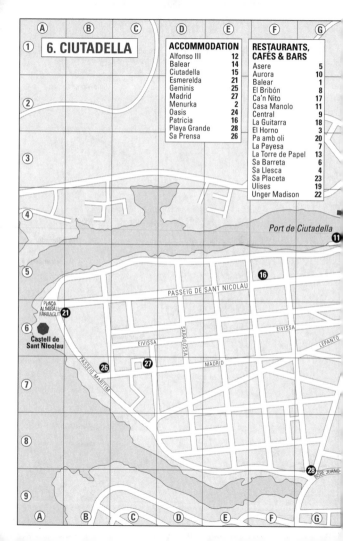

6. CIUTADELLA

ACCOMMODATION

Alfonso III	12
Balear	14
Ciutadella	15
Esmerelda	21
Geminis	25
Madrid	27
Menurka	2
Oasis	24
Patricia	16
Playa Grande	28
Sa Prensa	26

RESTAURANTS, CAFÉS & BARS

Asere	5
Aurora	10
Balear	1
El Bribón	8
Ca'n Nito	17
Casa Manolo	11
Central	9
La Guitarra	18
El Horno	3
Pa amb oli	20
La Payesa	7
La Torre de Papel	13
Sa Barreta	6
Sa Llesca	4
Sa Placeta	23
Ulises	19
Unger Madison	22

Port de Ciutadella

PASSEIG DE SANT NICOLAU

PLAÇA ALMIRALL FARRAGUT

Castell de Sant Nicolau

PASSEIG MARITIM

EIVISSA

EIVISSA

SARAGOSSA

MADRID

LEPANTO

BEBE JUANO